THE WAY OF DUTY

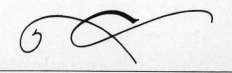

OTHER BOOKS BY RICHARD BUEL, JR.

Securing the Revolution (1972)

Dear Liberty (1980)

Mary Fish at the age of fifty-eight. By Reuben Moulthrop.
Courtesy, Fairfield Historical Society.

The Way of Duty

A WOMAN AND HER FAMILY IN REVOLUTIONARY AMERICA

JOY DAY BUEL

AND

RICHARD BUEL, JR.

W · W · NORTON & COMPANY

New York · London

Printed in the United States of America
The text of this book is composed in 10/12 Galliard,
with display type set in Garamond.
Manufacturing by the Haddon Craftsmen, Inc.
Book design by Margaret M. Wagner

First published as a Norton paperback 1985; reissued 1995

Library of Congress Cataloging in Publication Data
Buel, Joy Day.
The way of duty.
Bibliography: p.
Includes index.

1. Fish, Mary, 1736–1818.   2. United States
History—Revolution, 1775–1783.—Women.   3. Women—
United States—History—18th century.   4. Family—
United States—History—18th century.   5. United
States—Biography.   I. Buel, Richard, 1933–
II. Title.
CT275.F5586B83   1984   973.3'092'4 [B]   83-12176

W. W. Norton & Company, Inc.
500 Fifth Avenue, New York, N.Y. 10110
W. W. Norton & Company Ltd.
10 Coptic Street, London WC1A 1PU

ISBN 0-393-31210-0

6 7 8 9 0

For our daughter
Margaret

CONTENTS

PREFACE

UNTIL recently, the history of roughly half the Americans who have lived, the female half, was almost a blank. Within the last twenty years, the women's movement, in combination with a new social history, has touched off an avalanche of textbooks, monographs, biographies, journals, reference works, and university courses on women's history. Yet still the story is fragmentary, especially for the early period.

During the first century of settlement, most women had little time, ability, or incentive to record their thoughts and feelings. The work of the household, including child care and the manufacture of goods for home consumption, all but consumed their energy. Few had the benefit of formal schooling, and those who could read and write tended to exercise the first ability sparingly, the second hardly at all. Though the bits and pieces of letters and journals that survive have yielded some excellent studies of the general experience of various women, seldom do we have sufficient material to sustain an account of the varied experiences of one woman in particular. When a mass of evidence is available, it usually concerns women who have attracted attention by deviating from the expectations of their day, and of such women those who drew unfavorable notice outnumber those who stood out for admired achievements. The Anne Hutchinsons and Rebecca Nurses are more in evidence than the Anne Bradstreets, and the evidence comes more often from documents composed by male officials than from women's own writings.

In the early part of the eighteenth century, the boundaries to female accomplishment began to recede. The flowering of commerce in the North Atlantic encouraged a higher level of literacy in both halves of the population and gradually freed women from time-consuming tasks such as the production of all of the cloth for household needs. Girls began to have the leisure necessary for education. Literacy rates among women rose, and as time went on more of them began to leave behind enough material to support full-length studies of their lives. Biographies of nineteenth-century women abound, but of those who grew up a hundred years earlier only two (as far as we know) have received close scrutiny: Abigail Adams and Mercy Otis Warren. Both were notable women; nevertheless, a good deal of their interest for the historian derives from their association with public men. One was the wife of the second president of the United States and mother of the sixth; one was the sister of a prominent Massachusetts patriot and the wife of another. Their correspondence has been preserved because it sheds light not only upon themselves but upon otherwise shadowy corners in the lives of revolutionary leaders. Though it is true that Mercy Otis Warren achieved public recognition as a writer, her best-known work being a history of the Revolution, it is doubtful that she would have attracted so much attention had she not been exceptional among the women of her generation. None of them equaled her noble attempt to produce serious literature. Most only wrote and received letters occasionally; few kept journals, and those they produced were not often considered worthy of preservation.

The subject of this biography, Mary Fish, belongs to the generation of eighteenth-century women for whom, as a rule, the record is sketchy at best. But Mary, in the course of a long life, produced a large amount of written material, which has been preserved with unusual care by successive generations of her family. Much of it is now in the collections of the Yale University Library and the New Canaan Historical Society, but a considerable body of papers remains a cherished possession of direct descendants from both the Noyes and Silliman branches of Mary's posterity.

The material at Yale, the largest concentration of documents on which we drew, arrived there through the Silliman branch. The second son of Mary's second marriage, her lastborn child, was Benjamin Silliman, the most influential scientist in America during the early nineteenth century and the first professor of chemistry at Yale. He revered his mother as "a heroic woman" whose courage, devotion, and piety had laid the foundation for his own achievements. To ensure that a record of her life survived, he not only collected and kept as much of her correspondence as he could, but took the trouble to copy out her Reminiscences, into which she had incorporated parts of her Journal. He prefaced the document with a recommendation that all her descendants cherish her words and follow her example, and he took pains to circulate it among all branches of the family. One of the Noyes descendants also made a copy, but Benjamin's version is the most valuable for its amplification of Mary's original words with reminiscences of his own.

Where gaps occurred in Mary's writings, we have often (not always) been able to fill them by reference to letters and documents from other collections; to the correspondence of her parents, husbands, sons, and other members of her circle; and to the rich public records that exist for

eighteenth-century Connecticut. Altogether, these documents have allowed us to piece together a surprisingly
complete life of Mary Fish.

What follows is, however, an account of more than one
woman and her family. In telling their story we have found
that the nature of the material required us to juxtapose the
great public events of the period—the religious revival
known as the Great Awakening, the trials and perplexities
of the revolutionary struggle, the growing secularization
of society, the westward migration, the rise of Jeffersonian
democracy, and the advent of the Industrial Revolution—
with the persistent patterns and daily routines of family
and community life. It also enabled us to present, in pop-
ular, narrative form, some of the recent scholarly findings
in the fields of social and political history, and to show
how public and private spheres impinged on one another.
Since many of Mary's experiences were shared by her con-
temporaries, and she brought to them a set of values common to her time and place, her story illuminates the lives
of countless ordinary people who passed through an
extraordinary period of American history.

Yet her life would not merit full biographical treatment
were she no more than typical and representative. What
has attracted us to Mary from our first reading of her papers
(and probably accounts for the care with which her
descendants have preserved them down to the present day)
is that her life history and her character both ultimately
transcend the typical.

From a happy, sheltered childhood in a small Connecticut village, Mary went on to explore a wider world and a
variety of experiences uncommon to women of her background. After an unusually prolonged condition of filial
dependency, she passed through years of trial to achieve a
confident independence and personal strength that earned
her, in the eyes of her children and grandchildren, the status of a matriarch. The closest relationships of her life were
almost all with men, and were successful. Her father's ten-

derness, admiration, and concern that she be, first, educated and, later, loved and honored in marriage, influenced
her expectations of men and may have helped to give her
the good judgment that kept her safe from disappointment
in her choice of husbands. The ease and success of Mary's
intimacy with the authoritative figures of her early life led,
in time, to a comfortable assurance of her own authority,
not only with her sons, but also within a body of acquaintance that included many eminent men. The respect that
they accorded her derived from her embodiment of the
ideals and expectations of her day, for she performed to
admiration the duties of woman as society then saw them.

For all that, Mary's life did not run smoothly or follow
the path that would seem to have been laid down for her
at birth. She lived through personal tragedy; through the
tumultuous times of a war fought on home ground;
through periods of intense loneliness and fear of destitu-
tion; and through postwar social upheaval. Yet the culture
that bred her had given her a view of life that was essen-
tially religious, and her ability to yield to change without
surrendering that essence made her a powerful force for
the transmission of traditional values across the gulf that
separated the founders of America from those who achieved
America's independence. In Mary's hands, the family
became as vigorous an instrument as institutional religion
for the maintenance of the faith which, far more than secular ideology, provided a revolutionary generation with a
link to their origins.

ACKNOWLEDGMENTS

WE are indebted to the curators and staffs of the following institutions for their assistance in making materials available to us: the manuscript division of Sterling Memorial Library and the Beinicke Library at Yale University, in particular Judith Schiff and Patricia Stark; the New Canaan Historical Society, in particular Mrs. Mary Louise King and Mrs. George Durbrow; the Fairfield Historical Society, in particular Mrs. Catherine Boisseau; the Connecticut Historical Society, in particular Christopher Bickford and Ruth Blair; the Archives Division of the Connecticut State Library; the Dartmouth College Library; and the Watkinson Library at Trinity College. Special mention must be made of several individuals who gave us their help. Mrs. Judith Barlow and Mrs. Mary Jane Miller accommodated us in their house while we read materials in their possession. Mrs. Katharine Hewitt Cummin rendered us valuable assistance at a strategic moment. Mr. and Mrs. Philip English and their son James allowed us special access to

Benjamin Silliman's Reminiscences. We are also grateful to the Fairfield Historical Society and Sterling Memorial Library for permission to reproduce in illustrative form material in their possession.

Our thanks are due to Elizabeth H. Thomson and Louis Kuslan for their timely counsel; to Bruce H. Mann for his advice on the interpretation of legal documents; to the staff of the Godfrey Memorial Library in Middletown for assistance in genealogical matters; and to the staff of Olin Library at Wesleyan University, in particular Joan Jurale and Ed Rubacha, for support and assistance. Jane Muska-tallo's enthusiasm when typing the first draft of our manuscript gave us most welcome encouragement. She, together with Levena Tollison, introduced us to the wonders of computer typing. Frances Warren assisted in preparing Mary Fish's family tree.

Along the way, the manuscript has been improved by the critical readings of Chandos Brown, Richard Leighton Greene, Charles Royster, and Willard M. Wallace. A grant from the Colonel Return Jonathan Meigs First (1740–1823) Fund has helped us to meet some of the costs incurred in researching and writing the book. The Fund was created by Dorothy Mix Meigs and Fielding Pope Meigs, Jr., in memory of that soldier of the Revolution whose home was in Middletown, Connecticut, from 1740 to 1787. Finally, we wish to acknowledge our debt to our editor, Steven Forman, whose advice has been rendered with good judgment and with sensitivity to both the material and the authors.

THE WAY OF DUTY

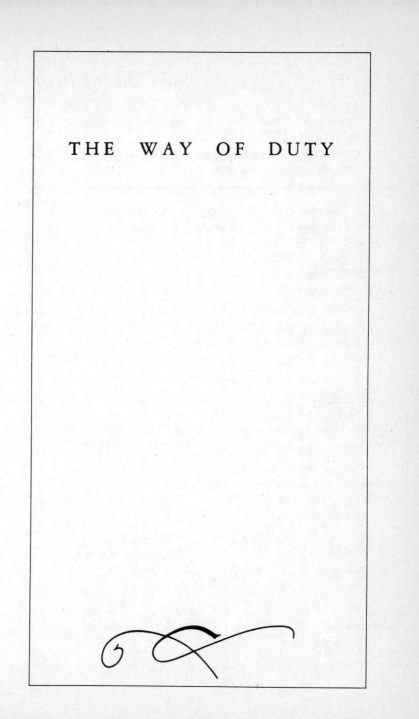

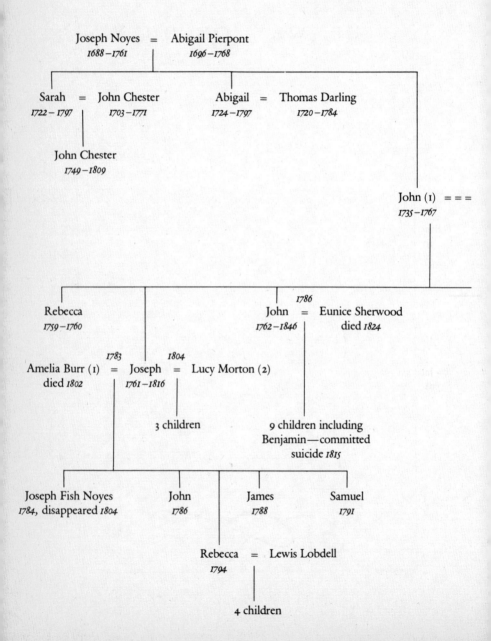

Joseph Noyes = Abigail Pierpont
1688–1761   1696–1768

Sarah = John Chester
1722–1797   1703–1771

Abigail = Thomas Darling
1724–1797   1720–1784

John Chester
1749–1809

John (1) = = =
1735–1767

Rebecca
1759–1760

1786
John = Eunice Sherwood
1762–1846   died 1824

1783   1804
Amelia Burr (1) = Joseph = Lucy Morton (2)
died 1802   1761–1816

3 children

9 children including
Benjamin—committed
suicide 1815

Joseph Fish Noyes
1784, disappeared 1804

John
1786

James
1788

Samuel
1791

Rebecca = Lewis Lobdell
1794

4 children

Family Tree

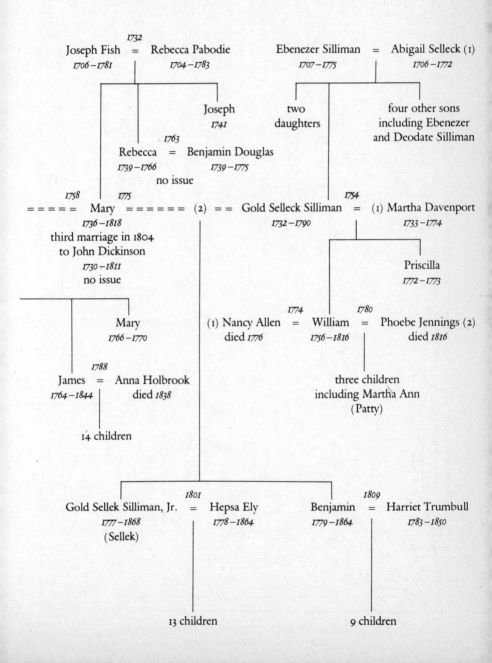

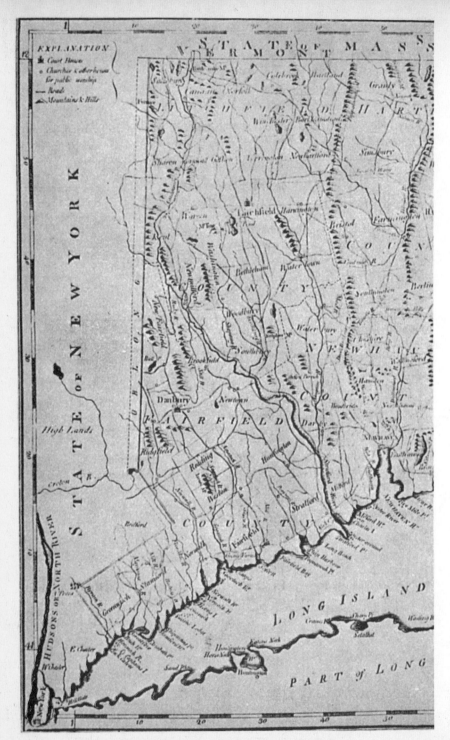

Map of Connecticut. Engraved by Amos Doolittle, 1795.
Courtesy, Yale University Map Collection.

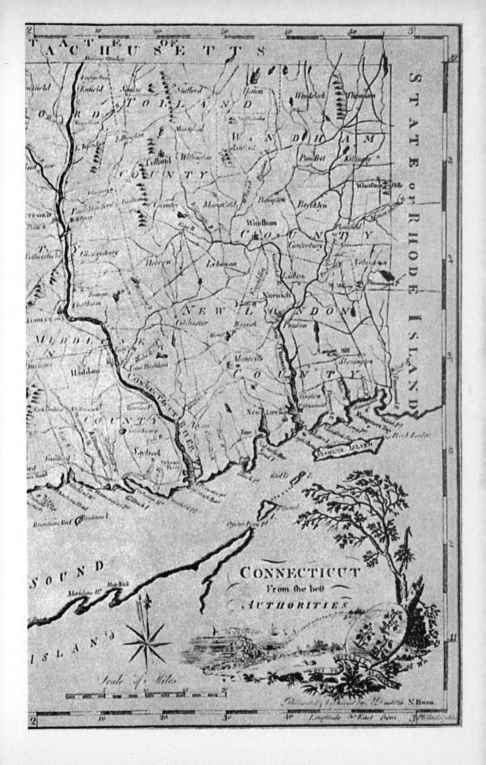

CONNECTICUT

From the best

AUTHORITIES

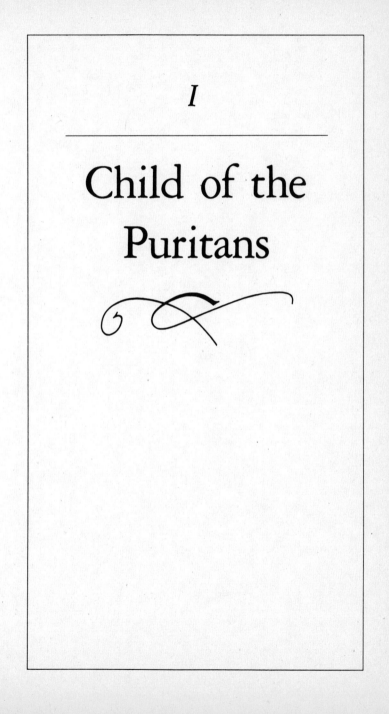

I

Child of the
Puritans

One

THE BEST OF
PARENTS

I

ON May 30, 1736, in Stonington, Connecticut, their first child, a daughter, was born to the Reverend Joseph Fish and his wife Rebecca, and given the name Mary. This is the story of Mary Fish, drawn from family correspondence; from a journal she kept intermittently from girlhood; and from the reminiscences she began to write at the age of sixty-four, in the hope, she said, that they would prove "instructive and entertaining to my dear children, when the hand that writes can move no more."[1] Her cheerful, practical approach to the prospect of her own death came from her long religious schooling in the remembrance of mortality and from the experiences of her life. But in 1800, when she wrote those words, death was farther off than she thought. Mary lived eighteen years into the new century, and before her eyes closed on this world, they saw it changed beyond anything her provincial young parents might have imagined on the day of her birth.

Joseph Fish hailed from Massachusetts. The third son of Thomas Fish and Margaret Woodward, he was born at

Duxbury in 1706 and was graduated from Harvard in 1728. It was then a frequent practice for a young divinity student to spend a few years as an itinerant preacher until he obtained a permanent position, and that is probably what Joseph did. In August 1732 he answered a call from Stonington, where the Reverend Ebenezer Russell had recently died. Though Mr. Russell's congregation had engaged young Mr. Fish to serve them only while they sought the right new minister, they soon reached a unanimous decision that they had found their man in him, and Joseph, who had his own reasons for wanting a settled position, agreed. On December 6, 1732, he married Rebecca, the daughter of William and Judith Pabodie, and one of ten children, at her home in Little Compton, Rhode Island. Three weeks later he was ordained and installed "By ye Solemn Imposition of ye hand of Presbetery" as pastor of the congregation known as the Second, or North Stonington, Society.[2]

Six years before, because the inland spread of the coastal settlement had put a large number of church members at a considerable distance from the meetinghouse, a second congregation had formed and built a church of its own. By 1732, when Joseph became pastor to the Second Society, further extension of the town along the shoreline had obliged the First Church to divide a second time, in order to provide a more accessible place of worship for the newly developed areas to the east of the original church. The First Church West continued under the ministrations of Eleazar Rosseter, pastor since 1718, while the First Church East engaged Nathaniel Eells, a fellow graduate of Joseph's from the Harvard class of 1728. Thus, there were three religious societies in Stonington when Joseph and Rebecca joined the community, though it was location alone that separated them. On all essential aspects of doctrine and church government, the people of Stonington and the ministers who served them were at one.

Young Mr. and Mrs. Fish moved into a large, two-story parsonage about a mile and a half from the church, an inconvenient distance yet a pleasant situation on a high hill from which they could see, on a clear day, Block Island Sound and the ships passing Montauk Point. Convenience of any kind was not among the advantages of their new position. The typical English village, a cluster of buildings centered upon a church, had set the pattern of development for many of the early New England towns, but not for outlying settlements such as North Stonington. The houses and farms that comprised Joseph's parish sprawled across the countryside, three to six miles from the church in all directions. Their inhabitants, less wealthy than the average family living along the more developed and more prosperous coast, would be correspondingly less able to provide him with the comforts and cultural appurtenances that were fast becoming customary there. Still, he could feel reasonably sure that he and his wife would never want for the necessities of food, fuel, and shelter. By 1735 they owned a small farm; in time they were able to employ a modest number of servants, and even to purchase one or two slaves. Beside these practical considerations, Joseph, being a man of ambition, might count himself fortunate to obtain a living in a society established long enough to have completed the basic tasks of building a meetinghouse and appointing the usual church officers, including a clerk, a treasurer, a committee, and the collectors of the minister's rate, yet sufficiently new and unformed to offer scope for his youthful initiative.

By all accounts, Joseph Fish had both a vocation for the ministry and the personal endowments necessary for success in that calling. His tall figure, upright carriage, and magisterial wig gave him an imposing appearance in the pulpit, and when he delivered his sermons he exercised another gift, one of inestimable value to a preacher, a particularly clear, carrying voice. According to one of his parishioners, he also had *"a wonderful way of noticing in his sermons the things which took place,"* in other words, of relating the everyday to the eternal.[3] And his strong constitution helped him to meet the physical demands of his work, which were considerable, for he had to make parish visits on horseback, in all kinds of weather and over many miles of country where the roads were often so bad as to be virtually nonexistent.

In his first few years as pastor at North Stonington, Joseph employed his talents to good purpose. Sixty-five converts joined the original thirty-nine members of the Second Church, a tripling of the congregation that both gratified the man of God and helped his people to fulfill their obligation to him. Though the law required all the inhabitants of a town to contribute to the support of the established minister, collection by distraint often proved both time-consuming and self-defeating. The larger Joseph's congregation grew, the easier it was for members to pay him the salary agreed upon, and to increase it if need be. When the depreciation of the colony's currency made it hard for him to live on his original stipend, the Society raised it; but even then he did not receive a salary sufficient for all his needs. Whatever a man's trade or profession, he had to be also a farmer, and his wife a producer of certain household items such as cloth, garments, candles, and soap. Joseph Fish farmed not only for subsistence but for sale. He sent sheep to the market at Boston, and sometimes paid for purchases there in kind rather than in cash. "I have purchased a Chair & an Excellent Horse for the Chair . . . and am to pay Mr. Holmes in the Fall in our Produce, such as Pork, Wheat, Rie, &c," he told his wife in a letter written on one of his occasional business trips to that city[4] In later years he added other sources of income, such as the supplementary posts he held in two separate missionary societies that employed him to teach the neighboring Indians. In general, however, his life followed a course prescribed by church calendar and agricultural season. For the first ten years at Stonington, it was a life of hard work, but little trouble.

A quiverful of children was not to figure among Joseph's blessings or his Society's burdens. In 1739 Rebecca gave

birth to a second daughter, named for herself; in 1741, one
sorrowful spring day encompassed the birth, baptism, and
death of a son, Joseph; and there were no more babies.
The two little girls, Molly and Becca as they were called at
home, grew up in close companionship to each other and
to their parents. The customs of the day fostered intimacy.
Home was still the place where the young received most
of their education, both religious and practical; where they
early observed and later shared in the work of farming,
spinning, and other domestic chores, steadily increasing
their knowledge of the adult world until they themselves
passed into it with unconscious ease. As always, there were
exceptions, but the general rule describes the Fish household quite accurately.

Joseph and Rebecca sent down their roots too deeply
into Puritan soil for the winds of change to move them
much. Rebecca impressed upon her children that, through
her, they were direct descendants of John and Priscilla
Alden, pilgrims on the *Mayflower*. She told them stories of
the Aldens that she had heard from the lips of their own
daughter, her grandmother. With her husband, Rebecca
both followed and transmitted a tradition of simple piety
little changed from the early days, as Mary's account of her
upbringing shows:

> They were very watchful over us in all our ways, and
> they had such a happy mode of governing that they
> would even govern us with an eye, and they never used
> severity with us at all.
>   They early put us to the best schools that Stonington
> afforded, but they did not depend on them for our
> instruction. My father's practice was every day to take
> us into his study, immediately after family prayers in the
> morning, and hear us read, and he would give us advice
> for the day. He would also enjoin it upon us to read our
> bibles by ourselves every day. . . . The sabbath we were
> taught to keep with the greatest strictness, both at home

and in the house of God and on our way to and from the same, not allowing us to walk or ride with those who would talk of worldly matters on the lords day. . . . They taught us also to call ourselves to account every night . . . to forgive injuries, and if any one spoke evil of us, we must examine ourselves and see wherein we had been culpable, and if we found we had done wrong, to be sorry for it, and resolve never to do so any more, but if we found [ourselves] innocent . . . never to return railing for railing [but] pray God to forgive our enemies . . . always to be glad if we could oblige even the most unobliging and to be thankful when it lay in our power to do any kind of office for any of our fellow creatures. They early taught us diligence—that we must always be doing something that would turn out to profit . . . and I feared that my father should at any time find me doing nothing, lest he should put the question, What? are you idle my child?[5]

Humility, self-searching, private Bible reading, strict observance of the Sabbath, and to be "always . . . doing something that would turn out to profit": these were teachings that would have met the standards of Old Plymouth Colony itself, as Joseph continued to call his birthplace long after it had become a part of Massachusetts.

That Joseph and Rebecca "never used severity" might, on the other hand, have incurred reproof. John Robinson, a seventeenth-century preacher of repute among the English Puritans, taught the parents of his day that "there is in all children . . . a stubbornness, and stoutness of mind arising from natural pride, which must, in the first place, be broken and beaten down; that so the foundation of their education being laid in humility and tractableness, other virtues may in their time, be built thereon."[6] A century later, though gentler methods had become more usual, some New Englanders continued to rear their children according to similar strict principles. But in this respect, Joseph joined those who diverged from old ways. He deplored "the (too common) Severity of Parents" as unchristian and ineffective:

> For if *Children* are of a tender *Make,* they neither *need,* nor can they *bear,* nor even be suppos'd to *deserve,* Severity. And if they are of a more hardy and stubborn *Make,* what so Likely, as *Goodness, Moderation* & Patience, to work them into a humane Shape, & mould them into a Gospel Temper?

His own children, he said, were "never treated with *Severity* of *Discipline,* nor *made* obedient by the force of austere parental commands, but governd by the gentle reins of *Love* and *Tenderness* accompanying the *Light* of *Counsel* and *Advice.*"[7] Perhaps that is why Mary remembered her childhood fondly, and why, long after she had passed from their control, she showed a degree of affection and respect for "the best of Parents" beyond anything that mere lip service to convention would have required.[8]

II

WHEN Mary looked back on 1741, the fifth year of her life, she recorded only the memory of her brother's birth and death. Yet for her father, the year marked both the summit of his career and the beginning of its decline.

Ten years before, when he first entered upon his ministry, the religious revival known to us as the Great Awakening had begun to send a fresh, strong gust of spiritual emotion across New England. The movement, which had swept Europe in the 1720s, caught up the young American divine, Jonathan Edwards, who had been graduated from Yale at about the same time that Joseph was graduated from Harvard. It was Edwards who opened the gates of New England to the evangelists, and they came pouring through. In 1740 George Whitefield arrived from England and embarked on a tour of the colonies. Others, including some native American preachers, soon followed his example. Faithful imitators of Whitefield's style, if not always his equals in ability, at first they succeeded in turning large numbers of people back to the active religious life. Joseph's own ministry, as he acknowledged, had benefited from theirs. Years later, despite the devastation of his church that followed in its wake, he looked back upon the revival as "the most wonderful work of God, that ever was known, in this part of the world," in which the "ministers of Christ were stirred up to preach, with uncommon zeal and solemnity, and the people as ready to hear, with unusual attention."[9]

The evangelists raised a question, however, that posed a recurrent problem for Calvinism: how is one to tell those truly gifted with the light of God from those who only deceive themselves that they possess it? They began to answer this question in ways that caused violent convulsions followed by permanent rifts within formerly cohesive congregations. Ever more insistently, they questioned the right of the established minister to his place; ever more frequently, they persuaded the flock to turn away from a shepherd whose power to guide and guard them seemed suddenly doubtful.

This pattern, with variations, was followed in many New England communities in the 1740s. Both George Whitefield and Gilbert Tennent, an evangelist from New Jersey, traveled through Connecticut preaching the revival. Tennent, whom Joseph lauded as "a son of thunder . . . by whose enlightening and alarming discourses, people were more effectually roused up," passed close to Stonington, but neither of the two great luminaries came there. It was left to the Reverend James Davenport, a lesser light, but, in Joseph's words, "a wonderful, strange good man . . . of undoubted, real piety, fervent zeal for God, love to souls, and ardent desire to advance the Redeemer's kingdom," to rouse that sleepy corner of the world.[10]

When Davenport arrived, Joseph admitted him without hesitation to the pulpit of the North Stonington church.

He regretted his hospitality almost immediately, and yet too late. Twenty years later, he recalled in graphic detail the spectacle of Davenport in action:

> He not only gave an unrestrained liberty to *noise* and *outcry,* both of *distress* and *joy,* in time of divine service, but promoted *both* with all his might,—by extending his own voice to the highest pitch, together with the most violent agitations of body, even to the distorting of his features and marring his visage: as if he had aimed, rather, at frightening people out of their senses, than, by solid argument, nervous reasoning and solemn addresses, to enlighten the mind, and perswade them as reasonable men, to make their escape unto Christ. And all this, with a strange, unnatural *singing tone,* which mightily tended to *raise* or *keep up* the affections of weak and undiscerning people, and consequently, to heighten the confusion among the *passionate* of his hearers.[11]

If Joseph disliked the manner of this ministry, the matter of it troubled him still more. Davenport encouraged people to induce *"visions"* by entering states of trance "in which some would lie for hours: and on their coming out . . . would tell of wonderful things,—that they saw, it may be, *heaven* or *hell,* and such and such persons, (if dead,) *there;* or (if alive,) going to one or t'other of those places; and upon it, the poor deluded people would be ready to *treat* those very persons, (if living,) according as they were seen in *vision."*

The possibilities for working off old scores inherent in such practices, and their resemblance to the witchcraft accusations of earlier times, need no elaboration. Among others, Joseph saw "a worthy minister of Christ [Nathaniel Eells] shamefully abused, by such a *satanical* discovery of men's future states."[12] Perhaps in an attempt to protect themselves against attack, some ministers voluntarily submitted to a private examination by Davenport. Though aware that they might be damned if they did, they knew that they would almost certainly be damned if they did not. With or without their consent to his proceedings, Davenport would arrogate the right to judge them; and such was the status this young man had acquired that many people, no matter how high their previous opinion of a pastor, would, when he came under Davenport's eye, act "as if [he] were going before the *judge of all the earth,*" wrote Joseph.[13]

It did not necessarily take a vision or a verdict to condemn a minister. For some of Davenport's adherents, the fact that a clergyman had received an education had already damned him. Joseph himself heard Davenport utter diatribes against *"letter-learned rabbies, scribes and pharisees and unconverted ministers:* —which *phrases* the good man would frequently use in his sermons, with such peculiar *marks,* not only of *odium,* but of *indication,* as served to beget a jealousy in many of the peoples minds, that *their* ministers were the letter-learned, unconverted teachers which he aimed at."[14] As, of course, they were. Soon enough, Joseph began to hear complaints that his quiet services and measured discourse no longer satisfied those of his parishioners who had acquired a taste for stronger stuff. "My soul is not fed by your preaching out of your head," he was told, and more to the same effect.[15] At last, inevitably, Davenport passed from innuendo to an open declaration that Joseph Fish must be numbered among the unconverted.

Joseph, who labored under the disadvantage of a genuine humility, and who was himself not impervious to the power of Davenport's preaching, took the verdict thus pronounced on him to heart. He wrote that he withdrew from pastoral duties for "five sabbaths" (by which he may have meant an interval of forty days and forty nights, in imitation of Christ), and his diary shows that he spent the time fasting, praying, and examining his conscience. At the end of that period, in February 1742, he found himself able to return to the church with renewed confidence in his vocation. He also found that "the zealous *exhorters*" had used his absence to promote their own manner of worship, and that they now "so filled the house with outcries, loud acclamations, prayers, praises, exhortations and voices of various kinds, that the word of God could not be heard, (many times), from the preacher's mouth."[16]

Much as he deplored these goings-on, Joseph could not immediately see a way to check them. "For want of clearer light, greater firmness, & resolution in *myself*," he acknowledged, "as well as for want of a *temper* of mind in *people* to bear it, very little was done towards purging the house of God, and clearing religion of those reproachful errors and mistakes which people had, unhappily fallen into." It was undeniable that Davenport had produced results, for 104 new communicants were added in one year. "A great draught indeed!" Joseph admitted, "but as in our Saviour's parable, *The net* (doubtless) *gathered of all kinds, good and bad.*"[17] How real were these hot, hasty conversions, and how lasting would they prove? Were they founded on a true understanding of God's word, or on a tottering pile of theological error?

Joseph examined some of his new church members on the ground of their belief, with far from satisfactory results. He then girded himself at last for "the difficult and dangerous work, of correcting the errors of . . . the . . . *children of God,* (as they called themselves . . .)" and preached a sermon in which he warned against construing outcries, ecstasies, trances, and visions as tokens of grace. "God's children, indeed, *may* have *these* things, but *these* are no evidences that they *are his children,*" he declared. An extraordinary scene ensued. "The house was fill'd with outcries *against* the preacher, or loud expressions of concern for him. He was, upon this, declared to be an *opposer* of the work of God, making the *hearts* of his children *sad* and strengthening the *hands* of the *wicked.*"[18] From that time on, the dissidents disrupted every service that he held. Women would "sit down in the broad Aisle with their knitting work in order to shew their contempt, and both men & women would cry out calling the minister a hire-

ling—a dumb dog that would not bark &c."[19] Separation
soon followed, and this time the moving force was not
convenience of access to God's house but contention within
its walls.

A former member of Joseph's church, Ephraim Clark,
completed the work that Davenport had begun. Clark, an
illiterate man with formidable powers of persuasion, proclaimed that self-ordination had endowed him with the
right to preach, and in the Stonington of 1743 he found no
difficulty in gathering a following about him. Joseph, who
would once have castigated Clark without hesitation, did
nothing for some time. Wary of inciting a rebellion against
the authority in which he no longer had perfect confidence, he felt compelled to heed the note of warning that
he heard in the rising voices of Clark's supporters. Not
until the spring of 1744 did he conclude that the Church
must discipline the man, and then he proceeded with
extreme caution.

On April 17, 1744, the Church made the moderate recommendation that Clark's "preaching without license
should be taken cognizance of." At the hearing that followed, the examiners contented themselves with the statement that Clark's conduct was not "Agreeable to ye Gospel
& . . . spirit of a Christian."[20] But if they thought that this
admonition would leave the offender contrite, they soon
discovered their mistake. Eventually they referred the matter to a special council of local ministers, preceded by a
Church meeting held in late August 1745 to which Clark,
his brothers, and their wives were summoned with a
demand that they explain their absence from communion
and worship. All the Clarks appeared except for Ephraim.
In late October the Council handed down the predictable
condemnation of his behavior, yet still the Church took no
further proceedings against him or the other would-be
separatists until they went so far toward their goal as to
compel reaction.

On September 11, 1746, two-thirds of Joseph's former
communicants met to discuss the formation of a separate

church. Joseph attended this meeting hoping to retrieve some of his former people, but whenever he attempted to speak he was drowned out by zealots shouting, "Don't hear him, don't hear him; 'tis the devil, the devil; a wolf in sheep's cloathing, don't hear him." During the two-hour meeting there were many who thus assailed him, and he later wrote that "not above *one* . . . treated me with anything of common civility, *decency,* or even with humanity."

The disrespect shown to his office, and the acquiescence in it of "*some* of the ablest heads that the separate churches then had, or have ever had since," who witnessed the scene, shocked Joseph almost as much as the act of separation itself.[21] He believed in the organization of society along familial lines and in paternal authority, originating in God and delegated by him to others, including his ministers. He believed that all persons, from heads of households to slaves, belonged within the bounds of some established family, which in turn belonged within the established church. He saw the separatists as a threat to both essential institutions, as the initiators of a train of events that would lead to "separations within separations, 'till some have separated from *all,* and sunk into a state of individuality," not a desirable state in Joseph's view. Many people, bewildered by the unaccustomed freedom to choose between one church and another, had begun to attend none; worse, they left their "*Children* and *Servants* . . . at liberty to go where they will to worship. . . . In these and many other instances of conduct, that might be mentioned, naturally resulting from the *separations,* the *order* of families as well as of churches and religious assemblies, is vilely broke, dissolved and lost," Joseph lamented. "The reins of government are thrown upon the neck, and nothing but anarchy and confusion reigns."[22]

The initial proceedings of the separatists appeared to bear him out. For a time it looked as if their determination to let spontaneity govern them in all things would keep them from taking even the first step toward a church of their own—the choice of a minister to serve them. Joseph could not forbear a certain wry satisfaction when he recorded their flounderings in the morass to which their "New Light" had led them:

> The brethren, at a meeting, appointed for the purpose, having an *impression,* that if it was the Lord's will that they should have a minister, he would shew it to them, and *reveal* the *man's* name, or shew them *the very man*. Upon *this,* one of their number, in a vision or swoon, had a revelation that he *himself* was to be their minister: but the brethren not having fellowship with him in that discovery, rejected *his* revelation, though he declared to me he knew it to be from heaven.

At the next meeting they had better success, for "under the like *impression,* in a trance or swoon, 'twas revealed to another brother, that such a man, by name was to be their minister; with which they had fellowship: and *him* they chose [and] ordain'd." But him, too, the brethren subsequently "silenc'd,—cast out of their church, and delivered up to satan, in less than a year."[23]

Nevertheless, their ability to agree on a leader at all, however fleetingly, carried the dispute to a new level, for it rendered the formation of a separate church inevitable and forced Joseph's congregation to act. On November 24, 1746, they voted to suspend Ephraim Clark from communion (in which he had long ceased to participate) until he acknowledged his errors. Then, on December 15, they voted to summon all the delinquents to come forward and give an account of themselves. Some answered; many did not. Still the church members could not bring themselves to abandon all attempts at reconciliation, and in early April 1747 they called a meeting at which they proposed to refute the arguments of those who had appeared and offered reasons for their separation, in the hope, they said, that "you may each of you return to us in Love."[24] That hope was vain. Nothing could alter the course of events now, not even the recantation of his former beliefs by James Davenport.

All but consumed by his own fiery zeal within three years of his first outburst, by 1744 he had risen from the ashes, in Joseph's words, "no longer the noisy, boisterous, rash and censorious *Davenport;* but the meek, humble, and yet the *fervent* man of God." In this changed aspect, he revisited scenes of his past triumphs, including Stonington, and confessed himself to have been deluded. What Joseph Fish wrote of his own lost sheep, however, was true of most others as well: "on the whole, they all *rejected his message.*"[25] Those of Joseph's congregation who had left him would not return. Never again would he bring more than an occasional convert into the church. For eight years after the "great draught," the net came in empty, and in 1758, when Joseph received his elder daughter into full communion, she was only the fourth to make profession since 1743.

Joseph continued to serve what remained of the Second Society because of the covenant he had made, but circumstances tried his faith in this particular too. Though his depleted congregation still accounted for seven thousand of the twelve-thousand-pound assessment of his parish, it could no longer afford generosity, and the bitter aftertaste left by months of accusation and backbiting sometimes provoked it to meanness. Several times in those years Joseph received offers from congregations able and willing to pay him more. In 1750 the call came from Little Compton, Rebecca's old home; in 1751, from Newport, Rhode Island, where they both had friends and relations. Pinched between rising prices and depreciation, on both occasions Joseph felt strongly inclined to accept, though when he sought guidance through prayer, he always emerged convinced that duty called him to remain with those who had bestowed their patronage upon his inexperienced youth. In 1756, when the Society's representatives took it upon themselves to refuse another solicitation (from New London) without consulting him at all, he expressed strong resentment of their high-handedness; but if they had asked him, he would almost certainly have refused it himself.

III

IF Joseph's congregation had disappointed him, both separatists and faithful, his daughters did not. They grew into personable young women: well-read, thoughtful, religious, handsome, and vivacious. The turbulence that rocked their father's pulpit and shook his conviction of his calling did not overwhelm the pleasantly circumscribed world of their childhood. By them the authority that tradition vested in their father was acknowledged, with love and without question. The example he had set them of honest (if not always successful) effort to obey God's law reinforced his own claim to be obeyed, while his gentleness in asserting paternal authority gave his daughters no reason to rebel. Yet he had taught them more than simple submission to his will. His passage through a great storm from which he emerged unshaken had also shown them the value of adherence to principle as a source of strength. It was a lesson that would nourish and sustain Mary's character throughout her life.

In 1751, when Mary was fifteen, Joseph took her to Newport, where she entered the school of Sarah Osborn, a well-known and respected teacher of young women. Born Sarah Hagger, she had lived in London until the age of ten. In 1722 her parents emigrated to New England, where in 1731 she married Samuel Wheaton. He died two years later, leaving her poor and wholly dependent upon her own efforts to support herself and their young son. A first attempt at earning a living as housekeeper to a scarcely known, newly emigrated brother ended upon his marriage three months later. After that Sarah sought employment without success until, one day, having prayed long and fervently, she seemed to receive an answer in the form of an unexpected call to serve as mistress of a small school. Thus began her career as a teacher.

In 1741, apparently because of ill health, Sarah closed her school. Her son was apprenticed and living away from home; she had only herself to keep, and for a few months she made ends meet by serving as an assistant in a shop. When she received a proposal of marriage from a man who was an established tradesman, a good Christian, and a congenial soul, it seemed another heaven-sent opportunity. In May 1742 Sarah married Henry Osborn, a widower with three children; but soon afterward it emerged that he was heavily in debt, and everything that he and Sarah owned was sold to pay his creditors. "From that time," according to Sarah's biographer, "he did but little or no business. . . . At the same time he had children who were poor, and wanted assistance."[26] In May 1744 Sarah began to keep school again, and kept it for thirty years to come, by that means maintaining her independence while retaining the dignity of one who labors in a worthy calling.

During the early years of the Great Awakening, Sarah had heard both George Whitefield and Gilbert Tennent preach at Newport. Whitefield "in some measure stirred me up," she allowed, but it was Tennent, with whom she had both a correspondence and a personal interview, who opened her mind to receive the full force of the revival. Moved beyond mere personal response, Sarah prayed to become herself an instrument of God's work, and sure enough "a number of young women, who were awakened to a concern for their souls, came to me, and desired my advice and assistance, and proposed to join in a society provided I would take the care of them."[27] The society was formed as proposed, and in it Sarah found her avocation. For the rest of her life she presided over its weekly meetings. Under her auspices its membership increased and was extended to include a group of young men, who met in a separate room of her house, as well as a group of blacks, both free and enslaved, of both sexes. As she grew ever more devoted to the cause she began to correspond with ministers all over New England, and among her correspondents was Joseph Fish. She was soon on visiting terms with him and his wife. He gave her the fullest account of the Davenport debacle that exists outside of his published sermons, and it may have been her church at Newport that solicited his services in the same year that she received his elder daughter at her school.

Unfortunately, though Mrs. Osborn wrote copiously on religion, she left no details of the curriculum followed by her students, but so redoubtable an example of female independence and accomplishment as she presented would surely have been an education in itself. Her life taught that a woman, no less than a man, could withstand adversity and even grow stronger by it. She reinforced the lessons of character instilled by Mary's father, and Mary regarded her with tremendous admiration and affection. In 1754, when Becca entered the school, Mary also returned, "leaving my parents in a lonely state," she observed, "but they grudged nothing for our improvement."[28]

Joseph and Rebecca did find their childless house lonely, as he acknowledged in a letter he wrote to Mrs. Osborn when he returned home after escorting the girls to Newport. "Our whole Little *Crop* is Under your Eyes," he told her, "Small Indeed, but precious to *us*."[29] Perhaps that is why an illness of their mother's, which turned out not to be serious, impelled him to bring them back before the year was out. As a result, they may have been present in the summer of 1755 when he addressed a gathering of Stonington's young men, together with their families, upon their departure to fight the French invaders at Lake George.

Long-festering hostility between the British and the French had erupted into war, so that local quarrels were for the moment forgotten. And if the snags that had recently broken the smooth surface of relations between colonies and mother country had appeared in the backwater of Stonington, they too were submerged in the common cause. In the minds of the men and women who spent

their lives in such small towns, the idea of French Cathol-
icism loomed as an unimaginable horror, a menace to all
their most cherished beliefs. In the shadow of that evil, the
distinction between church member and separatist, or
between British soldier and colonist, no longer appeared
so sharp or so important.

If Mary was indeed there, she saw many a likely young
man march away. Once they had gone, however, the war
receded with them, and her life resumed its even tenor. At
nineteen years old, Mary was an attractive young woman
with auburn hair, blue eyes, and a fair complexion. Her
memories of that year include nothing of the great battles
taking place to the north, but only the scrapes she got into
at home. She had a friend whose family had acquired a
carriage, a sensational luxury for the place and time. "In
those days we at Stonington knew but little about car-
riages," Mary wrote, "and we did not know but one horse
was as good as another to go in a carriage."[30] They took
an unfortunate animal who had hitherto known only the
plodding routine of a cider mill, hitched him up, and
stepped in. The terrified horse reared, kicked, and bolted;
both girls were thrown out, and the carriage smashed. One
would like to know what Parson Fish said to his daughter
on that occasion: at least he could not have reproached her
with idleness. She seems to have been somewhat reckless
with horses in general, for her Reminiscences record two
more riding accidents that year. Within the narrow confines of her world, these were tremendous excitements.

There was also an occasional excursion to the rich, cos-
mopolitan city of Boston, on one of which she attended
the marriage of the widowed Mr. Eells to Mary Dorrell,
herself married twice before, and apparently the product
of a more sophisticated background than that of Mary Fish.
"I was happy in the intimacy I formed with Mrs. Eells,
who instructed me in some things that respected delicacy
and elegance of economy in domestic arrangements," Mary
remembered. "These hints were very useful to me in after
life, when I had for my guests those that had received an

education like hers."[31] For Mary, that time was drawing near.

In September 1756, Mary joined the Eells family and some other neighbors named Cheseborough on an expedition to New Haven, where they planned to attend the commencement at Yale College. The Cheseboroughs were related to the minister of the First Church there, Joseph Noyes, who had been born in Stonington. His father, the Reverend James Noyes, had served the church from 1674 to 1719 and had met and married Dorothy Stanton, daughter of Thomas Stanton, an eminent interpreter of Indian languages. Joseph Noyes and his wife, Abigail, had hospitably invited the Stonington visitors to stay with them at their house on Elm Street, where they lived with only their twenty-two-year-old son John for company. Mary was subject to some predictable raillery about this eligible bachelor, and returned the customary avowal of indifference:

> When we were dressing to go to see the illumination, Mr. Eells said to me—perhaps you will see somebody this evening with whom you will spend your life; but I had then no attachment to any one there, or that I saw during the commencement.[32]

Nevertheless, in the following summer, when John escorted one of his sisters on a visit to Stonington, he took the opportunity to further his acquaintance with Mary; and before he returned home again he had made her a vow of love and a proposal of marriage.

In her Reminiscences, Mary followed her account of this event with the brief comment that she eventually accepted John because "he grew more and more amiable and agreeable to me and my friends."[33] This is undoubtedly true. It is also true that his ardor did not fire him to make an immediate approach to Mary's parents. For the moment, only two other people shared the secret: Mary's sister Becca, and John's cousin Grace Noyes, who was easily persuaded to undertake the delicious commission of receiving and passing on the letters that he began to send, clandestinely, to his "lovely Letitia."

Though John described himself as "not fond of Stuffing my Letter[s] with Protestations [and] pompious Declerations," they were for the most part the callow effusions of a youth as yet incapable of expressing love simply and directly. "How Savage that Breast! that's unsusceptable of those Soft Impressions, which in all Ages of the World, the *Virtues* & Beauties of your Lovely Sex have ever made upon the Hearts of Men," began his first letter.[34] In March 1758 he greeted the clearing of the way to Stonington, closed since early December, with the observation that "the Birds with their tunefull Notes warn me the Time is at Hand, when I should pay my Respects to the Lovely Charmer of my Soul."[35] But signs of genuine affection occasionally broke through this flowery surface, as when he supported a plain appeal to Mary for an occasional reply with the information that he had already taken the thoughtful, practical step of supplying Grace with money to pay for the postage.

In April 1758, John came again to Stonington, and somewhere about this time he and Mary at last revealed their attachment. John's parents made no objection; on the contrary, they were eager for the marriage to take place before another winter came down. Mary's parents responded with markedly less enthusiasm.

Since they admitted the mutual affection of Mary and John, the prospect of a son-in-law descended from three generations of eminent clergymen, himself an ordained minister and heir to wealth, might have been expected to please and even delight the country pastor and his wife. The one flaw that they perceived in John was a misfortune, not a fault. He suffered from epilepsy, severely enough to disqualify him for any permanent post, and certainly for the parish of his own that his abilities would otherwise have earned him. His repeated seizures had forced him to withdraw from his first appointment, that of rector of

Hopkins Grammar School in New Haven, and he had since occupied himself with occasional preaching and with modest dealings in the shipping trade. These activities did not provide him with a living, however, and he seemed likely to remain indefinitely dependent upon his parents.

Fortunately, Mr. and Mrs. Noyes had no lack of this world's goods, and of their three children John alone would need support, their daughters having gained substantial establishments through marriage. They had plenty of room in their house, as well as plenty of money to support not only John and Mary but also any children they might have. Yet even under these propitious circumstances, Mr. and Mrs. Fish displayed a deep reluctance to relinquish half their treasure. "I've often thought & said," Joseph once wrote, "that God had made us *Rich* in *Children,* tho *few* in number."[36] In August 1758, when John presented himself at Stonington with a formal proposal, a strong letter of support from his father's pen, and the free consent of the lady, Mr. Fish could find no reason to refuse, though his reply to Mr. Noyes showed a profound sense of loss. "The Request is for one of our greatest Favours, One of the most Valuable Presents that we have to make," he wrote; "you must forgive our Tears, extorted from us, by the Tender Thought, that She is no longer *Ours* (as heretofore) but *His,* whom, to fill the Gap, we now call our *Own.*"[37]

Less than eager, even so, to gain a son, Mr. Fish next procrastinated on the question of a wedding date. His first stipulation of December at the earliest brought a respectful but somewhat desperate protest from John, who elaborated so wildly upon the approaching horrors of winter that Mary could not resist the temptation to tease him about his "gloomy Apprehensions." He answered, affectionately, that he found her "merry banter" so delightful as to make him glad for what had occasioned it[38]; nevertheless, he would not abandon his argument that by December poor traveling conditions might necessitate a long postponement. Mr. Fish could not deny it, and at last he agreed that the ceremony should take place on November 16, 1758.

As the time approached for leaving her parents, and perhaps to palliate their grief, Mary performed a last act of filial piety. Her decision (noted in the church records) to make a formal profession of faith during her last few days as a member of her father's congregation may well have owed something to his influence. He would not, however, have forced her inclination, nor did he need to. Where a genuine faith already existed, no force was necessary to persuade so loving a daughter that before she departed from under his roof she should confirm the Christianity he had instilled in her. But her silence on this crucial event in her life as a Christian, and also on the subject of the conversion experience that should have preceded it, strongly suggests a spiritual condition more pliant than passionate.

Four days after she had made her first communion, Mary and John were married at her home in Stonington, probably by her father. One week later, accompanied by Becca, the pair set out for New Haven, arriving on Thanksgiving morning at the house on Elm Street to find a pleasant assembly of friends and family waiting to give them joy.

Two

UNCERTAIN
BLISS

I

THEN, as now, a newly married couple usually set up
house for themselves. Mary merely passed from one parental roof to another, but with no apparent sense of lost
opportunity. Happy and at ease in the position of daughter, she was content to retain it in her new sphere. Affection for John's father and mother followed as a matter of
course from her accustomed view of parents as kindly pro-
tectors, while she, as she serenely observed, "found favor
in their eyes, and we were mutual comforts to each other."[1]

In particular, the important relationship between
daughter and mother-in-law seemed likely to fulfill the
promise of its auspicious beginning two years before:

> I eat my meals at the Noyes [Mary wrote], and in the
> morning of Commencement Day I saw good Madame
> Noyes encumbered about many things, and, as my cus-
> tom was, whenever I was at a friend's house, I offered
> to help her; . . . she thanked me . . . and said, if I

would be so good as to put some buttons on a jacket, she would be obliged to me. This I did, and as she told me after I became her daughter, these little matters made an agreeable impression on her mind at the time.[2]

On the face of it, the incident may seem too trivial to merit notice, but such things carry more than their apparent weight when two women contemplate sharing a house.

After all, perhaps Mary did not miss the experience of taking charge as mistress over her own establishment, given the excitement inherent in the transition she had made from a small rural community to a busy seaport and college town. The Noyes household alone represented a striking change from the one she had left behind, being larger, liberally staffed with servants, more luxuriously appointed, and used to receiving as guests many of the colony's most distinguished residents, including the governor. Given so much that was new and bewildering to absorb, Mary might well have dispensed with independence more readily than she could have coped with it.

John's parents were persons of consequence in the New Haven community. Abigail Noyes was born and raised there. Her parents were the Reverend James Pierpont, who had preceded her husband as minister of the First Church, and Sarah Haynes, from whom she had received a substantial inheritance in the form of land at Hartford and Farmington. Joseph Noyes came of a family prominently associated with Yale College. His father, James Noyes, had belonged to the original board of trustees, while he himself was a Fellow of the college and had tutored there from 1710 to 1715. In 1716 Joseph Noyes played a major part in bringing Yale from its original setting at Saybrook to a permanent home at New Haven, and for the next twenty-seven years he counted the entire student body, which in due course included his son, among his congregation. Then he too had suffered the incursions of the Reverend James Davenport, heard himself denounced as unconverted, and witnessed mass departures from his congregation. For him, time brought no healing, only the wounding discovery that, even within the college whose interests he had so faithfully served, there were those who rejected his ministry as out- moded. In 1753, the year that John received his degree, Yale ended ten years of internal strife between the adherents and opponents of Mr. Noyes by setting up its own church and requiring students henceforth to worship there. Nor was this the final blow. Years of bickering followed, mostly over the legal obligation of the dissenters to continue their financial support of Mr. Noyes, and as the membership in his church diminished he was put to the humiliating neces- sity of going to law to collect his salary. In 1758 the First Church appointed the Reverend Chauncey Whittelsey as colleague-pastor with Mr. Noyes, who soon afterward vir- tually retired into private life.

Yet these vicissitudes did not diminish the social stand- ing of the Noyes family or deprive it of the consolation and cachet of wealth. Mr. Noyes possessed a flair for the entrepreneurial. According to Ezra Stiles, he parlayed an original investment of four hundred pounds into land holdings worth between four and five thousand pounds, which, added to his wife's inheritance, amounted to a property that would have conferred status even upon a newcomer. Though they had been less fortunate as par- ents, having buried four sons (three of them named Joseph) and two daughters, with John's marriage to Mary they had the satisfaction of seeing all the precious remainder securely established. Their daughter Sarah had married John Ches- ter, who was a member of a wealthy, influential Wethers- field family, a Harvard graduate, a colonel in the militia, and a judge. Their daughter Abigail had married Thomas Darling, who was a graduate of Yale, a successful New Haven merchant, a justice of the peace, and soon to be appointed a judge. Mary came from a family of compara- tively modest means, but Mr. and Mrs. Noyes did not need more money. They needed a faithful, affectionate companion for their son, and Mary was all that they could have wished. If they also hoped that she would bear him children, she pleased them in this respect too, for she was quickly pregnant.

II

THE fifty-odd miles between New Haven and Stonington, which present small problem now, made for hard traveling then. In the first few months following the marriage, bad weather, as John had predicted, kept Mary and her family cut off from one another. By the time the following spring had advanced far enough to clear the way, the pressure of work in the fields kept Mr. and Mrs. Fish from leaving home to visit Mary, whereas she was afraid to risk the journey to Stonington during the early stages of her first pregnancy. In June she did venture forth and returned none the worse, though carrying "a heavy load in my heart" at parting.[3] However kind John's parents, the separation from her own seemed harder in the face of her coming encounter with pain and danger.

In August of 1759, Mr. and Mrs. Fish shipped their daughter a quantity of furniture, linens, books, and other household effects, some of them former possessions, but the majority either new home manufactures or special purchases that they had made in Boston. These goods were probably intended to serve as a substitute in kind for the cash dowry they could not afford to bestow. Mr. Fish, who packed the chests, preceded the shipment with a letter in which he listed the contents right down to "1 ounce or 2 of Sewing Silk, Green" and supplied layer-by-layer instructions on the unpacking, concluding with an admonition to "be Carefull in Taking out the wool [raw wool used as packing] lest the small vessels, wh. are Dispersed through the Whole, should hang to it, & Receive Damage."[4] The loving detail of both list and instructions vividly conveys the preciousness of the homeliest articles in the days before mass production made so many of them cheap.

Better still, Mary's sister spent several weeks with her, the first of many happy summer visits; best of all, in early November, when Becca went home, Mrs. Fish took her place. She had come to attend her daughter's first confinement in spite of the danger that an early winter storm could have detained her at New Haven, no small sacrifice on the part of herself and her husband, whose anxious letters made his dependence upon her help abundantly clear. They took the risk for Mary's sake, and events gave them no cause for regret. On November 22, 1759, with a son-in-law beside her who had forever endeared himself by sharing in her attendance on Mary's unexpectedly long and difficult labor, Rebecca Fish held a namesake in her arms. Though Mary's robust constitution had barely carried her through, in John's words, "the Horrors of that Night,"[5] her customary good health reasserted itself in time for her mother to return home before the curtain of winter once more descended between the two households.

Early in 1760, impatient to display little Rebecca to the rest of her family and friends at Stonington, Mary seized on the first opportunity presented. Her father had been chosen to preach the election sermon on May 8, and John escorted her, with the child, to Hartford, where Mr. Fish would meet and carry them back with him. Mr. Fish had preached on the recent victory at Quebec and the institution of Protestant worship in Canada "where Saints & Images had been long adored," a happy occasion made happier still for him by the praise bestowed on his address.[6] Therefore, it was in an atmosphere of rejoicing both public and private that he returned home bearing with him his daughter and granddaughter. For two leisurely summer months, the small circle at Stonington was again to be complete.

Mary never forgot the meeting of the three Rebeccas. Years later, she recorded it in her Reminiscences with an immediacy that shows time had not smoothed the sharp edge of this memory:

> My dear mother was in raptures to see us arrive with the dear babe and said, "this is just as I would have it!" My dear sister, seeing my mother so much elated, said, "take care my dear mother, this is all uncertain bliss, and may soon be changed." I have often heard my mother reflect on herself that she was so stupid at the time as never to have once thought that the babe was mortal.[7]

That night, when Mary went to bed in the old room with her sister and her child, she fell asleep at once, tired from the journey. Becca lay awake, a prey to feelings of "unaccountable anxiety" that were too soon accounted for. At about midnight, Mary woke to find the baby in a burning fever. She summoned the doctor at once and in the morning sent an urgent summons to John. In those days the post was unreliable, the urgency of a message more a matter of feeling than a matter of fact, and Mary had still heard nothing from her husband when the child died, just four days after the homecoming that had promised such joy.

Though they kept the little body for three days, John neither came nor sent word; but when the weary, sorrowful family returned from the graveside, he received them at the door. "The calm, resigned frame in which we found him," Mary wrote, "shewed us that the Lord was with him and supporting him. We endeavoured to follow his example." Nevertheless, she had no heart to continue the visit as planned, and when John returned to New Haven Mary went with him.

In the days to come, she found the effort to follow John's example a fierce and bitter struggle. Never before having lost anyone so close and dear, she felt, she said, "like a bullock unaccustomed to the yoke." The culture that had bred her discouraged exhibitions of emotion and asked of the bereaved that they submit to God's will without com-

plaint, thus affirming their faith in his promise that the
dead had passed from this world to a better. Even as she
had followed her baby's coffin, her father had reminded
her of this. "These are melancholy steps," he said, "but the
path of glory leads through the grave, and it is well worth
while to undergo the pains of bearing and of parting with
children if thereby we people the redeemer's kingdom, for
of such does his kingdom consist, as he assured us when he
was here upon earth."

Mr. Fish was far from unfeeling, but he did less well
than he intended when he urged his stricken daughter to
suppress her sorrow. Death had carried off her firstborn
while it was still nursing at the breast, wrenching awry the
daily pattern of her life for some months past; yet she was
told not so much to solace her grief with hope as to deny
it altogether. The religion which ought to have replen-
ished her was presented as a demand she lacked the means
to meet. With the best intentions, and surely in the gen-
tlest manner, it was suggested to Mary that mourning for
her dead child implied the failure of her faith in the Resurrection. "Blessed are they that mourn, for they shall be
comforted" was a forgotten text, and it became almost
shameful for her to feel and show natural sorrow.

III

THIS time no great harm was done. Though Mary returned
to New Haven with empty arms, she returned to the
understanding companionship of a woman who knew what
it was to lose a child. Her young husband, too, though he
continued to strive for acceptance, openly shared her pain
at the death of the infant as he had shared it when she gave
birth. For him as for her, "every Object here brings to Mind
the Dear Child and renews our Grief," a grief that
demanded and justified release in tears. "We must have
Sunk beneath the Animal Creation," wrote John, "if we
don't feel the Pangs of breaking such a tender tie."[8]

The greatest sufferer on this occasion may have been Mrs. Fish. Beset by anxiety for Mary as well as by sorrow for the child, and perhaps restrained by her husband's wishes from indulging either as nature required, she sank into melancholy. In an August letter, Mr. Fish gave a description of her condition that suggests what modern medicine would term severe depression:

> Her pained Head & Mental Dejection is sometimes so heavy upon her that in a morning she can scarce recover spirit enough to undertake, or even look thro the Business of the Day. Although she is not unmindfule of those Comforts that are with her, yet she can't help pining after her Absent Child. Dear Molly! Dear Molly! is the frequent Expression of her Grief & tender Feeling for a Distant Object almost too deeply planted in a Mother's Breast to live without her. I think it is high time for her to leave her Business a little, & take the Air. We are meditating a Journey soon—& which way should she set her Face but towd. *N.Haven?*[9]

A week later, however, Mrs. Fish put off her visit. Heavy rain had prevented her husband from finishing his haying and harvesting, and she saw that, unless she returned to full partnership in the household, he would lose his year's labor. That recognition, together with a reassuring letter from Mary, ministered effectively to her ailment. In September, when Mr. Fish took Becca to New Haven for commencement, she cheerfully remained behind to oversee the work of house and farm.

The new year brought new life. With the cessation of the natural birth control that breastfeeding had provided, quite soon after her return to Elm Street Mary rejoiced, though with trembling, in the knowledge that she was again pregnant. Joseph Noyes (called Jose within the family) was born on February 14, 1761, but "with different eyes did I look on him," Mary remembered. "I always viewed him as mortal, and mine no longer than God was pleased to lend him, and every night I felt thankful that he was alive." These exercises heightened her sense of present happiness and hope, and the death in June of Joseph Noyes the elder, at the age of seventy-three, cast no more than a passing shadow on the bright days of that pleasant summer.

Though John dutifully remarked to Mary that "it seemed as if a stately oak had fallen, and a feeble sprout stood in the same place" [10] (by which he meant himself), in fact his father's death caused neither of them the conflict between passionate grief and required resignation that the death of their baby had raised. An old man had met a seasonable end, while their young son, though delicate, survived; and before long a third child was on the way. On August 27, 1762, Mary gave birth to a second son, John, a large and sturdy boy from the beginning.

In the same year, Becca, who had continued to make frequent visits to New Haven, received a proposal of marriage from Benjamin Douglas, a lawyer in that city. Benjamin, third son of Colonel John Douglas of Plainfield, had entered Yale in the class of 1760. During his student years he formed a friendship with John and Mary, which led in time to an acquaintance with Becca. She liked him, her parents were persuaded to consent, wedding preparations were made, and the sisters looked forward to reunion as neighbors. Then, in October 1762, Benjamin gave offense. Through a misunderstanding, he had had the banns called sooner than Becca or her parents had expected, and this, added to an afternoon when he had maintained, as they perceived it, a cold, proud silence in Becca's presence, gave rise to what Joseph termed a "Foreboding of future Sovereignty." [11]

The phrase may seem quaint, but the objection was serious. The legal subordination of women to men in the matrimonial relationship made it impossible, in the event of mistreatment, for parents to defend their daughters in the courts, and the proposed marriage would take Becca far enough from home to render personal intervention dif-

ficult. This had also been true of Mary's marriage, but her
prospective husband and father-in-law had both belonged
to the same inner circle of college-educated Congregational ministers as did Mr. Fish, and he had felt that he
could, if necessary, bring informal pressure to bear upon
them through mutual connections in the clergy. With Colonel Douglas and Benjamin, he would not have that
recourse.

His investigations of Benjamin's character, furthermore,
had not satisfied him. John and Mary had spoken highly
of their friend, but one informant said he was a Freema-
son, a brotherhood of which Mr. Fish disapproved, while
another labeled him a rake. The second of these charges
John dismissed without hesitation; the first he acknowledged as true, but pointed out that, in the opinion of many
respectable people, while Masonry might be superfluous
in a Christian society, it was not necessarily atheistic. As
an affectionate brother-in-law who would see the results
of Becca's marriage at close quarters and feel his responsibility should she prove unhappy, John had then been able
to reassure her parents. Now, their doubt sprang up afresh.

Last, there was the vulnerability of Becca herself. As Mr.
Fish described her, she had neither the constitution nor
the character to weather harsh treatment, being frail and
oversensitive. He and his wife had always demonstrated
even stronger protective feelings toward her than toward
Mary, and so they were especially alarmed by any hint of
arrogance on Benjamin's part. Once before, when Becca
had fixed her affection on someone they distrusted, they
had used their influence with her to oppose the attachment; on that occasion "her returns were answerably
Tender & yielding,"[12] and they stood ready to invoke
their power again if they saw fit. The letter demanding
satisfaction on the point of "sovereignty" came, signifi-
cantly, not from Becca herself but from her parents, and
Benjamin addressed his reply accordingly.

He had honestly believed, he said, that he and Becca

were agreed upon their wedding date. "We either did not Discourse so particularly as I have imagined," he wrote, "or her excessive Modesty forbids her to say the discourse we had."[13] Except for the gentle criticism implied in the word "excessive," his letter breathed contrition and produced his restoration to favor. But if he had hoped to bring a wife home to his house following his admission to the bar in November, he was to be disappointed.

By then, Becca had fallen seriously ill, and Benjamin's actions in the light of that fact may have done more to reassure her parents than the words of his apology. He paid her every attention possible given the distance, and on January 24, 1763, during one of his frequent visits to Stonington, he married her, though she was still too weak to remove to New Haven when his professional affairs called him back. The exact circumstances of the wedding are obscure, but it was clearly a sudden decision. John Noyes had accompanied Benjamin on the journey, and his announcement of the event upon return took Mary by surprise. From the letter she afterward sent her parents, in which she rejoiced with them at "the melancholy scene's so soon changing from extreme sorrow and distress to gladness and rejoycing," it would appear that she had expected, rather, news of a funeral. "I was much suppriz'd to see Mr. Noyes returne so soon," Mary wrote, but "much more so to here Him tell the many agreables that past while He was with you. Is my dear Sister alive? recouvering? and is she indeed married?"[14]

For many weeks to come, the patient Benjamin, as often as he could, rode back and forth over the wearying miles between his bride at Stonington and his business at New Haven, and on each of these occasions he carried letters between the sisters. Those which Mary wrote to Becca during this period are the best of the few examples of correspondence between them to have survived. They illuminate the relationship of the two young women as a flash of lightning illuminates: briefly, but with an astonishing clarity. Mary's tone toward Becca struck a note of playfulness reminiscent of the days when they were little girls together, blended with the occasional assumption of an important, older-sister air, like one whose longer experience as a wife has conferred the right to give advice. She shifted with perfect unselfconsciousness from teasing and gossip to discourse on the soul. On March 21, 1763, she wrote:

> My Dearest Sister, I am much oblig'd to you for your agreable Favour Pr. your other Self. And before I say a word more I must tell you He is now in the other Room.—But now you will ask and pray why do you leave Him to retire to convirce even with Me. Well I'll tell you, thers with Him the Gent. from Coledge. So that we cant have a word on our Darling Theme. you that know how well we Love you can easily Imagine what that is. . . . I trust you have fix'd on good and soled [solid] principles the Baces of rising esteem. And now I am sure your good sence will suggest and your Inclinations fall in with this which may be set down as a maxim, That a mutual desire of pleasing and being Pleas'd will render you desirable and make you happy in each other.

She next described, with evident enjoyment, a recent fashionable wedding and evening reception that she and John had attended. Then, with the brisk dismissal "So much for weding," she went on:

> Each passage of your dear Letter was very agreable but none equal to the observation you make that this Sickness has been a mercifull dispensation to your Precious Soul. Pray God accomplish what ever may be yet lacking. may you be a shining Example in Piety and Domestick Life that you may be an Honour to religion, [to] Our dear Parents who have been so unwearied in their good Counsels, To your Husband who is deserving your

Love and esteem, and to all your Friends to whome you
are so dear is the earnest Prayer of your most Affectionate Sister Mary Noyes.[15]

The "mercifull dispensation" to which Mary alluded was
Becca's conversion through a sudden sense of grace she
had experienced as she began to recover. In February, soon
after Becca's marriage, Mary had congratulated her parents
on the prospect of "my dear Sisters performing Her Vows
in the House of the Lord in that she publickly Avouches
the Lord Jehovah to be her God who has snatch'd Her
from the devouring Grave."[16] Becca was to make her
profession in April, but when the time came she hung back.
Mary had gone to service on the day appointed, and she
later wrote "I remembred you my dr. Sister at the Lords
table and pleas'd my self with the thought that it was likly
you were that day making a publick profession and performing your vows that you made in your distress. But as
our Hond. parents are silent about it in their's to me, conclude it was still omited. how is it with you my dear? are
you again sunk into the dark?"[17] Happily, if she was, it was
a brief declension. Six weeks later, on June 5, 1763, the Second Society of North Stonington recorded Becca's admission to full communion in the Church.

Becca's removal to New Haven followed soon after, to
Mary's joy. "Sister and I visit each other almost every day,"
Becca told her parents, "and are very happy together."[18]
Since their husbands were close friends already, and Becca's lively wit had won John's heart long before, all four
young people now entered upon a warm, satisfying relationship. For Mr. and Mrs. Fish, on the other hand, though
they were glad to have their daughters near each other, the
thought of them both so far away made the parsonage seem
desolate. The presence of servants and slaves was no compensation for the loss of the intimate companionship that
had existed between them and their children. Yet when
John and Mary offered to ease their adjustment by sending
down two-year-old Jose for the summer, to "divert you a

little in your lonely house . . . [and] to take the place as it were of your own dear little Son departed who if living would have been your support when your daughters had remov'd their habitations," they were surprisingly unwilling.

"I know your reasons for hesitating in the affair are weighty," Mary replied, "Tho that one you offer (that his conveniences with you wont be good) has not given me any concern."[19] What were the unwritten reasons she implied she understood? The most obvious was a fear of the past repeating itself. One grandchild had died in their house. They could not bear to risk it happening again, especially with themselves in sole charge, as Mary and John proposed. Mary herself lived always in the shadow of that moment when her childhood home became her baby's tomb. On the first visit that she and John had made to Stonington after the birth of Jose, a fragile baby, they had gone without him even though this meant the employment of a wet nurse. And their pleas for the Fishes not to suppose "that [the memory of] our leaving behind us at Stonington a pleasant Child on a former visit, Deters us from coming down with Our present Blessing"[20] would tend more to raise than to allay that suspicion. Even with the first loss three years behind her, as Mary set forth plans to make a brief expedition with her husband and the baby John, she added a prayer that "the Lord be gracious unto us and suffer the precious little one to live" and a confession that she had the "wormwood and gaul . . . still in remembrance."[21] It is not likely that her parents' memories were less vivid, or their apprehension less keen.

Pressure of work may have contributed to their hesitation over adding the care of a two-year-old boy to their other responsibilities. Mr. Fish was in the midst of an attempt to mount a revival, prompted perhaps by the hope that the separatists of fifteen years ago had grown disillusioned and would now be ready to hear his call and return to the fold. His efforts had begun in 1761, when, as he informed Mrs. Osborn, "I have been all the summer

Engaged in setting forward a *Reformation* Among my People. To Effect which I have been leading of them to *Renew Covenant,* & am like to Accomplish it, at the Expense of much writing & Conversation . . . what takes much of my Time, & wears me, I think, the most of all, Is *Visiting Every house,* Catechizing, Instructing & Exhorting the Children, youth & Servts. with a particular & solemn Address to the Parents & Heads of every Family."²² Church records do not show that any overwhelming surge of new members ensued, but he persisted in the face of all discouragement, including some from the pen of his elder daughter.

"Must you spend the remainder of your days among those that have no appetite for spiritual food tho' daintys are set before them?" asked Mary, with uncharacteristic belligerence, in a letter of March 27, 1763, "[and] is their no other way to open their Eyes and ears, but the sight of an empty Desk or some other Man of God to administer there?" She admired the "noble example" her parents set her "in your patiense, in your resignation in your faith, in that you'r content yet to suffer by the gainsaying and perverse among whom—You, Sir have spent so much of your strength for nought." She had also come to question it. Five years in a sophisticated, urban environment had taught her that there were easier and more rewarding livings to be had, and she could not forbear wishing that her father "were remov'd into some other part of Gods vineyard" where he might "be much happier." Nevertheless, knowing that he would probably disapprove of such worldly sentiments, she hastened to promise that she would "strive to hush every uneasy thought and dwell on this quieting one, that the Lord reigns and will order all for the best, and . . . [so] be comforted and with you wait on God."²³

These dissatisfactions aside, the summer of 1763 was glorious. The long war with France had ended in victory for Britain and her colonies, and on both sides of the Atlantic the people celebrated a triumph. For the mother country, it was just one more confirmation of her long-established power. For the Americans—and it was during this war that they began to call themselves Americans rather than colonists—it was the source of a new self-confidence. No longer the mere inheritors of a land won by others, they had proved their right of possession by their courage and competence in defending it. Though the British officers had often shown contempt for the colonials they led, the men themselves knew that they had rendered indispensable service. The insults rankled, of course, and returning soldiers had stories of British arrogance to tell that angered their hearers at home, where attempts to assert the imperial power continued to annoy. For the most part, however, Americans felt more pride in being part of a conquering empire than resentment of past wrongs, which, in any case, a grateful mother England would surely now redress.

The two young couples undoubtedly attended many a public celebration of the victory, happy in each other's company. If only happiness had brought health, 1763 would have been a perfect year for them. But with the autumn came a return of illness to Becca, and a serious deterioration in John's already poor condition. Becca became a prey to what her father called "violent fitts," never more precisely described, though he said that at one point she teetered on the edge of a plunge into madness. In this extremity Benjamin again proved the sincerity of his earlier vows; Becca praised him to her parents as "unwearied in his care and tenderness of me," and by the end of the year she was restored in mind and body.[24]

John Noyes was not so fortunate. The epilepsy that had plagued him since childhood had grown worse. "Those fits, so distressing to him, kept me always in an anxious state, for they would come upon him without any warning," Mary remembered. "Sometimes he would be taken in a fit when he was at prayer in the family, and we had to run to support him, or he would have fallen down. He would then sit a little while in his chair, and, what was

very remarkable, he would when he came out of his fit rise
& begin where he left off and finish his prayer with propriety."[25] In later life, she could speak of these episodes
with a certain detachment; at the time, as one letter to her
parents shows, they terrified her. Even so, John continued
to give Mary sexual companionship, to judge from the regularity with which the children came. On August 4, 1764,
she gave birth to a third son, James, and in the summer of
1766 she was again blessed with a daughter, this time named
for herself.

Mary was now the mother of four living children, the
eldest barely five. In addition, John's inexorable decline left
him increasingly dependent on her care, but she had many
hands to help. Madam Noyes kept a sufficient number of
servants to free her daughter-in-law from all concern with
the kitchen, while she herself, as an ever-present grandmother with no husband to claim a share of her time, could
lavish attention on the children. Becca and Benjamin, still
childless after three years of marriage, played uncle and
aunt with all their hearts. Mrs. Fish spun, wove, and sewed
diligently to keep the children well supplied with clothing,
besides which she and her husband, as grandparents without daily access, would take them almost completely off
Mary's hands whenever they made or received a visit. Mrs.
Fish spent more than two months with her daughter following the birth of little Mary, though her husband found
it harder than ever to do without her. Now her absence
not only added to his burdens but increased his loneliness.

That penalty of age was about to be remitted. In mid-
July, when Mr. Fish went to fetch his wife home, he carried young Jose, now five years old, back to Stonington as
well. Once more, the parsonage received a child within its
walls; once more, Joseph and Rebecca Fish entered upon
the tasks of teaching and nurturing. Time and the addition
to the family of four healthy children, three of whom had
already passed beyond infancy, had removed the specter of
fear that had haunted Mary and her parents since the death

of her first baby and left the way clear for Jose to begin his education where his mother's had begun.

IV

ON a Saturday evening in the summer of 1766 John received a request for his services that he found as welcome as it was unexpected. Twenty years before, the dissidents who separated from his father's congregation had formed a new one, now under a Mr. Samuel Bird. On this particular evening some of Mr. Bird's parishioners paid John a visit. Mr. Bird had been called away quite suddenly, and his congregation, having first endeavored to find someone else, came as a last resort to John with a request for his temporary services. When the men had gone, his mother asked in amazement, "Are you going to preach there, my son!" "Yes, madam," he replied, adding, with gentle irony, "There are no people too bad to be preached to."

Mary did not share Madam Noyes's feeling of affront. She considered that the episode illustrated John at his best, "unfluctuating in principle, but no bigot." Though another fifty years would pass before the two societies achieved full reconciliation, John saw at once that his demonstration of Christian forbearance had encouraged both sides at least to close the chapter of active antagonism between them. "That event always affected his catholic mind with uncommon satisfaction," wrote Benjamin Douglas of his friend and brother-in-law.[26] It was the last time John preached. A short time after, when he had been more ill than usual, his doctor ordered him to give up the ministry entirely. "Oh! must I quit this delightful work!" was his sad response. He had long abandoned hope of settling in a parish, but to be denied even the occasional practice of his calling sank his spirits low indeed.

One day later that summer, after the doctor had made a visit, he took Mary aside and told her that John's fits had brought on a consumption that had progressed so rapidly that he would not live through the autumn. Mary wrote in her Reminiscences:

> This was a dagger to my heart. I had been manufactur-
> ing some linen for him with which he had been pleased,
> and in the evening I went to bring it in from out of
> doors. But how sad did everything look; it seemed as if
> the Glory was departed from this world as I feared that
> my other self was a-going to leave it, for with him will
> expire my happiness. While I was immersed in these
> gloomy apprehensions, it seemed as if I was asked, what
> I would think of my children, if I thought it best to take
> away something they valued among their playthings, if
> they should be angry and should throw by all the rest
> and say they would have nothing to do with them.
> Should I not think them undutiful children and that
> they needed the rod? This silenced my murmurs, and I
> resolved to enjoy my husband's company with thank-
> fulness while I had it, and endeavour to exhibit a cheer-
> ful countenance; which I did, and every night felt
> thankful that he was loaned to me another day.[27]

Contrary to the doctor's expectation, John did live through the autumn. He was alive in December, to share sorrow with Mary one last time. In November, soon after Becca returned from a pleasant holiday at Stonington, a brother of Benjamin's had arrived to stay with the Douglases. Just back from a sea voyage, he brought with him a Negro servant boy who soon afterward fell ill with smallpox. The first symptom to appear in Becca was a sick headache, cause for concern, but not necessarily a sign that she had taken the disease. Nevertheless, "we think proper for me to Diet," she told her parents, "which I do so effectually that I am almost Faint by turns. I find myself more calm on this Occasion than I ever before thought I should be. Don't distress yourselves, my Dear Parents, about me. I am in the hand of a good and kind God."[28]

The news spread quickly through the community at Stonington. At the time, it was not unusual for a person to open a letter addressed to someone else if he thought it might contain news of general interest. Mr. Eells, pastor of the First Church East, had heard of Becca's illness, and so, when a letter from John passed through his hands, he read it and wrote some words of sympathy on the paper before he sent it on. The contents called for sympathy. Mr. and Mrs. Fish had earlier allowed themselves to receive reassurance, first from Becca's own letter, and second from the opinion of a doctor, passed on to them, that the sick child had left the Douglas house before his illness became communicable. John's letter, which described her symptoms so plainly as to allow no room for further self-delusion, "left us broken-hearted," wrote Mr. Fish. He reproached himself for surrendering to the charm of false comfort, which had caused him to put off answering Becca in the expectation that better news would arrive at any moment:

> It grieves me to reflect that I did not *write her,* perhaps my last advice, to excite, encourage & strengthen her, by the next Post (as I was about to do, but thought I'd wait the next still), that we might have exchanged Another pledge of mutual Affection—But so it is! I must be silent! . . . But O! who can tell our sorrows! *Others* may *hear, see* & *imagine,* but *Parents only can feel* the *Arrows* that are levelled at their *Child!*[29]

For a week after this exchange the unhappy parents grieved, prayed, and waited for word that never came. On December 12, Mr. Fish was called to perform a marriage. "Just as I finished the service, the Letter was put into my hand," he told Mary. "But oh, the Seal!—Expected, or greatly feard, yet beyond Conception sinking!—I said to my Friend, there is Death! With an aching heart and trembling hand, I opend, and found it so—Upon my Return with the News, my Silent Steps & Soft Approach to the Door a little prepared the mind of your Dear Trembling Mother. . . . She was Dumb, and opend not her mouth in any unchristian complaints. We slept but little."[30]

The letter put into his hand had come from Benjamin Douglas and began:

> Reverend Sir, God in his Righteous providence.—Oh, my rising heart, impatient of a due resignation to his will. How Insufficient for the struggles of nature. But God give me fortitude and patience to submit. Infinite wisdom has at one blow suddenly bereived you of a dear and dutifull daughter and me of a most tender and affectionate wife. Becca, so near to each of our hearts, *is no more*.

Benjamin, too, had clung to the hope that his brother's servant had not infected her, up to the moment when "we discovered the fatal Pock which now began to rise in her face." In a populous city like New Haven, the doctor who made such a discovery had no choice but to order the patient's removal to the pesthouse. Though pesthouses were often dirty and rat-ridden, friends who inspected the New Haven house assured Benjamin that it had been cleaned and repaired only the week before. Nevertheless, for fear that the mere mention of the place would strike terror into her heart, he told Becca that she was going to a farmhouse in the country. She knew the nature of her illness, but felt so sure of recovery as to worry about scars, and to ask that her parents receive no further reports until they could be told that she was out of danger. That moment never came.

For the last time Benjamin showed himself worthy of the trust Becca's parents had reposed in him. As death approached, he remained steadfast at his post beside her bed. "She was never easy when I was out of her sight, saying, wher is my dear Husband? . . . don't leave me, my dear—which she repeated hundreds of times," he recollected. After agonies of pain, vomiting, and diarrhea, she slipped into unconsciousness, a state that, under the circumstances, most people today would term a blessing. Not so then: "I could not be easy without attempting to make her in some measure sensible of her danger," Benjamin wrote. "I awoke her and asked her if she did not [know] that she was on the very verge of Eternity. And was obliged to use more forcible expressions, shaking her at the same time before she would seem to regard it. At length, as waking from sleep in an air of supprise, she said, 'Am I dieing, my dear?' " She asked the nurse for a pinch of snuff to help keep her conscious while her husband prayed. "When I had ended," he told Joseph, "she calld me to her opening her arms and embraced me with a tenderness not to be expressed, and after saying a few endearing words, she put her hands in a decent posture of supplication, and distinctly uttered a prayer worthy to be engraved in letters of Gold." She comforted him, and added to her prayers a petition that God would send him another loving companion. Then she slept. On waking, she blessed him, commended her soul to God, and, after a short, brutal bout with "most shocking pain," died at seven in the morning of December 8. Benjamin obtained permission to bury her within the city limits provided the coffin was "Well secured by tar," and at eleven o'clock that night Becca's tainted remains were huddled into the earth.[31] Such was the fear of smallpox that not even a sealed coffin could make her body safe to pass through the daylight streets where the living walked.

All this time Mary had fretted and chafed under her inability to perform the least service for her sister. She had no immunity to smallpox and could not go to Becca's side without risking a life on which five people, a dying man and four young children, depended for their care. Her exclusion from the deathbed and the poignant knowledge that Becca's final agonies had taken place within the walls of an institution rather than in her own room, surrounded by familiar things and familiar faces, were experiences less common in the eighteenth century than in our own time. Mary dared not even attend the burial. She sat beside the

fire with John, listening to the solemn tolling of the funeral
bell and waiting for the night to pass.

   In the early hours of the following morning, having first
changed his clothes and bathed, Benjamin came to them.
As Mary absorbed his account of Becca's last moments, she
blessed him for all his attentions, but above all for having
forced the dying girl to wake from peaceful sleep so that
she might prepare her soul. "This was a balm to my
wounded heart," she wrote, "for the night before her death
I heard that she was senseless; and although if she had died
in that condition I should have had reason to think she
was saved, yet we wish for ourselves and our friends that
we may have our senses in a dying hour."[32] The power to
pray was worth any suffering entailed in restoration to
consciousness. Bodily ills were transitory, the good of the
soul an eternal good, and the condition of the soul most
surely determined on the threshold of death.

V

BENJAMIN remained at the Noyes house for the time
being, an arrangement that Mr. and Mrs. Fish approved as
better for him than mourning in a solitary house. For their
own part, they were thankful for the presence of Jose. Caring for the child, teaching him, and comforting him helped
them find comfort themselves. They did sometimes feel
that, making all due allowance for Jose's tender years, he
had on occasion expressed "such Ardent Love for you [all],
especially his Mamma, that we are a little concerned [lest?]
his Affection should overcome his Manhood," Mr. Fish
told Mary, a rather strong criticism (if gently worded) to
come from two firm believers in the value of the tie between
parent and child.[33] On the other hand, Jose also showed a
proper boy's relish for seeing the year-round work on a
farm, as well as applying himself to his lessons about as
much as might be expected at his age. "Dear Jose is very
well, active & busie as the day is long," his grandfather

reported. "Go's out with me night & morning to tend Creatures . . . reads very handsomely in his Bible, except when a little careless—studies his Catechism (generally) every day—has learned to recite, with a good deal of readiness, as far as the Fifth Commandment—Could soon get through, but we are afraid of burthening his Memory, by crowding too full—he has also learned a number of excellent hymns from Dr. Watts."[34]

Besides Jose, Mr. Fish had his writing to solace him. He was preparing a set of sermons for publication and had begun writing a memorial to Becca. Benjamin, who was composing an epitaph, asked his advice on style, and received the best. "I fear the *Language,* tho indeed *Poetical,* is too *high* to be Instructive to *Common* Readers," Mr. Fish commented; " *'Whom gentle Hymen's Lure'* I'm apt to think is speaking in an Unknown Tongue to the Unlearned. I should think it best to keep as near as you can to plain Scripture Language, which cannot be mended."[35] His own sermons, when they appeared in print, showed this principle in practice, and his work on them proved salutary, for by March he had achieved a measure of the resignation he prized. "[I] think I can as heartily bless god for the Gift . . . now it is *gone,* as when it was present with us," he told Mary, adding, with insight and honesty, "at least, I can *rationally* do it."[36]

Mary's labors had less restorative power. John's illness had reached a stage that necessitated constant attention to him; though Madam Noyes did all she could, since she was over seventy the greater burden rested on the younger woman. Unable to lend more practical help while the winter lasted, Mr. Fish directed a steady stream of advice toward New Haven. From "old Doctor Gray (Florid & active at 70 e'en as a young man of 30)" he had heard of "the, almost, unfailing success of a *Milk Diet* & Constant *Riding* on Horse Back"; from a former epileptic, of the miracle cure wrought in his case by "Taking the *Filings* of *Pewter.*"[37] But Mary knew that John was past remedy, and that summer, when Mr. Fish brought Jose home to New

Haven, he too saw to his sorrow that "every Visit now Appears, more likely than ever, the *Last*."[38]

Though John had already lived almost a year beyond the time when the doctor had predicted his death, Mary felt that he would not live much longer. She balked, however, at performing that duty for which she had commended Becca's husband:

> I could not talk to him of his approaching dissolution as I feared it would sink his spirits, but one day he was more ill than common, and as I was sitting by him I was overcome, and hid my face behind the curtain to conceal my tears, but he, perceiving it, said, don't weep, my dear. I do not doubt your affection for me, but if my friends look sorrowfull, I shall go the sooner, as it will grieve me. . . . I then asked him if he could leave me and our dear children with god; he said, yes, he will be a husband and a father.

She had begun to approach the limit of her physical endurance and "anticipated the time with sorrow when I feared I must go and leave him a part of the night with watchers, but as God ordered it, I did for him to the very last." At about midday on November 5, 1767, while Mary was helping him to lie down, John said "that his breath grew shorter and shorter, and that he had almost done breathing." Composedly, he made arrangements for his mother to be fetched home from Wethersfield, where she had gone to visit his sister, and sent for Mr. Whittelsey, who prayed with him and asked him "if his hope stood firm." He answered that it did. "These were his last words," wrote Mary; "soon after, he threw himself back and expired as one falling into a calm sleep. Thus died that dear, good man."[39]

Three

IN THE
VALLEY

WHEN the family returned from the funeral, it was five-
year-old Johnny who, with a child's directness, put Mary's
thoughts into words. "What shall we do?" he demanded.
"We have no father now. Shan't we send and ask Grandfather Fish if he will come and take care of us?"[1] Mary,
who would have liked nothing better, knew that it was not
as simple as Johnny supposed for Mr. Fish to set aside his
responsibilities at Stonington and rush to assume fresh
ones. As it happened, however, he was already on his way,
and arrived shortly afterward. Having heard that the end
was imminent, he had come of his own accord both to
comfort his daughter and to inquire how she was left.
Nevertheless, he dared not tarry for fear that ice would
clog the river and prevent his return. In a few days he was
gone again. Yet Mary was not alone: she had the companionship of Madam Noyes, no stranger to bereavement; and
when the initial shock of John's death faded only to reveal
a vast new range of tasks a widow must surmount, Mary

found in the older woman a guide who had traversed that territory too.

I

SINCE John had died intestate, the probate court appointed Mary his executrix. Under the laws of the colony, she had first to post bond for the honest and equitable settlement of the estate and then to arrange an impartial appraisal of the assets. After she had paid John's funeral expenses and reimbursed the appraisers, her next task was to notify all of John's creditors to file their claims. They had two years in which to do this, and only after all legitimate demands had been met could the remainder be distributed. Mary would receive a life interest in a third of the lands and an absolute interest in a third of the chattels. The rest would go to the children, with Joseph, as the eldest, receiving a double share.

"I was left under circumstances comparatively comfortable, but the estate of my children lay principally in land & afforded me no immediate profit,"[2] Mary wrote, a statement amplified by the four-page inventory of John's assets in the probate records of the state library at Hartford. Of the £2,182 14s. 5d.* he had left, £2,015.10.0 was in land. Not until 1783 would the Fairfield County Court approve distribution of what remained after all of Mary's charges had been paid, and not until 1788 would the final settlement take place. Most of the expenses she recorded were incurred within a year of John's death, such as the £1.13.9 she paid for his coffin. Otherwise, except for a composite charge of £27.17.9¾. "To finding Cloathing for Jos. Noyes, John Noyes & James Noyes from the first of Decm. 1767 [to May 1775] . . . & for Mary Noyes Jun.," her major disbursements were made to John's creditors.[3] His largest

* £2,182 14s. 5d. indicates 2,182 pounds, 14 shillings, and 5 pence, hereafter noted as £2,182.14.5.

outstanding debt at the time of his death was the £25.0.3 owed to his doctor.

Though John's personal property would have covered the expenses incurred in settling the estate, Mary was undoubtedly advised by Madam Noyes and Benjamin Douglas not to waste her dower right by consuming the chattels in this way. She disposed of things for which she had no use, such as a gun for £2.5.0, a yoke of oxen for £14.0.0, and thirty-two sheep for £8.0.0, but her largest transaction was the sale of sixty acres, which fetched £74.10.0. The major purchaser of John's land was Benjamin, also one of his principal creditors. Yet she could not employ that means of raising money without the permission of the probate court, nor could she resort to it often without jeopardizing her future and that of her children.

In her Reminiscences, Mary wrote "my chief anxiety was for the education of my children, which I thought of the first importance,"[4] and one of the first entries in her account as executrix, dated January 5, 1768, reads "to Mrs. Teal for Schooling 14/-."[5] Madam Noyes evidently shared her concern, for she promised that "if the income of their father's estate should not prove sufficient to give them a college education, then the estate which she had or should leave them in her will should be applied toward their education," Mary wrote. "My own parents were no less solicitous."[6] Mr. and Mrs. Fish could not contribute a great deal of money, but they would board and teach the children as they reached the appropriate age, which would save Mary considerable expense. For the moment, however, she could not bring herself to part with one of them. That winter she instructed them herself, guided by her father's precepts. "Always view them as *Children*, —Flowers just opening— Reason & all their Faculties but in the Bud, to be tenderly and Discreetly handled," Mr. Fish advised, "and wait patiently, in the Way of *repeated* Instructions (giving Line upon Line &c.), hoping & looking for full, ripe Fruit, but not *before the Season*."[7]

Mary and Madam Noyes had always enjoyed a strong

mutual affection; now their common widowhood and
shared bereavements drew them closer than ever. With her
own parents at a distance, Mary clung to the older woman
as to a rock. Alas, Madam Noyes was flesh and blood. In
the autumn of 1768, a year after John's death, she went
again to visit her daughter at Wethersfield. She had planned
to travel home on November 10, and went to bed in apparent good health the night before, but the morning found
her dead. When Mary returned from her funeral to the
diminished house on Elm Street, she felt "more than ever
desolate."[8] In less than two years, three of the dearest people in her world had gone down into their graves. And for
the first time, she found herself alone: alone with grief, and
alone to shoulder the responsibilities of household and
family head.

At this critical juncture, Mr. and Mrs. Fish stepped in to
take Jose and John to Stonington for the winter, while
Mary and the younger children remained at Elm Street.
Mary described herself as convinced of the necessity for the
separation by her father's "weighty arguments," which
probably had to do with the fact that the maintenance of
the establishment at New Haven now rested entirely in her
hands. She could not abandon the house to the servants,
especially since it represented an opportunity to bring in
cash by taking boarders. Besides occasional students from
the college, Mary boarded some of the notable men that
Madam Noyes had formerly entertained during the quarter
sessions, the general assembly, and at Yale's commencement.

Despite the advice and attention of the Darlings, Benjamin Douglas, and Joseph Noyes's successor Chauncey
Whittelsey, who Mary said behaved toward her "as a kind
and tender Father," she found her new situation both tax-
ing and troubling.[9] Among the problems she confronted
was the discovery that Madam Noyes had also died intestate. Mary's circumstances were not altered for the worse
by this. Under the law, Madam Noyes's property was distributed equally among her three children, with her dower

right in the house reverting to John's heirs. The hope of special provision for the boys' education had vanished, however, while the difficulty of obtaining ready cash remained.

Bewildered by the succession of losses and the tangle of complications that seemed to have become the ordinary course of her once untroubled life, Mary was ill prepared to confront the events that occurred at the Elm Street house in February 1769. Soon after the death of Madam Noyes, a servant named Thankful Garden, a woman who had numbered among her household tasks the intimate one of occasional wet nurse to Mary's children, had given birth out of wedlock. One morning, with no prior illness to account for it, the child was found dead. Though Thankful swore she had done no wrong, Mary felt obliged to have the corpse examined; the panel of women, assisted by a doctor, who performed that task concluded that the child had been strangled. When Thankful came before the magistrates, the violence of her grief convinced them of her innocence, and charges were not pressed. But the tragedy had left its mark on Mary. She began to feel death-haunted. Her letters dwelt on the dead, and on her fear that some fresh bereavement would prevent the hoped-for reunion with her parents and sons that spring, while she proclaimed her gratitude to God for their present health so often and so anxiously as almost to suggest a superstitious act of propitiation rather than a religious exercise. A passage from one long and emotional letter written to her parents in March 1769, shortly after the inquest on Thankful's baby, shows her state of mind:

> I don't know that since I first left you I have ever been so impatient to hear from you as I have of late; finding I had no Letter by the last post, I was ready to imagine, yea I greatly feard that you, or the dear Children, were ill and that you feard to distress me with the news before you knew the event. . . . I hope I am very thankfull that God has restored my dear Johnne . . . I long

once more to see my dear father's house. But o what
tender sensations do I feel when I only visit it in thought.
What pleasing satisfaction have I taken in my Tender
Childhood with Her, *that dear creature* with whome I
was nurs'd up with Paternal tenderness surpassing what
is common. Since her shadow has ceas'd I have visited
that dear Place and mournd its abscence in every room.
But then the dear companion of my joyes and sorrows
was in *time,* whose tender sympathy was ever ready to
take more than his shair of my sorrow.—Alas, my tears
blur my sight on the recollections of those departed
hours of social converse I have had with *that dearest* of
Creatures in my dear Father's House, wher our intimate
acquaintance first began. How will every room afresh
be covered with a gloom, and revive the Ghost of my
departed joys.

In conclusion, she repeated the hope that she would be
"permitted" to visit them in the spring, and "that our little
remains may be gathered together once more."[10]

I I

MR. FISH had continued to receive calls from other
churches which his own forbade him to accept. In 1763 the
church at Mount Carmel, a community not far from New
Haven where both his daughters were then living, had
called him, but when he consulted his people they refused
to let him go. Since then changes in both their circumstances and his own gave Mr. Fish reason to think that
they might now view his departure more complaisantly.
Accordingly, in early 1768, when the church of White Haven
made a tentative approach to him, he renewed his appeal
for release.

In 1767, Mr. Fish had published a collection of sermons,
The Church of CHRIST a firm and durable House, which

attracted considerable attention for its critical yet not unsympathetic account of the Great Awakening. Among its admirers were many members of the church of White Haven. Originally formed by those who had separated from Joseph Noyes's congregation in 1742, White Haven had since moderated its demand for religious purity and had reinstituted halfway membership. Halfway members were those who, while they could not claim to have experienced grace, were willing to submit to church discipline. This allowed them to have their children baptized, though they themselves could not participate in communion. Against this background, Joseph Fish, a friend to piety though an opponent of excess, appeared an ideal choice of minister.

For his part, Mr. Fish was more than ever ready to consider "retiring into winter quarters after struggling with howling sectaries in this wilderness."[11] Further separations from his own church had made it progressively more difficult for the parishioners to pay his salary. A dispute between him and his people had led to the summoning of a council of ministers and a recommendation in 1764 that his compensation be increased. Now the financial straits of his Society might work to his advantage. Since his departure would negate their obligation both to support him in old age and to hire a younger man as his assistant, it would save them a good deal of money. And the compassionate reasons for allowing him and his wife to make their home in New Haven had increased. The loss of one child; the plight of the other, the sole remainder, bereaved of all who might have helped her in the struggle to raise four fatherless young ones except for her own father and mother; and the difference it would make to everyone concerned if they lived near each other instead of at several days' distance: these were new and powerful arguments in favor of granting Mr. Fish his request.

Mr. Fish had in fact secured the consent of his parish when he learned that White Haven had dropped his candidacy and given the post to Jonathan Edwards, Jr. Then,

several months later, the church resumed communication
with him, this time inquiring if he would consider a co-
pastorship. A substantial minority had objected to
Edwards's appointment, not wishing to see a return to the
uncompromising stance of 1743, and the rest were seeking
to appease them by adding an older, more conservative
man to the pastorate. Mr. Fish was willing, and it seemed
pleasantly appropriate for him to play such a role. Unfortunately, it now emerged that the dissenters already had
another candidate in mind for the second position. Nevertheless, they consented to interview Mr. Fish, and in early
1769, when he brought his two grandsons back to Mary's
house, he went to see them. There is no record of what
passed on that occasion, or of the letter that he sent the
group just before he returned home. But their next move
was to request a gathering of the whole parish for the purpose of dividing, citing that letter as their authority. For
in it, they claimed, Mr. Fish had "given them all the
encouragement they could expect or desired that he would
lead them" if they separated.

Mary had taken an active part in all these negotiations,
transmitting communications to and from her father, and
promoting his interests in conversations with church representatives on both sides of the controversy. When the
rumor that he had encouraged a division began to circulate, certain other ministers, including Chauncey Whittelsey, questioned her, observing that "he above all men they
did not think would head a separate party." Though Mary
tried to suggest that the case might be "quite different
respecting these People" since their fear that the church
would rescind halfway membership was forcing them to
leave, Mr. Russell of Windsor answered sharply that "the
world would not make that distinction." It is not clear
whether Mary had spoken in the belief that her father had
indeed made the statements attributed to him, but it seems
unlikely. A more plausible explanation is that she spoke
out of pure eagerness to resolve the dispute in his favor.

Feeling as she did that "things are represented much to my Fathers disadvantage," perhaps she had sought to correct the balance.[12] It pained her, she confessed, to hear his reputation traduced by both sides and say nothing in his defense. Yet she continued to hope that the controversy would end in his appointment, right up to the day when the dissidents began to build a church without deigning to debate the matter further.

In the autumn of 1769, another prospect appeared for her father's removal nearer to New Haven when the First Church of Milford, its pulpit left empty by a death, looked to Joseph Fish as a possible future occupant. They wanted to examine him in person before they made a firm offer. Benjamin Douglas thought this reasonable, and Mary too urged him to agree since "tis very probable this may be the last door that may be open for your removal."[13] In mid-December he journeyed to Milford to meet with the Society, but no acceptable offer ensued. Though the family correspondence does not reveal what might have gone wrong, it is a fair guess that the aged appearance of Mr. Fish, now sixty-three, caused Milford to reconsider. How much service could they hope to receive in return for their commitment to him before they had to support his years of decline? It is also possible that the publication in 1768 of a vitriolic attack upon him, *A Fish Caught in his own Net,* in which Isaac Backus tried to associate Mr. Fish with the worst of Old Light repression, had dimmed his reputation for theological moderation and with it his chances of removal. Whatever the cause, this new rejection of her father, the second within a year, left Mary both hurt on his account and disappointed on her own.

I I I

DURING all this time, Mary had contended not only with the worry and burden of her multifarious tasks, but with a troublesome tendency to violent swings of mood. For example, in early June she entertained her mother with a cheerful vignette of herself as head of the house, but her next letter spoke of "the many pressures that have of late set uncommonly heavy upon me" and of herself as having been "in the valley, a valley dark and dismal, I could not see light in either world, was sometimes ready to faint because of the way."[14] Though she professed to see in this "the hand of God . . . pleas'd to prove me by various trials," the proof did not always turn out to her advantage.

One trial from which she did emerge the stronger was the measles epidemic that struck New Haven in the summer of 1769. Though Johnny was among the first to take the disease, he recovered as promptly as he had succumbed and did not seem to have infected the other children. Five weeks later, symptoms appeared in Jose that gave Mary far graver concern than Johnny's illness had done. One Sunday, he had a fainting spell in church. A glass of madeira revived him, and on Monday he went to school, but that evening the symptoms recurred. Badly shaken, Mary saw "reason to fear his disorder was *hereditary*. But to my joy next day the measels appeared."[15] That she should welcome the measles, which had claimed the lives of many children, as an alternative to epilepsy, showed how deeply John's disease had troubled Mary, and how she dreaded its reappearance in his offspring. Nor had she any reason to change her mind. Jose recovered quickly and completely, while her other children escaped altogether. That death had visited so many houses and passed hers by seemed to lift the curse under which she had existed, and in the midst of the epidemic Mary could write that "this morning [I] feel in a sweet calm trusting frame, & may it continue and all remains of unbeliefe be done away." Other problems, however, brought less constructive results.

It was at about this time (though it is impossible to date the incident precisely) that something happened which left Mary so little satisfied with her performance that she obscured all references to it in her correspondence and journal. Still, it is possible to discern an outline of events. Someone made her a proposal of marriage, someone known to and supported by John's sister, Abigail Darling, and the offer found her vulnerable. Though it was many months since the death of Madam Noyes had ended the long, sheltered period of her life, she had as yet achieved no sense of her ability to handle business matters. That summer, she wished more ardently than ever that her parents lived nearer, since "none feels for me nor my dear Fatherless as they do," she wrote. "Our intrest suffers extreemly for want of someone to guide our affairs with discretion."[16] Perhaps it was that want of someone which led her to keep her suitor dangling longer than either kindness or propriety allowed; long enough, in fact, to draw down public criticism on her head. Perhaps, though she had not much enthusiasm for the match, she had so little confidence in herself that the prospect of having a man take charge presented a temptation difficult to resist. She knew that she was acting shabbily, and the knowledge gave her pain, yet she could not bring herself to set matters right by answering yes or no.

She had not resolved this dilemma when the blow fell that brought her to her knees. There is true pathos in the account that Mary left us in her Reminiscences:

In the month of May, 1770, my dear and only daughter, Mary Noyes, was taken ill of canker and worms [diphtheria?]. She was then a little more than four years old, and although so young, would take anything that was given her, if ever so bad to take. She would first taste it, and then would say, it is not good, Mama. I told her the Dr. said she must take it to make her better. She would then open her little mouth and take anything, and would foment her throat over hot steam with great discretion. She died on the 10th day of her illness . . . I closed her eyes myself; and felt in some measure

resigned, knowing that God could give a good reason
why he had thus afflicted me.[17]

Resigned or no, the loss of her little daughter broke Mary's
spirit. She lapsed into depression, and felt that her faith
had died with the child. That autumn, afraid for her sanity,
Mr. and Mrs. Fish suggested that she and the boys remove
to Stonington for the winter. On November 5, 1770, Mary
returned, a weary, disheartened woman, to her girlhood
home, and that same day she began the journal she would
keep, with varying degrees of regularity, for the rest of her
life.

Though she opened it with a factual account of the journey from New Haven to Stonington, in general it is less a
record of external events than an introspective chronicle of
a spiritual odyssey. She did observe, however, that conversations with her father on the subject of the mishandled
suitor had enabled her to end that unhappy business. "I
blamed myself that I had not been more wise in some matters that had taken place," she wrote, "and although I had
acted an honest part, in some things I had not acted a wise
one, and I thought my character would suffer. My father
told me that perhaps my character had been my idol, and
that I ought to be willing to give up even that, if called
for."[18] His counsel helped her decide to send a final negative, which relieved her mind of one trouble. Yet her damaged self-esteem, the fear of a lonely future, and the
"spiritual deadness" that resulted from the crushing weight
of sorrow she had borne in recent years continued to make
her miserable.

Many years later, when Mary looked back on that winter
from the perspective of old age and long experience, she
could still describe it as "the most gloomy and vexatious
one I ever passed in my life." A few extracts from the journal she kept at the time will show why:

December 5, 1770. Distressed in my mind and know not
what to do . . . I found myself a poor weak and helpless

creature, could do nothing but lie at the foot of mercy and look for direction.

December 6. Kept a day of fasting and prayer, but kept on my knitting, that it might not appear to the family what I was engaged in.

December 7. This day resumed somewhat of my wonted cheerfulness; felt willing to wait until I knew God's will respecting my future circumstances in life.

January 1, 1771. This day begins a new year. O! may I be prepared for the events of it, whatever they may be.

January 8. Spun, read . . . feeling in a measure resigned to the lord's will; found that of late I had been in a good school, and hope I have profited.

January 13. Sab[bath]. So stormy I could not go out and had a comfortable day in my mind but in the evening my burden returned. O when will it please the lord to set me free!

January 16. Found some comfort in reading God's word, but all the day pensive, fearing it was all wrong with me. . . . My conduct has given people reason to suspect my stability of mind.

January 21. In the morning, distressed with an unre-signed frame of mind & a proud heart. Not willing to bow, not willing to have my character roughly handled.

January 25. Much distressed with my stubborn will and proud heart.

January 26. More composed. . . .

January 28. O May this calm frame continue, and I never more dishonor God by distrusting his goodness.

January 29. A very comfortable day, sweetly resigned to God's will.

January 30. Oh how changed from yesterday—a distressing day! Thoughts on my errors in judgment . . . pressed me sore.[19]

The fluctuation between good and bad days continued for months, with Mary "sometimes calm and trusting—sometimes ready to sink." In April she returned to New Haven, "all my journey home looking to the hills above for more strength to encounter the trials which I had reason to think awaited me." She did have reason, and soon enough found herself "a little discomposed by hearing reports to my disadvantage." But in time, she wrote, "God caused me to get far above my trials, and I was not ashamed to look everyone in the face."[20]

Indeed, the twinge of hurt pride proved easier to overcome than the pain of loss, both loss of loved ones and loss of faith. One Sunday in May, Mary wrote "I mourn that I had no more communication with God. . . . Oh, this dreadful deadness of heart!" She marked the anniversary of her daughter's death with the words: "A day never to be forgotten by me!" After that her mood briefly improved, and on September 8 she exclaimed "How good it is to feel awake and alive!" Then, on an evening in November 1771, she once more described herself as "Dead, lifeless and blind this day."

Again she sought the shelter of her parents' house, where on Christmas Day she gave thanks that "my mind enjoys a steady calm," a state in which she continued so long that she began to think herself cured of despondency. "It seems to me as if last winter Satan had desired me that he might sift me as wheat," she recalled, "for I was tempted and was ever ready to give up every thing and to question everything as I thought I had been entertaining false hope." By contrast, "I every day this winter experienced in my mind what I would have given the world to obtain last winter, that is, resignation to God's will." Then came a night in March when she recorded wearily that "as I was going to bed, my sorrows came afresh into my mind, the last wound bleeding again, even the death of my little Mary."[21]

I V

MARY'S inward journey continued in this halting, sometimes even regressive fashion, with no great leaps forward
to encourage the pilgrim; but if her progress was unsure,
her effort was steady. Once in a while the recollection of
grief gave her a pang, as in September 1773 when drought
sent a wave of sickness and death across New England:

> The young, the gay, the beautiful Polly Austin in the
> darkness of night was committed to the grave. She died
> of the smallpox at the pesthouse. It brought fresh to my
> mind my own sorrow when in the like circumstances
> my dear and only sister was committed to the dust.[22]

But this was the soldier's old wound, the reminiscent ache
that would never entirely leave her. Five years of patient
endeavor had rewarded her with strength to withstand the
storms from within that had once "a little unhinged my
mind," and to cry "blessed be his name that has not scattered darkness in my way as in times past."[23]

Almost unawares, Mary had taken the first steps toward
independence in mundane matters, too. In the summer of
1772, in New Haven, she resumed her practice of receiving
as boarders boys from the college, and in addition some of
the men who attended the quarter sessions, among them
Major Wolcott, Colonel Williams, Major Phelps, Colonel
Huntington, and Governor Trumbull. Benjamin Douglas,
now remarried and risen to heights of professional eminence remarkable for a man hardly more than thirty, often
joined the company together with his wife. Not only did
this bring in money, it brought Mary back from her retreat
to the safety of Stonington and into renewed association
with some of Connecticut's most prominent citizens.

In the winter of 1772 a new suitor presented himself, this
time known to us as the Reverend Naphtali Daggett, professor of divinity and acting president of Yale. Mary seems
never to have given him much encouragement, but in early
1773, aware, apparently, of the influence wielded by Mr. Fish,

he took it upon himself to go to Stonington. When he arrived, finding only Mrs. Fish at home, he chose not to disclose the topic of his visit. Instead he waited until her husband returned, when he requested a private interview. This was a blunder, compounded by a clumsy letter of apology in which he also asked indulgence for other "Puerilities, Flights and Foibles of Expression, which are difficult to be intirely avoided by Persons of my valatile Make," hardly a description to recommend him to either parent.[24]

Oblivious to the bad impression he had made, in March, when Mary sent him a final refusal, he again addressed her father. "Sir, I do not, I cannot, I will not take your daughter's complaisant letter as a real, much less a decisive negative to my proposal," he wrote. "I view it only in the light of female Play, & have taken the Liberty to treat it accordingly."[25] It is a pity that Mr. Fish's reply is not extant; we may be sure, however, that it confirmed Mary's refusal in such terms as not even the confident Mr. Daggett could mistake for female play.

Within a few months a third candidate for Mary's hand (again anonymous) appeared. This time she declined even to consider a proposal until after her winter's retreat to Stonington. "At present, can only observe I am under no engagement," she wrote on October 11, "but hope to spend the winter with you, my dearest Parents, at whose fireside these matters may be more freely talked upon than by writing." What passed in those conversations she did not record; nevertheless, upon her return to New Haven in the spring of 1774 she discouraged further advances. When they continued, Mary, ever careful to disguise her meaning when committing a delicate matter to the post, reported renewed "attacks from the Norwest." Unimpressed, her parents predicted that "the 'Northwest attack' will be increased to a close siege" and advised that she arm to withstand it "thirty years at least."[26]

Whatever the reason for their unfavorable verdict on these applicants, it is not likely to have been that Mr. and Mrs. Fish opposed their daughter's remarriage in princi-

ple. Apart from the consideration of companionship for
Mary, still only thirty-eight, her widowed state imposed
burdens on them, and particularly on her father, that they
would have welcomed an opportunity to relinquish.
Despite her growing competence, Mary could not handle
all the work entailed in supervising the Noyes estate without help from Mr. Fish. When he advised her to make her
Farmington lands more profitable by purchasing a house
and barn in the vicinity so that she could install a tenant,
she confessed that she felt unequal to the task; and in the
end, at some cost to himself, he undertook the business for
her. Another, perennial, problem was that her sex put her
at a disadvantage when the necessity arose (as it frequently
did) to dun a defaulting tenant for his rent. On the other
hand, her own creditors did not hesitate to press her hard
if she fell behind in her payments. In May 1772, the Waterbury collector made his way into her house to demand
payment of a bill that she had overlooked. Pleading that
she had not sufficient money in the house, she asked him
to wait until she received her rents from Farmington, "but
he unpolitely insisted," she wrote, "and what could a feble
woman do[?]"[27] She went out, borrowed money from a
neighbor, and paid the collector, thus ridding herself of
one embarrassment but acquiring another.

She was often in difficulties of that kind. Neither John's
estate nor his mother's had yet been distributed and Mary
rarely had enough cash on hand to meet her obligations.
Not that she feared insolvency, but she never grew accustomed to indebtedness, or ceased to lament her inability
"to fullfill one of God's most reasonable requirements, even
that of doing justly to my fellow-men.—and they are apt
to wonder why it is not done, such an estate and not able:
strang[e]!"[28] Occasionally her parents had to assume temporary responsibility for a bill, which they confessed put
them to hardship since "Money is not in these parts as it
used to be."[29] Their daughter's remarriage could provide
her with help and protection, and themselves with relief
from such demands.

They had to remember, however, that it could also put Mary and her children at the mercy of one who might ruin the Noyes estate, either by mismanagement or by appropriation to purposes in which their welfare did not figure. Sarah Osborn's second marriage may have come to mind. The chances of someone's courting Mary for mercenary reasons were considerably greater now than when she had been the daughter of a clergyman who could give her only a modest dowry. Mr. Daggett was especially suspect in this regard, for his first marriage had left him with seven children, four of them sons, and all of them minors.

Yet if ever Mary were tempted to marry just for the sake of gaining a protector, it would have been in the autumn of 1774. Jose, a credit to his grandfather's teaching, had gained admission to Yale College at the early (though not exceptional) age of thirteen. If Mary now pursued her usual course of removal to Stonington at the end of November she would have to leave him at New Haven alone. Although he could board with some decent family, as other boys had boarded with his, in case of accident or illness many days of travel would stand between him and his mother's care. Mary could not bring herself to take that risk. She decided that, for the first time since 1770, she would see the winter through at Elm Street. Ten-year-old Jemmy (James) would go alone to Stonington (where his grandparents had just retrieved and forwarded the last of the previous winter's leavings, a Latin grammar abandoned in some odd corner of the house). Johnny would remain behind and study with a tutor.

V

IN that year, Mary showed a growing interest in the discussions of current affairs that took place among the guests who filled her house during the quarter sessions. She and her parents had never before paid much attention to politics in their letters. Families not actively engaged in the business of government rarely fill their private correspondence with public affairs unless one begins to intrude upon the other. In 1759, John made reference to the strong general resentment of the British soldiery only when they caused a disturbance that directly affected his family. One night, the inhabitants at Elm Street, who had "Imagin'd Our Selves free from their Insults,"[30] were wakened by gunfire, which proved to be an assault on the jail by British regulars bent on rescuing two comrades imprisoned for infractions of local law. In 1766 John described New Haven's festivities marking the repeal of the Stamp Act, an event greeted with wild acclaim all over America. In 1770, however, neither the repeal of the Townshend Duties nor the Boston massacre was mentioned. The death of Mary's daughter and her subsequent struggle with depression occupy the letters and the journal to the exclusion of all other topics.

This makes all the more striking the sudden emergence of the imperial controversy in a letter from Mr. Fish to Mary of May 1774:

> I don't remember any Time, since I liv'd, so alarming as *these,* on Acct. of the Tyrannical Measures which the Ministry at home have taken & are designing to take agt. the Colonys. They seem (by accounts sent over) determined to distress us to the last degree, if not to destroy us, unless we submit to the yoke of slavery they have prepared for us. The united Forces of France, Spain & all the savage world in the last War appeared not so terrible as *Those* that are now engagd against us. For *then* we had our Gracious King & all his Powers in strictest Friendship, & Resolute to defend us: and what was more, God fought on our side. But now we have our British Brethren to encounter, Our King & his mighty ones to contend with, & nothing short of our Liberties & Invaluable Privileges will satisfie their Thirst

or answer their Demands. And unless our Gracious God, beholding our Sinful ways, is pleased to glorifie his Mercy in *healing of us,* he will surely cast us down.[31]

He could not have shown more plainly how one man, accustomed all his life to upholding the standing order, experienced the first stirrings of that revolution which a later president would locate in the hearts and minds of the people. The suggestion that a spiritual sickness at home might call down the wrath of God sprang from an old conservatism, for, almost since the first pilgrims landed, American divines had lectured their descendants on their loss of original purity. In phrases such as "our gracious King" and "our British Brethren" Mr. Fish also voiced the traditional pride in America's association with a great empire. Even so, in this letter the rhetoric of rebellion, new to his pen, drowns out the echoes of the past. Dissonant words like "tyrannical" and "slavery" break in; the assertion that "nothing short of our Liberties & Invaluable Privileges will satisfie their Thirst or answer their Demands" implies no remaining hope for reconciliation; and even the expression of fear at the prospect of war with Great Britain suggests that such a course, though appalling, is no longer inconceivable.

In November 1774, Mary took up the subject. She had entertained a large number of guests during the general assembly and had enjoyed "hearing so many worthy People of sense converse on affairs so interesting." One of them had given her a copy of the resolutions passed by Congress opposing further importation from Great Britain and urging abstention from the use of dutied articles such as tea. This she transmitted to her parents with the comment, "There has not one drop of Tea been drink'd by any one of our family but only two afternoons when I had very particular company."[32] Her father was prompt to follow suit. "Your little Son & I began yesterday the Disuse of Tea," he answered, "& doubt not of our perseverance."[33]

Still, the grand trivia of family life continued to receive

the greater share of their attention. Johnny's scarlet fever, Jemmy's bout with canker ("in wh. time he could not content himself without action, so his Granne teached him to *Make Garters,* wh. pleased him much"), and Jose's first solo venture to Stonington (which he described for his mother down to the last detail of where they stopped to give the horses hay) engrossed their pens. To Mr. Fish, the great question of the day remained how Mary and the two boys would weather the hardest part of the year alone, for, as he admitted, "you all lie so near our hearts that we want Faith to trust you with god."[34]

II

Revolution

Four

A NEW SCENE
OPENS

THE spring of 1775 found Mary debt-free, healthy, and self-possessed. On March 8, she sent her parents a letter that caused them considerable surprise and some discomfort. After reporting Johnny's return to health and listing the guests currently under her roof, who included the governor and several of the Assistants, she announced that she had received yet another proposal of marriage. And this time, though she asked their advice as usual, her tone betrayed that she had her heart set on the man. She wrote:

A new scene now opens which calls for direction from heaven and my earthly friends. "Tis a delicate subject that I don't love so well to write upon, but hope this will go safe and the contents be kept to yourselves.— Know then, my dear Parents, that I have a proposal made me, by one whose person and address are exactly agreeable to my taste. . . . And I doubt not, by what appears, I could be very happy with [him]. His age, 43; has but one child, and he married; well of it for things

of this world, and doubt not but he would render himself very agreeable to you. I have but one objection,
which I know will be yours; that is, he lives 25 miles
from here. And tho he shows himself very obliging, he
can't see how he can remove here. . . . Was my sons
through Colledge, I should not hesitate (with your consent), for a person more agreeable to my wish I could
not desire. . . . My friends here not only advise me to
accept, but even congratulate me on an offer so prom-
ysyng. I have been made willing to sit alone the remainder of my days if it was the will of heaven, but if it
orders it otherwise, and gives me pleasant society, I
hope I shall be thankfull and fill my place with honour.

In case the letter should not "go safe," by which she meant
unopened, she withheld further detail, but promised that a
friend would soon call at the parsonage to "tell you many
things you may want to know, and among others the name
of the above Genlmn."[1]

I

THE name that Mary's emissary pronounced to Mr. and
Mrs. Fish was that of Gold Selleck Silliman. This gentleman lived at Holland Hill, near Fairfield, where three generations of his family had lived before him. The first
Silliman arrived there in the mid-seventeenth century. Born
Daniel Sillimandi, the descendant of Italian Protestants, he
grew up in Geneva where his family had sought refuge
from religious persecution. Eventually he emigrated to
America, settling on a hill just to the east of Fairfield village, which was later called Holland Hill, some said after
the place in Europe from which Daniel had embarked.
    Daniel's descendants followed a pattern repeated all over
New England. When his sons married, they built houses
on their father's land. The third generation did the same,

and by Gold's time the Sillimans had become one of Fairfield County's most influential families. His father, Ebenezer Silliman, born in 1707, was grandson to Daniel. In 1728 Ebenezer married Abigail Selleck, and on May 7, 1732, she gave birth to Gold Selleck, the first of seven children. Ebenezer struck out a distinguished career in public service, holding office as justice of the peace, probate judge for Fairfield County, delegate in the general assembly for the town of Fairfield, major in the 4th militia regiment, and, beginning in 1739, as Assistant, or member of the upper house of the colony's legislature. In 1743 he became one of the five Assistants annually designated by the general assembly to act as judges of the Superior Court, a position he occupied for the next twenty-three years.

In 1766 the smoldering fires of colonial resentment, still on the outer edge of lives like those of Mary and her parents, attacked the heart of his. In that year Ebenezer failed to win re-election as an Assistant because he had joined in administering the oath to enforce the Stamp Act to Governor Thomas Fitch, who also lost his place for having sworn it. Without an Assistantship, Ebenezer could no longer hold a place on the Superior Court. Nevertheless, he remained an important figure on the Fairfield scene. He retained his appointments as justice of the peace and judge of probate until his death, and served as one of Fairfield's delegates in all but two general assemblies between October 1766 and May 1774.

In 1773 Ebenezer became Speaker of the House. As such, he held a place on the nine-man Committee of Correspondence, constituted by the general assembly in May 1773 in order to maintain communications with similar committees in the other colonies. Then, in May 1774, he was inveigled into an unsuccessful attempt to restore both himself and the unpopular Fitch to their positions on the council of Assistants in place of the patriot leadership. As a result, the assembly dropped him from the Committee of Correspondence and Fairfield refused any longer to

honor him with its suffrage, which brought his speaker-
ship to an end.

Long before the dawn of revolution closed his own
political career, Ebenezer had begun to pave the way for
his eldest son to succeed him in it. Gold, who was graduated from Yale in 1752, had followed his father in choosing
to study law, and the elder Silliman's influence appeared in
the son's designation, probably in 1768, as king's attorney
for Fairfield County. In 1769 Gold became a captain in
Connecticut's prestigious corps of horse, and in 1772 he
received a commission as justice of the peace, an honor
which was to be renewed every year by the general assembly for the rest of his life. It was at about this time that the
political views of father and son began to diverge, fortunately for the son. In May 1774, the assembly raised him to
the rank of major in the colony's 4th regiment, and in the
following October to lieutenant colonel, the post that William Samuel Johnson had resigned because of his Loyalist
sympathies. By May 1775 he had attained the rank of colonel. He also placed twenty-fifth in the nominations for
Assistant submitted by the freemen at their September
meetings, a sure sign of his growing reputation.

While his public career advanced at a steady pace, his
private life had met with frequent checks. In August 1774
his wife of twenty years, Martha Davenport, daughter to
Deodate Davenport of East Haven, granddaughter to the
Reverend John Davenport of Stamford (and, incidentally,
niece to the notorious James), died after a protracted illness. Their marriage had been unfruitful by eighteenth-
century standards. The first child, a daughter, lived less than
a day; the second and only surviving child, a son named
William, was born in 1756; then, in June 1772, after almost
eighteen barren years, Martha gave birth to a daughter who
died seventeen months later. The reason for the long gap
is nowhere hinted, but it may be that Martha's first two
pregnancies had so endangered her health as to enjoin some
attempt at birth control. Certainly she did not long survive
her third. She never completely recovered after the con-

finement, and in August 1774 she followed her baby to the grave.

Silliman was thus a recent widower when he met Mary Noyes. Though his profession had brought him often to the quarter sessions in New Haven, it does not appear that they knew each other before late 1774, when someone took him to her house. Any one of Mary's frequent guests might have made the introduction, but it is both pleasant and plausible to suppose that Benjamin Douglas did them that good turn. An old friend of Silliman's, Benjamin carried letters between him and Mary and showed such an interest in the progress of their courtship as would befit its promoter. At the same time, to judge by comments from various other quarters, more than one mutual friend had conceived the notion that the newly widowed Mr. Silliman would make an excellent match for Mrs. Noyes. Not only were they temperamentally compatible, but practical considerations would set no obstacles in their way. Mary's three children by her previous marriage would place no financial burden on Silliman, thanks to their inheritance; on the other hand, since Silliman had substantial means of his own and but one son, grown and married, to draw on them, the Noyes estate would present as little temptation to him as to any man. Nor did the recent date of his bereavement constitute a hindrance. In days not so long removed, prompt remarriage had often been a strict practical necessity, and it was still frequent. Ebenezer Silliman had taken a second wife, Abigail Hall, little more than twelve months after the death of Abigail Selleck, to whom he had been married for over forty years. Mary had remained a widow longer than usual for a woman of her age and attractions, while Silliman's loss of his mother, baby daughter, and wife, in the space of little more than two years, so far from making him ineligible in Mary's eyes, may have served to encourage her initial interest.

Interest soon increased to strong attraction, but Mary would not lightly relinquish her hard-won independence. Soon after Silliman broached the subject of marriage, Mary presented to him a document she had composed in August 1773 entitled "Portrait of a Good Husband." In it, she described the qualities "which, if ever I was settled again, I should wish to find in the person, and without which I wished to live as I was."[2] He must be "one who shall feel my griefs, and endeavour to redress them, and participate with me my joys; and who shall be willing to gratify my reasonable inclinations." He must be equally generous with money. "May he love to see his table furnished with the good things of providence," she wrote, "and not only with the necessaries of life, but sometimes with the comforts and delicacies as his income may allow. . . . May his cabinet [library] be ever free for my perusal and improvement, and may he not be too tenacious of the money key, for surely she to whom he gives his heart may reasonably think she may have access to his treasures, and he fear no want." She would not submit to jealousy, "that bane to conjugal affection"; or to husbandly reprimand in public, or to a double standard of behavior. "Let a mantle of love be drawn over my imperfections," she wrote, "and let them not be adminiverted on in company, but told me in private with all that tenderness and faithfulness that becomes a husband and a Christian, and may he in every point set me an example worthy of imitation."

The rights and the needs of her sons by John Noyes must receive the same consideration as her own:

May he be indeed a father to my fatherless children. . . . May he look on the inheritance of their deceased father as sacred, never to be converted to his own use or in any way to augment his own estate, but let him put it under the best possible advantage to be profitable as well for their future good as for their present education. Above all, may he take care to cultivate their minds, instructing them in the grand principles of religion, and may he see to it that his example corresponds to the precepts of the same: that he be kind and tender, which

will bind them to obedience, while the reverse conduct
. . . would excite in them not a filial but a slavish fear.

Nor should he forget the common humanity of servants
and slaves:

> May he be willing that I should be kind to his servants,
> knowing that we have our master in heaven. May he
> have a happy talent at governing, and let severity be his
> strange work. Let each that has an immortal soul be
> dealt with as a rational creature, and not be treated as
> the brutal creation.

Last, she turned to the world outside the family. The man
she married must be "one whose heart is open to the cries
of the poor and needy, and [who] is kind to the evil and
unthankful, thereby imitating the divine pattern who causes
his rain to fall on the just and the unjust. . . . One who is
just to all he deals with, and punctual to fulfill his engagements; one who endeavours to owe no man anything but
love." Anticipating the charge that she expected too much,
she concluded firmly that "I once knew a dear man that
was possessed of all these accomplishments so far as he had
opportunity to shew them . . . and sweet to me is the
memory of that just man."

So far, indeed, all Mary's intimate relationships with men
had inclined her to think well of them. She had known a
kind father, a considerate husband, and a brother-in-law
who had made her sister as happy in marriage as she was
herself. But her "Portrait" reveals that she knew it was not
necessarily so. Each stated characteristic of her "Good
Husband" implies the recognition that the obverse existed.
A bad husband was one who would abuse a wife and step-
children, waste their inheritance through mismanagement
or dissipation, make their lives miseries of pinching and
scraping, and disgrace them publicly by mistreating his
servants and reneging on his business obligations. Mary

had led a sheltered life, but not so sheltered that she did not know such men existed, and that their wives were wretched, with little power, as the law then stood, to redress their wrongs.

Yet there was one course open to women who wanted more protection against the consequences of a bad marriage than the common law afforded, a course that widows of property took more often than girls contemplating a first marriage. A woman could insist upon a prenuptial agreement according to which she would retain some rights in whatever property she brought to the marriage. Mary, who could draft and present so detailed a moral agreement, apparently never considered asking Silliman if he would bind himself to a legal contract. The omission is not likely to have been inadvertent. Apart from her own and her father's probable awareness of the law, Benjamin Douglas would certainly have known about it and advised her on how to proceed had she so desired. It seems reasonable to assume that Mary's silence on this point signified a conscious choice, based upon both her religious and her emotional inclinations. If she took Silliman, she would take him on trust: a trust founded as surely as possible on an informed and considered assessment of his character, but otherwise with no props to sustain it save the vows each would make to the other.

Silliman's response to the "Portrait" appears nicely calculated to assure Mary of his intention to aim at the standard she had set without displaying Mr. Daggett's offensive certainty of success. "The next time he came, he looked pensive, and said that the paper which I had put into his hands had given him trouble," wrote Mary. "When I asked him why, he said he was afraid he should not be the character there described, although he had a wish to be." Upon this, Mary had not the slightest difficulty in perceiving that "his diffidence of himself plead in his favor." In other words, she meant to marry him, and only some truly glaring display of fault would change her mind. How much she already trusted and cared for Silliman showed in her letter to her parents. No trace of her former indecision appears, and the parenthetical reservation "with your consent" sounds unmistakably pro forma amidst the vigor of the surrounding phrases, "Was my sons through Colledge I should not hesitate . . . for a person more agreeable to my wish I could not desire." Mary's maternal responsibilities did not allow her to count the world well lost for love; she would certainly have heeded any strong objection by her parents, but she hoped they would raise none.

For her own part, if their advice confirmed her inclination, the only remaining obstacle to the marriage was, as she had said, the removal to Fairfield that must follow. If her parents, now past seventy, should need help, the journey to Stonington would take considerably longer from Fairfield than from New Haven even at the best of times, and winter weather might make it altogether impossible. Also, since Jose would re-enter Yale in the fall, while John was to study for the entrance examination under a local tutor, the miles between Fairfield and New Haven would put two of Mary's sons, the eldest barely fourteen, at more than a day's distance from her. Experience had taught her enough about the ever-present danger of serious illness and sudden death to give her pause about that.

II

SO that she could think through these problems without distraction, Mary asked Silliman to refrain from further visits until she had heard what her parents had to say. He complied, but used the period of interdiction to write his first letter to her, worth quoting at length for its revelation of character:

Dear Madam,

I hope you will not think it strange that I interest myself very much in whatever appears to me to give you either Pain or Pleasure. The two last Times, but especially the last Time I had the Pleasure to see and converse with you, my Dear, I remarked to you that I feared from a visible Alteration in your Countenance that you was unwell. You then hinted to me that the importance of the Subject on which we were conversing produced that Appearance. This, my Love, tho it convinces me of the Goodness of your Heart, and your great Prudence in thoroughly considering a subject of so much Importance to the Happiness and Comfort of ourselves and our Dear Children . . . has ever since given me a good Deal of Pain and Anxiety of Mind. To think that the very Method I have taken, and the Proposal which I have made to you with a View and Hope of making the Remainder of your Life as happy, my Dearest Love, as by the Blessing of Heaven I believe my own would be, should yet nevertheless fill you with melancholly Ideas and troublesome & uneasy Thoughts! Why should it have this Effect, my Love? It is my most sincere Desire to render your Life happy and easy, & to participate your Sorrows & Troubles as well as what is delightfull & pleasant. Why should the grand Obstacle in the way of that dear Connexion which, by God's Blessing, I hope might & would be our mutual Happiness, be considered as any Obstacle at all? You will say, my Love, that you have Children to educate and take Care of. So you have, my Dear, but will it not be easier for you to discharge this and every other relative Duty in the Dear Connexion I am soliciting for (assisted in every thing by another Self) . . . than it would be to go through these things alone?

But methinks I now see you lay down the Paper and ask, but ah Sir! How do I know that you would treat me and my Children in this kind Manner, if you had us in your Power? I have Nothing but your Word for it. Very true, my Love. I freely own there is a Risque in it. God has endowed us with the noble Powers of Reason: we must in such Cases make the best use of it to form a right Judgment, and rely upon him for making the Event

Happy. But in such a Case, my own Happiness would be so absolutely & inseparably connected with yours that I could not make you unhappy (if I should be so lost to all Sense of the Charms of your Dear Person, and the yet more valuable & endearing Charms of your Conversation) without at the same Time distroying my own Comfort. As to your Children, so deservedly dear to you, I think there being so to you would be a sufficient Motive to make them so to me, and to engage me to do everything in my Power for their Good. . . . You will also please to consider that I have a Child that I hope would find in my Dearest Mrs. Noyes another Dear & tender Mother. So that, on the whole My Love, you have some Security beside my bare Word.

This will, I doubt not, get safely to your hands by means of our common Friend, Mr. Douglass, and my Dearest, if you will be so kind as to favour me with an Answer, he has engaged to send it safe under Cover. . . . Pray, my Dearest Love, assure yourself that you are writing to a Man to whom you are very, very Dear, and who values himself on being a Man of more Honour than to abuse a Lady's Confidence, which I hope will induce you to express your Thoughts without Restraint. . . . With my most affectionate Compliments and tenderest & and dearest Regards to you, my Love, I am your Most Obedient and affectionate, Hum. Servt., G. SELLECK SILLIMAN.[3]

The warmth and charm of this communication, with its masterly progression from "Dear Madam" to "my Dear" and then "my Love," so that "my Dearest Love" falls into place with the ease of a familiarity sanctioned by long usage, leaves us in no doubt about why Mary "should not hesitate" but for her minor sons. The content, however, acknowledged the seriousness of that reservation. To paraphrase Silliman's own words, if Mary married him she would put herself and three others *in his power*. He sought to show her that she could base that decision on something more solid than his word and her desire to accept it: she could use her God-given powers of reason to make a right judgment. But to the three arguments he offered for believing in him she might have replied that a son who, though still at home, had reached the age of nineteen and had recently taken a wife would stand in no such vulnerable relation to her as her sons would bear to Silliman. And the statement that love for the children would follow from love for herself returned to the starting point; how could she know that he truly loved her until she had risked their future happiness and security along with her own? As for the suggestion that the mutuality of marital happiness would guarantee his regard for hers, it bore a curious resemblance to the argument that the interdependence of mother country and colonies would prevent the power of one being used to the disadvantage of the other. The imperial controversy, and the existence of unhappy marriages, disproved the theory in both cases. In fact, the relation of wife to husband, or of colonies to mother country, was not so much interdependence as the dependence of one party on the benevolence of the other. For Mary, this meant that reason gave her no more reliable measure of Silliman's integrity than instinct and affection would provide. Wisdom advised that she employ all three in making her decision, but ultimately, as Silliman admitted, there remained "a Risque in it."

Recognizing that her abstracted manner at their last meeting and her request for a moratorium on further interviews had caused Silliman to fear that she was growing cool to his proposal, Mary reassured him with a candor that would have amazed Mr. Daggett. No one had better reason to think well of friendship (as she termed married love) than herself. It was "originally intended to aggrandize, not to debase the rational soul . . . the greatest happyness mortals can enjoy, and the more refined, the more like Him who has said he is *Love*." Nevertheless, all human enterprise "has its dark and its light side . . . and whatever inclination I might have to dwell on the light side, and

walk by that, my reason bid me look also on the dark—
and there I happened to be at our last interview." She saw
no reason to expect that her parents would object. They
would share her regret that Silliman lived so far from Stonington and from New Haven, but "as to person and character, they are too much prejudic'd in favour of a beloved
child, not to rely on her judgement," she wrote.[4] This was
as much as to say that she had already rendered her own
verdict in his favor, and paused only for her parents to
confirm it.

Silliman waited a week in the hope of hearing that Mary
had received the desired sanction before he wrote to thank
her for her letter and "for that dear and charming Frankness of Expression, so much like yourself, which graces
every Part of it." In return, he put one simple, plain question that went to the heart of the matter:

> Do you think you could be happy with me in the Dear
> Connextion I am so earnest for or not? . . . is there no
> Way, my Love, in which a second Marriage founded in
> the principles of true Love, vertuous Tenderness & pious
> Friendship can consist with the Good & Happiness of
> the dear Pledges of a first Love & Marriage? Surely there
> is: . . . only remember, as I have often told you, that if
> I am blest with your dear Company, whatever you think
> best as to your Children shall be done.[5]

Could she be happy with him, and could her children be
happy with him? All their elaborations on the subject of
marriage came down to this.

"I answer in the affirmative," Mary replied on March 26,
"And will not be ashamed of the confession, were the correspondence to end here."[6] She had received, and here
transmitted, her parents' answer. "The ardent Love, Tenderness, deep Concern we feel, perhaps above what's common," Mr. Fish began, "are, on such an Ocasion especially,
pregnant of Doubts, Fears and Enquiries or Questions
about —— O the Dear, Dear Children!" he burst out, "Our

Life, while we live! —— Our hopes, when dead! —— in their present situation & stage of learning —— Where their Shelter? Who their protector, Watcher, Counsellor, Guide? —— In the midst of snares, Temptations to go astray, at an age the most susceptible —— &c &c —— Thus we are in a strait betwixt two —— having desire for the Happiness —— of both —— shall endeavour to leave it with the Allwise Disposer, who orders all things right —— shall expect to see you, while *yet* a Daughter of *Liberty,* if it may be consistent." The disjointed phrases of this passage, linked only by long dashes untidily scrawled across the paper that Mr. Fish would ordinarily have filled with economical care, appear in the letter only where he referred to the children. He concluded in a calmer tone, acknowledging, as Mary had predicted he would, that he had "no reason to doubt of the Taste, Discerning Judgement, Wisdom, Prudence, and deliberate procedure of the Dear Person who (in the present Question) is most greatly concerned."[7]

Mary deferred comment on this letter until she had heard Silliman's response. He had no hesitation in interpreting it as consent. "Words are wanting, when I attempt to express the Feelings of my Heart, on reading the gratefull Contents, grateful indeed to my very Soul," he replied; "shall I wish you, my Dearest, the greatest Happiness that I at present know as to this World? Then I wish your tender Heart filled with the same warm & tender Feelings that overflow mine." Yet his heart had room for sympathy with the feelings of Mr. and Mrs. Fish. "[O]nly one Dear, Dear Daughter, justly & most deservedly the Delight of their Eyes and the Darling of their Hearts," he wrote; "already at a great distance from them, and now solicited in Marriage: with whom? A Friend? A Neighbor? An Acquaintance? No, a Man that is a Stranger; and not only so, but instead of carrying her nearer, is aiming at carrying her farther off; and alas, if she consents—should she be unfortunate, should she be unkindly and illy treated—how naturally must these Apprehensions arise." As for the children, " 'tis askt: where shall be their Shelter, their Protector, their

Guide, their Counsellor?" he echoed. "Give me Leave to say their Shelter shall be where their Dear Mama's is, if she pleases to accept the proposed One. Their Counsellor, their Guide, their Protector, shall still be their Dear Mamma, assisted by One who will delight to make her and them happy."[8]

The barrier to visits being down, Silliman called on Mary without further delay, and they agreed that when she went to Stonington in April he would follow her and present himself at the parsonage. In the meantime, given her parents' acquiescence, he saw no need to conceal their engagement further or to put off setting a date for the wedding. With the evident design of removing any possible doubt that friends and family at Fairfield would welcome her, he told Mary that in recent days "My Dear Mrs. Noyes is as much the subject of Conversation here as at New Haven." The Reverend Mr. Eliot, the local clergyman, "lately said in Company, I am informed, that he would give me a Lecture for undertaking to form such a Dear Acquaintance without consulting him for he had had it long in Design to have advised me to it, and was pleased to add, that it was a *sweet Match*." This was by way of reassuring Mary that nobody's sense of propriety would be offended by an announcement. On the contrary, "considering the known Situation of our Connexion . . . it would be no Disservice if the great Point was known to be fixed," suggested Silliman. "Happy, Happy Hour will that be, my Dearest of all created Blessings, that shall unite our happy Souls & Bodies in the blessed Bonds of Marriage and enable us to walk through all the Scenes of this Life mutually supporting, blessing & assisting Each other in the Way of Duty, untill we shall at last be called off the Stage to enjoy an Eternity of Happiness in the World of blessed Spirits above." In conclusion, he told her that "it is almost Eleven at Night, and so I wish you a good Night's Rest, and hope I shall have the same myself, if you don't keep me awake to[o] long as you do almost every Night."[9]

When Mary received this letter, she found the messen-

ger who brought it almost more interesting than the contents:

> Well, Sir, I have now passed a period that I have lookd
> forward on with no small degree of anxiety. I have
> anticipated a certain future day, and viewed him, your
> dear only Child, on a certain occasion, exerting all his
> resolution (out of filial duty) to put on a pleasant or
> perhaps an air of cheerful countenance to welcome a
> new inhabitant. But O the tender movements of his
> soul!—which, notwithstanding all his philosophy, must
> vent it self in soliloquy, in such silent language as this:
> Here comes one to possess the place of my late, dear,
> indulgent Mamma! Did I think, on that fatal day never
> to be forgotten, that my dear Pappa would ever think
> of another. *My* wound is *recent*. Why does it so soon
> close with him? Can it be that another finds a place in
> his affections as did *she* I shall always lament? Ah! He
> may imagine his loss made up; mine never will be.[10]

Mary's description of her first meeting with William Silliman, or Billy, as he was called within the family, reveals an
understanding of his situation which suggests long reflec-
tion on that of her own sons. It intimates that, as she had
observed its effect on other families, the remarriage of a
widowed parent could cause an unhappiness to children
quite apart from any violation of their property rights or
ill-treatment. To see a stranger successfully "possess the
place" in a parent's heart of a dead mother or father who
is, no matter how excellent the replacement, irreplaceable
to the child had some potential to inflict pain on even the
best disposed. While Billy's manhood removed him from
the dangers faced by minor children, it presented a possible problem for Mary. If he resented her intrusion, and his
father's acceptance of her sons by John Noyes, Billy might
give his displeasure sufficient expression to spoil Mary's
chance of happiness with Silliman however genuine their
love. It was with relief, then, that she observed in the young

man "a disposition at once to be pleased and give satisfaction." Her own boys in turn had met him "with that
friendly affability I wish'd them to do," she wrote, "and
what do you think was the observation of one of them
after he was gone? Says Jose, What a pritty young man
that is, Mamma. He looks like his D---a—to whom I now
advert, least he should think my affection has got to be all
Maternal."

The answer Mary sent to the letter that Billy had carried
gave Silliman every reason to expect that she would end by
naming the wedding day. Instead, she asked him to
acquiesce in her continued deferral of that decision. Two
explanations suggest themselves. First, Mary knew the dark
side of marriage, the responsibilities, problems, and pains
that attend even the best of human relationships. She had
come by a rough road to a place where she could stand
alone without fear, and she now felt as hesitant to leave it
as she had once felt reluctant to stay. Second, the pleasure
of Silliman's courtship, which may be inferred from his
letters with their engaging mixture of sobriety and playfulness, would incline any woman to prolong that period.
The almost youthful passion of his words to her, and the
answering tenderness and gaiety of her replies, become all
the more moving when a reversion to business reminds the
reader that they were not first lovers but seasoned veterans
of marriage and parenthood, their sorrows as well as their
joys. Nevertheless, Mary let Silliman know that she did not
mean to put him off indefinitely. "I dare not tell you what
time of night it is, or rather morning," she concluded. "That
you, Sir, and I, may reform and keep better Hours is the
desire and resolution of your Accomplice, Mary Noyes."

III

ON April 19, 1775, the day on which Billy set out from
Fairfield to carry his father's letter to Mary, the train of
events began that would change all their lives in far more

fundamental ways than the projected marriage, for better or worse, could possibly have done. While Silliman and Mary wrote love letters, others had been more grimly engaged at Lexington and Concord in the first skirmish of the war to come. On April 22, Mary received a letter from Silliman in a wholly different style from his usual elegant periods, and carried not by Benjamin Douglas but by a militia captain come to New Haven on urgent military business:

> The doleful News from Boston puts all into Confusion here, and I am now in the Midst of the Confusion of Arms what will be the Event I know not, God only knows, whether I shall go, I yet don't know, I am distrest for my Dearest, is it prudent for you to go any nearer to the Scene of Distress as yet pray releive my Mind by a Line this Evening and have it ready for the Bearer Capt. Abell so that he may get it tomorrow when he returns from Hartford where he is now going Express, leave it so that he may have it tomorrow if you are at Meeting when he calls at your House; pray write me more fully than my Hurry will admit me to write now. If I go, I shall take my leave of you as I go. . . .[11]

Two days later, still at Fairfield, he wrote at greater length. He advised her to make no further plans for a journey to Stonington "before the unhappy affairs at Boston are settled," which he thought would not take long. "I doubt not but they will be near determined before Election Week comes on; perhaps you will go then," he suggested. "I shall be happy, my Love, to have the Pleasure to wait on you down . . ." Meanwhile, his militia duties continued to engross his attention. "Such a Sabbath as yesterday, I never before knew," he told her, "as to my own Part, I attended Meeting as much as the extraordinary Business of the Day would admit, which was but a part of Each half-Day's exercise." The rest of his time, from sunrise to sunset, had been taken up with the tasks of assembling and equipping soldiers for the march to New York and Boston, where the patriots were gathering their forces in response to the news of Lexington and Concord. Forty men "well armed & mounted on Horses" had departed at three in the afternoon; another forty-six stood ready to go at a moment's notice.

"But from these publick Transactions in which we are intrested, I will now turn to our own Dear Concerns," continued Silliman. Once more, he urged her to set a date for the marriage, enlarging her own modest description of initial goodwill between herself, her sons, and Billy into a full-scale portrait of the happy family to be:

> [H]ow shall I express the Satisfaction & Delight you give me in so frankly joining me in my most sincere Petition for our mutual Happiness in the married State, & giveing me also an Account of the dutiful & filial Behaviour of my Son to my Dearest Love, and of that friendly & fraternal Complaisance which appeared in the Behaviour of our Dear Children to one another and . . . their Parents? Give me leave, my Love, to use the Expression. Dear Jose, I thank him for his fraternal Sentiments toward his Brother (permit me, Dear Love, the Expression) as well as the benevolent Sentiments which his Comparison shewed that he entertained of me. When I figure to myself the dear Mamma siting with her four Sons around her, viewing and conversing with her . . . what Scene here below (one only excepted) can my Imagination paint to itself that would fill my Soul with such inexpressible Satisfaction & Delight.[12]

"You must not expect much of an answer to your very affectionate letter in this," Mary replied. "I don't know how it is at Fairfield, but here they take the freedom to open every letter that comes by the Post, in search of News."[13] Talk was safer, and he would find her at home to receive him on May 1.

She wondered, however, if by then the swift movement

of events might not have carried them past the point of making marriage plans. Her father had recently observed to her that, in his own experience, "when I have been greatly delighted, or too much pleas'd, with raised Expectations of happiness, from the prospect of approaching but (as yet) distant worldly Good, I have generally, if not always, met with some Disappointment or Keen Trial from the quarter, which, indeed, should not stop a rational procedure; yet should serve to qualifie our Temper & Dependence."[14] Though he had written those words before the present trial had arisen, they fitted Mary's situation more precisely now, changed as it was from the hope of a second spring to the apprehension of a cataclysm. "What God is about to do with us and our land he only knows," she warned her lover. "Perhaps far other scenes await us than what has lately been in view."[15] But when their meeting took place, Silliman seems to have used his formidable powers of persuasion to convince Mary that they need not stand helplessly by while public events dictated their destiny. With no further discussion, without waiting even to attend the wedding of Deodate, Silliman's youngest brother, which was to take place at Fairfield on May 25, they made their arrangements, traveled down to Stonington, and were married there on May 24, 1775.

They lingered at the parsonage for a week, which allowed Mary's parents to assess the son-in-law they had so suddenly acquired. Before the visit was out, Silliman had gained their affection and calmed their fears; if any shadow of a doubt remained, he dispelled it by demonstrating that, with all won, he would continue to cultivate their good opinion. Because Mrs. Fish had told him she admired the hymns and psalms of Dr. Watts, he paused at Hartford on his way home to buy and send her a handsomely bound copy of the complete works. Then, though both his law practice and his responsibilities as a colonel in the militia demanded that he first return to Fairfield, as soon as he had dispatched the work that had accumulated there in his absence he turned to the business of the boys' inheritance.

He planned to visit Waterbury "to have some more of the Lands there brought under Improvement," he told Mr. Fish, whom he took care to inform of all matters pertaining to the estate. "And from thence I expect to go again to Farmington . . . to have the Fence around the Home Lott New Made, which it very much wants; and for company I take with me our little Son Jemmy, who is very fond of the Ride."[16] Before the summer ended, he completed his survey of the scattered Noyes estate with visits to Amity (Woodbridge) and Bethany, saw to necessary repairs, ordered "an exact Map or plan . . . for the Benefit of the Children" of the large farm at Waterbury,[17] and found tenants for it who bound themselves to develop the land in certain specified ways that would enhance its value in exchange for the use of it over a limited period. Though such leases would produce no income during the short term, the Noyes estate included enough improved property, immediately rentable for cash, to cover the costs of sending Jose to Yale and preparing John for college. By the time the larger expense arose of keeping all three boys simultaneously at Yale, the improved lands at Waterbury would be bringing in money too.

The measures that Silliman had taken were designed to secure and enhance the inheritance as a whole, and Mr. Fish responded to his carefully detailed reports with the simple statement that "It relieves my mind of a burden of thot and care that *one* so able and likeminded, who will naturally care for their [the children's] Interest, has undertaken to provide and secure it."[18] In that brief, plain sentence, however, the words "likeminded" and "naturally" carry a power of meaning. He had seen in Silliman a man after his own heart in every respect, but not least in the reverence for the sacred ties of family, which made his extension of paternal feeling to his stepsons natural indeed, and therefore dependable.

Shortly after Silliman and Mary returned from their wedding trip, though they had not yet found tenants for the Elm Street house, they moved Mary's entire household, including Peter, a native-born African slave who had lived with the Noyes family from boyhood, to Fairfield. Since Silliman had just been named colonel of the 4th regiment, an appointment that necessitated his presence there, they could hardly do otherwise, but it was a difficult undertaking. Silliman's house, by the standards of a later age not a particularly spacious one, already held a number of people. Billy and his bride, the former Nancy (Ann) Allen, continued to live there, along with nine-year-old Amelia Burr, the daughter of Silliman's sister, who had made a home with her uncle since her father's death seven years earlier. Another inhabitant, described as "a single woman of great integrity and devotion to the family . . . [who] had a sharp temper [but] was prompt and efficient," was Esther Lord.[19] Esther, who received wages, was nevertheless more a friend than a servant, and her twenty years of previous residence with the Sillimans made her a presence to be reckoned with. Mary's new neighbors, Ebenezer with his second wife and the newly married Deodate with his bride, also counted as a peripheral part of her new household since they were close relations and frequent visitors. All in all, the potential for friction in this merger of two large and formerly independent groups, including three generations of adults and children and two sets of servants accustomed to different routines, was considerable. That it was not realized does credit to everyone concerned, but particularly to Mary. In her multifarious roles as wife, mother, daughter, sister-in-law, and mistress over an establishment with which she had no previous acquaintance, she touched the lives of all those affected by the change her marriage to Silliman had wrought, and their adjustment to some extent depended upon her.

On July 12, Silliman sent Mr. and Mrs. Fish an account of the amalgamated families guaranteed to please them. "[O]ur Children seem happy in a mutual Esteem & Friendship for each other & in a visible and apparent Design by Acts of Benevolence & Kindness to secure each other's Friendship; after this Short Description I believe you will hardly ask the Question whether we the Parents are happy in our children or not," he wrote. "So great a Similarity has there been in the Mode of their Education, and so great a Similitude is there in their Manners & general Behaviour, that I believe a Stranger would be inclined to think them all Children of the same Father and Mother: the same happy temper hitherto subsists among the Servants also." Mary soon afterward added that her sons had taken spontaneously to calling Silliman "Dadde," while Silliman's own son and daughter-in-law had requested inclusion in the roll of the grandchildren who, at the close of every letter to Mr. and Mrs. Fish, "present their duty to their Grand Father and Grand Mamma."[20]

IV

RELIEVED of their long anxiety over Mary and her sons, her parents began to pay closer attention to the profound upheaval now sending tremors even into their retired neighborhood. Indeed, it forced itself upon their notice. The British defense of Boston had driven many homeless families to take refuge at Stonington, a first intimation for Mr. and Mrs. Fish of the terrible suffering that a war fought on home ground would entail. To add to their distress, an early dispatch from the scene said that John Chester, Sarah Noyes Chester's son, lay dead on the battlefield at Breed's Hill. "We mourned for him with bitterness, near a week," wrote Mr. Fish, "till yesterday were assured that he was spoke with alive and well since that Engagement."[21] It was not the last time that a false report would cause them needless grief, the inevitable result of news-gathering by verbal transmission. Meanwhile many of their friends and neighbors had in truth fallen, and many families mourned without remission.

On every hand, Mary's parents found fresh reminders of the impermanence of earthly attachments, which jolted them into awareness that within Mary's new happiness lay the seeds of new sorrow. Sooner or later, if the conflict continued, Silliman himself would meet the mortal dangers of the battlefield. They remembered Mary's former struggles with depression too clearly not to fear for her stability of mind if she should find herself again bereft. "So far as creatures . . . are able to make you happy, we are much mistaken if the ingredients are not before you," Joseph acknowledged; but he cautioned her to remember the lessons of the past, and to "let God have all the praise; live upon *him,* & not upon *them.*"[22]

At the time, however, Mary was too busy to brood over possibilities. The house that Silliman had brought her to may have reminded her of the house she grew up in, for it occupied "an eminence which commands a view of the Sound of Long Island for forty miles."[23] She had to learn the workings of this establishment and its home farm, and also to acquire some knowledge of her husband's financial affairs, for, though he had taken momentary charge of her interests along with his own, she knew that whenever the tide of war swept him away both responsibilities would shift back to her shoulders. At the same time as she addressed this necessity, she had to provide for a steady stream of visitors. Besides her former guests, most of them already known to Silliman and accustomed to visit his house at Fairfield as frequently as hers at New Haven, she had to feed and accommodate an increasing number of officers and soldiers traveling about the countryside who looked, as a matter of course, for hospitality under Colonel Silliman's roof.

Mary found that the enterprise on which she had embarked, though she felt more and more confident that it would fulfill the brightest promise she had dared to see in it, did show a dark side. In mid-July Ebenezer Silliman suffered a stroke that paralyzed the left side of his body. His mind remained clear, but it seemed unlikely that he would ever regain his physical health. Worse still, Billy's young wife, unwell for some time, had developed unmis-

takable symptoms that soon declared their cause. She had
fallen victim to a consumption that devoured her so fast
that even his hopeful eyes could see no hope. Mary had
come to care for Nancy, a lovable girl whom Silliman
described as "blessed with a Temper calm & unruffled as
the smooth Surface of the unruffled Summer Sea," as if for
the daughter that death had twice denied her.[24] Now she
found herself once more presiding helplessly over the dis-
solution of someone close and dear.

Outside the family, too, death and disease seemed to
clog the New England air that summer, with epidemics
ravaging one small town after another. Besides smallpox,
there was dysentery, or camp distemper, so-called because
the crowded, unsanitary army camps had bred it and the
soldiers on the move had contributed to the spread of it.
Dysentery in particular "prevailed greatly & proved very
mortal in some of our neighboring Towns," Silliman told
Mr. Fish,[25] so much so that at one point he and Mary went
to the length of moving the family, servants and all, back
to New Haven.

Another sort of plague had descended upon Stonington. A crop infestation of white worms, "the Army Under
Ground" as Mr. Fish termed it, threatened the supply of
food for both household and livestock, and the effort to
control the pest kept him and his wife tied to their fields,
unable to make their planned visit to Mary's new home.[26]
As a result, they were present when Stonington came under
attack from the navy above ground. "Our Long Point has
been most terribly & cruelly Cannonaded for most of a
Day," Mr. Fish wrote on September 5, "but (wonderfull,
even to astonishment) not one human Person killd; only
one wounded, now almost well; not one house or Building brot down, nor greatly damaged . . . nor any dumb
creature killd or hurt, save one *Cat,* I am told."[27]

Autumn brought a brief respite on all fronts, and in mid-
September Mary's parents made the long-deferred journey
to Holland Hill. They spent a month there, and on the

return journey they visited, among others, the Chesters and the Douglasses, who had a newborn daughter. John and Becca were long gone, but their going could not loosen family ties once formed. Mr. and Mrs. Fish went home happy in all their connections, but especially the newest. "Tho' the Distance [between us and you] is sensibly increased, yet have reason to be thankfull, that we see you so comfortably resettled, That God has provided such a *Friend* for a Husband, & such a Tender Father for your Fatherless Children," Mr. Fish told Mary. And yet, perhaps because of the many deaths they had seen or heard of in recent months, in battle or from illness, they felt unusually melancholy at the prospect of the winter's separation. "Our parting at the Ferry, where you stood looking after us with Filial Tenderness," he wrote, "was doubtless accompanied with mutual Reflections, that as *we* are aged & *your* life, like ours, a vapour, 'twas very uncertain, if not unlikely, that ever we should see each other's faces again in this world of change."[28]

Though no such final parting lay in wait for the two families, the next few months brought partings enough. Soon after Mr. and Mrs. Fish set out for Stonington, Ebenezer Silliman died. His son had little time to mourn him, for a few days later Mary was stricken with the dreaded dysentery. She lay at the point of death for so long that, even after she had passed the crisis, her weakness and emaciation left her no more than a tenuous hold on life. Just as she began to take the first steps on the road back to health, a letter from John and Jose at New Haven brought grievous news. Benjamin Douglas had contracted a bad case of "St. Anthony's Fire," or erisypelas; so bad that his death was hourly expected. "If your dear Uncle Douglass is no more, in him your Mamma has lost a kind and tender Brother," Mary lamented; "We have often known one another's souls in adversity, and mingled tears as we have felt each other's woes."[29] About to leave for the Superior Court at New Haven when the message had come, Silliman hastened his departure, but still arrived too late. Keenly as he felt the death of his friend, on Mary the blow fell with a double force. Benjamin represented "all that was left of my dear sister," she wrote, "and his brotherly kindness to me rendered him very dear.[30]

Grief retarded her convalescence, and not until December 22 did Silliman report to Mr. and Mrs. Fish that for the first time in almost two months Mary had "left her room . . . and moved out into the common Dwelling Room." On the same day an urgent message from John sent him posthaste back to New Haven, where he found Jose seriously ill with sore throat, eruptions from the ear, "a constant Buzing Noise in his Head, a Stiff Neck, and a constant severe Pain in his Head."[31] Recognizing that, come what might, Jose would be in no condition to attend college for some time, Silliman sent him home to Fairfield. Within a few days of his return, the gentle Nancy died; and Mary, barely recovered herself, now had Jose to nurse, Billy to comfort, and her own sorrow to bear.

Silliman, meanwhile, had more than family crises to confront. During all this time, as he hurried between one sick person and another, he had also to cope with increasingly complex and troublesome military responsibilities. Just as the difficulty of distinguishing rumor from fact added to the tribulations of civilians, so it often caused those in command of the soldiery to run an obstacle course before arriving at a decision on many apparently simple questions. In the autumn of 1775 Silliman received more than one urgent request for the help of the forces under his command. He knew that New York harbored an active Tory element supported by the *Asia*, a sixty-four-gun man-of-war, and that Connecticut's extensive coast invited attack. He also knew that a signal of distress, no matter how desperate or plausible it seemed, might arise either from panic in the face of some erroneous report or from a deliberate intention to draw off his men from that part of the coast which was marked out for the real attack. Each

call that reached his ears consumed an enormous amount
of time, thought, and energy even before he acted upon it,
for he dared not send away his men before he had established its genuineness; those that he answered cost him still
more anxiety until he knew that he had not misjudged the
case.

V

IN the first few months of the war, the colonists had kept
alive a hope that a resolute display of American unity and
prowess in arms would deter Great Britain from pursuing
a military solution to their dispute with her. Bunker Hill
and the conquest of Canada had seemed to be steps in the
right direction. Since then, however, the failure of the
Continental Army to dislodge the British from Boston,
combined with the defeat at Quebec, had given the British
ample reason to fight on. That winter, Congress asked
Connecticut once again to supply men for the campaign
that the spring of 1776 would now assuredly bring, and
once again Silliman helped to raise them. But both he and
Mary knew that if the war widened, as it was almost bound
to do, he must expect to take a more than administrative
part.

Perhaps the same foreboding impelled Mr. Fish to renew
the question of provision for the Noyes children as the
spring approached. "Am concerned, how you . . . command a sufficiency of Cash out of the Incomes of the Estate,
to defray their College Charges," he wrote. "I would freely
send them a little Recruit, out of my Small Support, for
their present relief, were it possible to collect my Dues: but
we find it even impracticable to get a sufficiency for our
own necessities: and I have done with my *Indian Mission*
at Narragensett . . . which used to be a pretty Resource."[32]
In March, Silliman made him a lengthy reply. He had

recently revisited the Noyes estate in the course of a journey that he and Mary had taken together. "We were absent two weeks," he informed Mr. and Mrs. Fish. "The first I spent principally in attending the Superior Court then sitting at New Haven, which ended on Thursday; the Rest of my Time that week I spent in waiting on my Dear Partner to see her Friends, and a very Busy Week she had of it as you will easily imagine."[33] They had stayed with Elizabeth Douglas, "she and dear little Betsy well," wrote Mary, "But O the vacancy, how did I miss my dear departed Brother."[34] On the journey home, they spent three days with Abigail Darling, and Silliman had ridden out to inspect the Bethany and Farmington lands.

Immediately upon his return to Fairfield, he set to work to prepare a full report for Mr. Fish. Though he did not say so, Silliman probably meant to ensure that if he were suddenly called into action Mary's father would possess a written statement of all that he had done, and of how matters stood when he left. He acknowledged that, though he had spent a good deal on repairs, he had not yet succeeded in renting out the land on the terms he wanted. He felt confident, nevertheless, that "tho I have not been able to collect Cash quite so fast as I have paid it out, yet it will come by & by, so I hope you won't give yourself any Uneasiness about it," he told Mr. Fish; "pray don't think of doing anything with Respect to Cash that will in the least incommode Yourself, or our Hond. Mother; for, if you should, you would give Pain where you intend the Contrary." He hoped, he said, if "the State of Publick Affairs will allow of it," that when he went to Hartford for election week Mary would accompany him with two of the boys and the whole party would afterward go on to Stonington. "[I]f we do come, we hope and design to tarry with you over the happy 24th May," he concluded. "Dear Parents, do you recollect the Spectator's History (Vol. 8) of the Manner and Design of bestowing the Flitch of Bacon on married People a year and a Day after Marriage, on

certain Conditions? * I hope my Dear Wife & her Husband
will have the Pleasure to do Honour to that ancient Institution with our Hond. Parents, if God spares our Lives
and Healths."[35]

*This custom, which originated in the thirteenth century, persists in
the village of Dunmow, Essex, England, to this day. A flitch of bacon is
awarded to the couple that has neither quarreled nor regretted the marriage within its first year.

Five

GLORIOUS
TIMES,
DISTRESSING
TIMES

ON March 19, 1776, Mary began a long, chatty letter to her parents, mostly about the boys. Two days later, she added a postscript:

> I tell you with a heart most tenderly affected that this morning an express comes in with orders from the Governor for my dearest Beloved to march forthwith to New York with a part of his regement, there to wait the arrival of General Washington. What I have long feard is now come upon me; I endeavour to commit him to the care of a kind providence, hopeing he may be returnd in safety.[1]

The summons to New York followed from an event that the patriots had prayed for. On March 17, the eleven-month-old siege maintained at Boston by Washington's army had at last forced General Howe to withdraw his troops. But a new and sharp anxiety qualified the sweets of this victory, for no one knew where Howe would next appear. He might mount a fresh assault on Boston, or he might sail down the coast to attack New York; Washington would have to guard against both contingencies. The moment he heard of the evacuation he ordered that six regiments from the army at Boston march south to reinforce New York. Since he knew that men traveling on foot during mud-time might not move as fast as Howe's ships, he also asked that Connecticut send some of her militia to swell the ranks of the city's defenders until the Continentals had arrived. It was in response to this that Silliman had received the order to muster and command his share of these temporary forces. When the men had assembled, Mary accompanied him to town to review them "as well that I might have as much of his company the few precious moments that remained as I could, as to see the regiment," she said,[2] and the moments were indeed few. Mary recorded his and Billy's departure on March 27, together with a heartfelt prayer that "the great happiness we have enjoyed may not end here—may they be returned in safety to the rejoicing of us all—how happy have we been—such a husband, such a father few can lose!"[3]

I

SILLIMAN arrived in New York at five o'clock in the morning on March 29 and embarked on a grueling daily round that kept him in a "Constant Hurry" from the pre-dawn hours till dusk, though the comforts and congenialities of urban life relieved the rigor of his duties.[4] He and Billy had found a comfortable billet with some other officers in "an Elegant House" cared for by a staff that included three Connecticut men "who . . . are extraordinary good Cooks."[5] On his second afternoon in New York Silliman went to a dinner where he met Doctor Franklin, other members of the Congress, and several high-ranking offi-

cers of the army, the first of many social engagements which
lent his accounts of the days almost an aura of gaiety.

His lighthearted tone owed even more to his belief in
the impregnability of New York. The arrival of the first
regiments from Boston on March 30 relieved his mind of
any fear that he and his men would bear the brunt of an
attack alone, and a day-long tour of the fortifications
increased his sense of security. He described them to Mary
in the voice of a man overawed by what he had seen. There
were "strong Breast Works raised across every Street that
leads down to the Water," formidable batteries on the East
and Hudson rivers, and a fort, almost complete, posi-
tioned in the rear of the city to give protection against
attack from the interior.[6] Such was the confidence inspired
by these precautions that the incessant speculation concerning the whereabouts of Howe's force and its next
objective seemed to infuse him with more excitement than
alarm.

Silliman was quick to warn Mary that the arrival of reinforcements would not mean his immediate discharge, and
indeed he showed no impatience to return. Change had
stimulated him, and though his letters frequently expressed
fatigue and homesickness, a note of almost boyish enjoyment crept in too. Perhaps he relished the idea of joining
the victorious Continentals. Billy and his Uncle Ebenezer
certainly did, for both had asked Silliman to use his influence in procuring commissions for them. If he succeeded,
"Neither Uncle nor Nephew will be seen at Fairfield for
some time."[7] Since, however, the original plan had called
for Billy to return as soon as his father was settled, presumably in order to supervise the spring planting for Mary,
Silliman consulted his wife before acting upon his son's
part of the request.

Mary professed herself "content with respect to dear
Billy's tarrying as his heart is so much set on it," but
acknowledged that she felt "as if a prop was taken from me
on which I hop'd to lean in the absence of my greatest

earthly support." For while the men savored the new and
piquant taste of army life at a post of danger, Mary toiled
at the bleaker service demanded of those who stand and
wait. The burden of extra work, though it taxed her endurance, was not without psychological benefits. She took
pride in the discovery that she could cope unaided with
the work of overseeing the farm chores, keeping the
accounts, and dealing with household repairs, responsibilities for which widowhood in New Haven had only par-
tially prepared her. "The negroes are now bringing the Hay
you order'd from the other house; I will give the [Noyes]
estate credit when they have done," she informed Silliman,
with a happy air of conscious efficiency. "I have sent and
got what little cupper [cooper] work I wanted done, &
have got home the window shuts; if you think best to send
some Hinges by some private hand, will get them put up.
I have sent N. H. chaise to be mended, it is to be done
today."[8] The very diversity of the tasks that rested on her
shoulders helped to keep her days as interesting as they
were busy, and the elements of her situation that most
afflicted her were of another order.

Foremost among them was the loss of her husband's
companionship. As a substitute for conversation with him
she reread his earlier letters, but there was another lack for
which there was no substitute. When the woman who had
dealt competently with a damaged chaise responded to a
damaged quill with the complaint that "I wish you was
here to mend my Pen," Silliman could read between the
lines. "Want me to mend your Pen, Love! Is that all?" he
retorted. "No, I hope not indeed; had I been there, fond
Arms would have been in the way of your Writeing, I
guess."[9] As constant as her longing was her fear. Like the
men at New York, Mary could not foresee if or when an
attack would come. But while they knew at every moment
where they stood, each report that Mary received was
already a day or more old, not to mention unreliable. She
had always to think what might be happening even as she
heard that all was well. Bad news, on the other hand, car-

ried instant conviction to a mind prepared by fear to hear
it.

On April 2, as Mary sat writing to her husband, she broke
off to greet Jemmy. When she resumed, it was in handwriting suddenly ill-formed and smudged. "This minute
Jimme comes in from school and says Mr. Elliot says the
Fleet are sail'd from Boston for New York. O my trembling hand!" she wrote. "What can I say, what can I do
but commit my dearest Husband and dear Son to the care
of that God that directs the lightning under the whole
heaven, and can preserve you safe, tho instruments of death
fly thick around you. Goodby, my dear one, pray God protect you and restore you to my longing arms."[10] Yet in a
letter from Silliman to Mary that crossed with hers to him,
he calmly relayed the quite different news that, according
to information just received by General Putnam, Howe
had sailed for Rhode Island. Silliman certainly thought the
report reliable or he would not have ventured the request
that followed. "Can't you contrive to send Jemmy down,
my love?" he suggested. "I wish to have the pritty little
fellow here to gratify his curiosity; I dare say he would be
all Eyes & Ears for a Day or two at least."[11]

The remainder of the reinforcements from Boston arrived
soon after this exchange and, since it had by then become
clear that Howe was not advancing on Rhode Island either,
Putnam dismissed the militia. Mary passed quickly from
wretched apprehension to happy preparation for Silliman's
return, but first she hastened to grant his wish for a visit
from Jemmy. On hearing that Silliman had invited him,
the boy seemed "as tho he would almost fly out of his Skin
till he got away," Mary said. He arrived at New York on
April 9 and for two days made himself, as predicted, "all
Eyes and Ears."[12] Silliman and Billy (apparently disappointed in his request for a commission) accompanied him
on the journey home to Fairfield, where he lost no time in
setting down, in a fine, italic hand, his own observations
on the grand proceedings going forward at New York:

My dear and Hon. Grandmamma,
I want to see you a great deal to tell you something that
I have seen. Dadda sent for me to come down to New
York, and I went with a very kind man. We set out in
the afternoon, and got to Horseneck [Greenwich], about
34 miles that night. Next day we got to Dadda's house
about 4 o'clock, found him and My dear Brother Billy
well, and very glad to see me. I see four large Ships
there; one a seventy Gun Ship; and I saw the kings
statue, and he sat on a great Horse, both covered over
with leaf Gold; and the King had one bullet hole
through his cheek, and another through his neck, and
they talk of running his Majesty up into Bullets for he
and his horse are made of lead. The houses most all join
together; and I never see such a fine place in my life.
. . . and now I have got home well is not my dear
Grandmamma glad I have been? . . . P.S. I heard this
week from my dear Brothers at New Haven, I don't
know what they will think when they hear I have been
to New York.[13]

II

SILLIMAN'S absence had lasted less than three weeks and
he had seen only the preliminaries for battle, not the face
of it. Even so, he returned to find his affairs in disarray.
He had lost business to lawyers who had stayed at home;
at the same time, he had accumulated a daunting backlog
of work. He had returned in time for the county court
sessions, an important period in the lawyer's year, but he
could not attend them regularly because he had still an
unmet obligation to his men. Within a few days of his
homecoming he rode again to New York in order to collect their wages, only to find that he could immediately
obtain no more than their marching money. As for the
rest, Washington bluntly informed him that he could not

pay. Disconcerted, Silliman felt that he should not leave without at least some indication of when and where the money would be forthcoming, and as a result several more precious days elapsed before he could start back.

Nevertheless, by the middle of May he had dispatched his work at both New York and Fairfield and could accompany Mary to Stonington in time to keep their first anniversary where their marriage had begun. They left Billy in charge of the farm, a responsibility for which he showed little relish at that particular moment, though he reported dutifully on the progress of work and mustered the generosity to praise the servants and slaves. Job and Peter had labored so diligently in the field in spite of an unusually wet spring that, though less advanced than usual with their planting, the Sillimans were ahead of their neighbors, while the faithful Esther had kept "busy as a bee at the Cloath and Yarn & had almost finished it."

Billy's heart was not in homely chores. He reserved his enthusiasm for another topic. When intelligence revealed that, in the coming campaign, the British intended to hurl an expeditionary force of unprecedented magnitude against the colonies, Congress asked that Connecticut raise several new regiments, and Billy had heard a rumor that his father would be given command of one. He also told of a sinister increase in Tory activity at Fairfield, a phenomenon that struck almost more fear to people's hearts than the open aggression of an outward, visible enemy. "Oh Dear Sir! The Prospect before us is dark and gloomy indeed, & Daily seems to grow Darker," he lamented. "Our own Countrymen & those whom we Valued as Friends are riseing against us & concerting the most Horrid & Diabolical Schemes for our Subversion & entire Ruin, while a British Army is on the Borders of our Coast." Yet through his assumption of alarm and despondency there gleamed an unmistakable elation at the thought of joining the fray. "I put my trust in the God of Armys & am ready & Desireous to meet & Attack the Bloody foe," he declaimed. "If I am

called to March forth to Battle, to Battle I'll go, & fight for
the Citys of my God: for if God be for us, who shall be
against us?"[14]

Silliman and Mary returned to Fairfield in early June to
find confirmation of his new post awaiting him. The British were already gathering their forces for an assault on
New York, and Silliman did not linger over his preparations. On the morning of July 7, when the household gathered for family prayer, the master's horse stood ready at
the gate. The service concluded with a heartfelt reading of
the Ninety-first Psalm:

> Thou shalt not be afraid for the terror by night; nor for
> the arrow that flieth by day;
>
> Nor for the pestilence that walketh in darkness; nor for
> the destruction that wasteth at noonday. . . ;
>
> There shall no evil befall thee; neither shall any plague
> come nigh thy dwelling.

And when the last amen was done, Silliman rode away.

The second parting cost Mary an even sharper pang than
the first. This time, she knew, her husband would almost
certainly see action. On the next day, when she sat down
to finish his most recent letter to her parents, her eye lighted
on the concluding sentence: "God only knows what may
be the Event with Respect to our Country as well as to me
in particular, or whether I shall ever see you again in this
world or not." She wept as she went on to praise him in
terms that confirmed his correspondence to her "Portrait."
"As a husband how tender, as a Father how indulgent, as
a Master how kind, as a child how dutifull," she wrote. "O
my dear Parents, how highly are we favored in this dear
connection . . . but God only knows what is before us."
Yet Silliman's fatherly indulgence had not extended to his
war-enamored son. Poor Billy! "He wanted much to go,
fier'd with the importance of the cause, but as his Dadde
thought not best, is content to stay," explained Mary comfortably.[15]

A few days later, a letter arrived for Silliman from General Washington. Mary opened and read it before she sent it on, for even military dispatches were subject to the practice of garnering news from all the correspondence that passed through one's hands, a practice that may on occasion have aided Tory subversion. In this particular letter, for instance, Washington revealed that he had so far received pitifully few men. "I think the General writes rather gloomy; but hope the arrival of so many of our worthy Officers and soldiers with a blessing will give him spirits,"[16] Mary wrote. Silliman, however, who had reached New York in time to hear "the Proclamation for Independence . . . published at the Head of the Troops, which was received and welcomed with Huzzas," agreed that those troops numbered less than they should have done.[17] "I have no more than 430 men in my Regiment instead of 744; I am much concerned that our People have been so backward in inlisting," he confessed. "[By] the Paper sent herewith you will see that our Forces here & hereabout are said to be 50,000; depend upon it my Dearest that they are but little more than half that Number."[18] Subsequently it emerged that even Silliman's estimate was twice as high as the reality.

Silliman also saw a sobering change in his surroundings. "Everything wears the face of a Garrison Town, very few Inhabitants are left here," he wrote.[19] The British fleet, considerably increased by the arrival of Howe's transports, now presented a formidable appearance to his eyes, the ships lying "so thick together that they cannot be counted." The conviction of impregnability that he had carried away from his earlier sojourn was shattered when, on the afternoon of July 12, two men-of-war and two tenders ran up the Hudson River right past the city's defenses. The Americans fired on them, but the sole result was the loss to themselves of "Seven Men killed in the Action, and several wounded, all by our own Cannon and not by the Enemy's Shott."[20]

The reason for all these vexations appeared plain to Silliman. They were, he said, "certainly designed to bring us seriously to consider our awfull Declensions from an holy God."[21] This view of events, widely held by both clergy and laity, did not preclude full confidence in America's ultimate victory. If Americans were lacking in that virtue which would go further toward winning the war than numbers, equipment, or skill, they were nonetheless more virtuous than the King's men, their reformation more assured, and their cause the righteous cause. Without contradiction, therefore, at the same time as Silliman decried his country's degeneracy, he could proclaim his faith that she would ultimately triumph through superior moral force. "Yesterday 11 more Transports and Men of War arrived and joined the Fleet, which we are told is their whole Reinforcement; so now, as soon as they get a little recruited, there can't be anything to hinder their attacking us," he wrote on August 13. "And I hope we shall be able to give them such a Reception as shall show Mankind that there is a difference between Troops that fight only for the Mastery and 6d. Sterling a day, and those that fight for their Relligion, their Laws, their Liberties, their Wives & Children & everything else that is dear to them."[22]

Mary may not have shared her husband's absolute assurance of righteousness. The entries in her journal at this time betray a certain conflict between the new loyalty to her native land and the old attachment to the image of England as nourishing mother, between adherence to "the glorious cause" and abhorrence of the war as "unnatural" because those against whom Americans turned their swords were "bone of our bone and flesh of our flesh."[23] The imperial relationship had so often been described in familial terms that now, along with the empire, the very bonds of family seemed to be giving way.

None of this turmoil appeared in her letters to Silliman, but enough escaped into those she addressed to her parents to alarm her father, for he cautioned her against such introspection. "Hardy Souls may do well to think much

on the affecting subject, to excite a Feeling, but your *spirits*
are p'rhaps too tender already—they won't bear to be raised
higher," he suggested.[24] He tried to brace her with an infu-
sion of his own millennial hopes. "The times are, indeed,
alarming, & in some views very distressing—But still in
my apprehension they may in other respects be called Glorious Times, pregnant (I hope) of happy Events to the
Churches, & to the Commonwealth of our Israel," he
wrote. "Behold how the Sons of America, armd and furnished with every Article for the Field, by heavens Indulgent Care, do flock together from every Quarter. They run,
they fly to the place of Danger, in double Numbers, determined, under God, to repluse the guilty Foe, and not suffer their Shackl'd Feet, to burden the Shores of America,
Sacred to Liberty & the Rights of Conscience."[25]

Mary could no longer contemplate so roseate a picture
in the same naive spirit as her father. Her husband's letters
from New York, despite their confidence in the eventual
triumph of divine justice, had cast too bleak a light upon
immediate events there to leave her the comfort of illusion.
In their more personal passages they did comfort her with
the undiminished warmth of their affection. "[I]t is now a
Pleasure to me to converse in this the only way that I can
with my beloved Wife," he told her, "placed as we are by
an holy Providence at the Distance of almost 70 Miles,
deprived of that Dear, inexpressibly Dear Delightful Converse & Intercourse with Each Other which the blessed
Father of Spirits sent down our Souls to communicate Each
to the other; happy it is for us in this State of Separation
that the Quill can be taught articulate Sounds." Still, Silliman did not gloss over the precariousness of their present
situation. "[P]erhaps [God] has measured out our Portion
of Delight & Happiness in Each Other; certain it is he has
poured out an Abundance of it upon us in the Course of
about Twelve Months," he acknowledged. "Certain it is, it
must have an End as to this World, and my present
Engagements are such as do most expose me, therefore my

Dearest Love let us both rely on the protecting & preserv-
ing Mercy of that God that has never yet forsaken us; but
if it has been as long extended to us as may serve the Purposes of his Glory and he sees it proper no longer to extend
it to us, let us endeavour sincerely to say Amen."[26] "True,
my dearest, we was—was, most Bless'd," Mary returned.
"May we be restord to one another's longing arms as Isaac
was to the arms of his resign'd father."[27]

Silliman told her that he saw no hope of such a restoration "till we have had our Dispute with our Red Coated
Gentry,"[28] but though her loneliness and her fear grew
as the days of his absence lengthened, so did her competence to do the work that filled her waking hours, even
with Billy to help. In that work she found a prop and stay
to sanity stronger than any reassurances her husband or
her father offered. One duty in particular gave Mary
immense satisfaction: that of keeping Silliman supplied with
the essentials he could no longer afford to buy at New
York. Requests for sundry domestic articles often mingled
with reports on weightier matters: for brown thread stock-
ings to save his good ones; for pins, cheese, and butter;
and for a hogshead of Billy's best cider "for I have no Doubt
but that Cyder will be 5 Dollars here within a Fortnight,"
he complained. "We buy everything here at the most
extravagant Rates."[29] In response, Mary sent all that he
asked and offered what he had not. "Pray let me know of
anything that may be contributed to your comfort; you
shall have anything in our house you want for, even tho it
is for your *Wife*," she hinted.[30]

"I thank you, my Dearest, for your dear Kindness, that
you will send me anything I want, even my beloved Wife
if I send for her, you say," Silliman replied. "If God pre-
serves our Lives to see the present Cloud scattered, so that
I can ask it with Prudence, I shall, you may depend upon
it, I shall certainly ask you to send her down, but I dare
not trust her here yet."[31] Apart from the ever-present
danger of attack, there was dysentery at New York, and

where Mary's well-being was concerned he feared the second as much as the first. Yet, though he could keep her out of the city, he could not keep the illness in, and in July it appeared among the scholars at Yale.

When Mary received a message from John to say that Jose had fallen sick and had no one to nurse him, their landlady having fled the town, she had not a second's hesitation in setting out to meet face to face with "the pestilence that walketh in darkness." She arrived at New Haven in the late afternoon to find her son sorely in need of her ministrations. At about eleven o'clock, almost exhausted, she retired to bed, though not to sleep, for she was unexpectedly "beset by numbers of those nocturnal blood thirsty enemies which have heretofore attack'd you, my dearest," she told Silliman. "I stood my ground, and fought and slew, but reinforcements came so fast I was obliged to quit the field, and thought I would set up the rest of the night, but finding a Creek Bedsted without a bed, I lay down on that with a Coverlid folded up for my Pillow, and by and by forgot my hard lodging and got to sleep."[32]

Mary might have been less able to laugh at the loss of a night's rest to bedbugs had she not wakened to find Jose better. As it was, she mustered the energy to conduct some business in addition to caring for him. She found a tenant for the New Haven salt meadow and collected her rents, though she chose to make no demand on a woman tenant who had both husband and brother in the army. She showed no sign of succumbing to the infection; on the contrary, her health and spirits seemed better than before she left Fairfield. Her persistent failure to regain the weight she had lost earlier, during her bout with dysentery, had prompted Silliman to ask, in a letter which reached her just after she returned home, if anything he had written had spoiled her appetite. "I want to whip you with my lips for having such a thought," she scolded. "I dont expect to grow fat till I have the pleasure of seeing you." Short of that pleasure, her expedition to New Haven, though hardly recreational, had oddly enough refreshed her, "and if I dont hear any bad news I believe I shall soon regain my flesh."[33]

III

MARY returned to Fairfield on Monday, August 19, bringing both sons with her. During her stay at New Haven the scholars had succumbed to dysentery in such numbers that the president had closed the college. She and Johnny had escaped, however, and Jose recovered so fast that on the following Sunday he attended church with his brothers. In their absence Mary received a visit from a Mrs. Gay, wife of Colonel Fisher Gay, who had been hurrying to her sick husband's side in New York when word of his death turned her back. "[W]hen our children came from meeting, they brought me your dear affectionate favour of 21 and 22 Inst.," Mary told Silliman. "I observ'd to the Children what reson we had to be thankfull, that we had such good news from you, while poor Mrs. Gay was mourning . . . but while we were refreshing ourselves with these sweet Ideas, we hear you my dearest and regiment are orderd on Long Island, where I view you in the situation I expected . . . [on] that trying day when I parted with the darling of my Soul."

Shortly afterward another visitor brought word that heavy firing had been heard coming from the direction of Long Island on the previous afternoon and had lasted until early that morning. "If so there has been a dreadfull Battle and . . . my dearest without doubt was in it," Mary wrote. "And have you surviv'd it my dear? . . . yes, I will still think so, and endevour in patience to possess my soul, till I know what tidings God has in store for me; at least let me O indulgent heaven have the pleasure one evening more of thinking and hoping my best beloved still lives."[34]

Mary endured many days of uncertainty before she learned that, on the day of the battle, the regular rotation of troops had led to the timely relief of Silliman and his men from duty at an exposed outpost. At the moment when the enemy attacked, they had been in the relatively safe position of manning the fortifications behind the front line of American troops, had suffered no casualties, and had joined the successful retreat to New York. But even as Mary gave thanks for his safety, she faced new and unexpected trials. "The prisoners here vaunt over us, saying the day is their own, and if it had not been for them D----d contrary winds they would have been in possession of New York before now," she wrote,[35] disgusted to find that some prudent townsfolk were taking the precaution of wining and dining the enemy officers in detention at Fairfield in case of a sudden British coup. Worse still, she soon witnessed the degrading spectacle of militiamen hastening home in droves, some claiming to have been dismissed, but many admitting their desertion. To cap all, some of them, aggrieved by Silliman's refusal to discharge them, began to spread rumors calculated to damage his reputation. The knowledge that he had survived, and survived without dishonor, outweighed such petty malice; yet Mary, with a wife's partisanship, felt hurt and angered when she heard him abused.

"You seem affected, my Love, at some Malevolent Things which the Militia say of me; my Love, I am not at all, I should be really more concerned to have Men behaving as they did speak well of me as an Officer," Silliman assured her, "for as well the Officers as the Men belonging to the Militia, behaved extreamly ill; and Officers of all Ranks, & privates, kept deserting & running off, in a Most Shamefull Scandalous Manner." Some of those who had obtained their discharge on grounds of illness were reported to have arrived home in such good health as to make it clear that they had never seriously ailed. This had prompted a novel form of epidemic among the remainder of Silliman's men, "for if they felt the most Slight Indisposition they would be directly after me to get Discharged," he wrote: "there were such Crouds of them constantly following of me . . .

thronging into my House & filling my Room when I returned home, that my Life became almost a Burden to me. . . . There behaviour here was such, that they have done us a great Deal more Hurt than good, for their deserting in such Shoals as they every Day did encouraged the Enemy, who were informed of it, and much disheartened our own Army."[36]

Far from feeling bruised by the militia's mishandling of his character, Silliman was pleasantly exhilarated at having stood the test of his first encounter with danger and hardship. Following the battle he and his men had spent two days in the open field exposed to the full fury of a northeaster, yet he had returned to New York City "in as good Health as ever I was in my life," he told Mary, with all the pride that a middle-aged country lawyer might be expected to feel in having proved his strength and stamina. "In short I don't know but that if I live to get Home I must sometimes take a Tour out in the Woods for a Week or so with my Blanket, and lie on the Ground through stormy Nights &c if I intend to be healthy."[37] "And won't you be willing to take Company with you, Love?" responded Mary, restored to cheerfulness by her husband's good-humored example.[38]

At the beginning of September her spirits plunged again when Silliman sent home his chest, his bed, and her letters to him, with the explanation that he foresaw another engagement with the enemy at any moment, under which circumstance "a Soldier must not have any more things with him that he can carry on his Back or his Horse."[39] A few days later he also returned all but one change of clothes, along with his bayonet, gun, and ammunition. "I am, my Dearest, in a Station now when all my Movements must be on Horseback except a very few, therefore can use no other Arms but my Sword and Pistols," he explained.[40] Mary remonstrated that he had been too quick to strip himself, but in fact he had acted only just in time.

On September 15 he broke off in the midst of a letter to

her with the words, "I must Stop news is come that the Regulars are landing." He thrust the letter in his pocket, and finished it the next day in sadly changed surroundings. "My Love, the Affair of Yesterday was Most unfortunate," he wrote from the temporary camp at Kings Bridge to which the Americans had retreated. "[T]he Enemy are in Possession of N York and all between here and there. My Brigade was left in New York the last of all, and the Enemy landed between me and the Rest of the Army, and out of all Communication my way was hedged up, but the Lord opened it; I brought in all my Brigade except a few."[41]

Mary received the news more philosophically than Silliman had expected. In a passage from one of her father's letters, she had found a reason for believing that "the way of duty is the way of safety"[42]:

> Where should *our Friends* be, and where are they safest, but *there,* where the Lord calls them, where their Duty lies? There only may we hope for & expect protection, even where we are serving God, according to his Will. I therefore look on Mr. Silliman safer *now,* in the Army, where calld, than at home, in his Chair, while his Call abroad continues.[43]

Nevertheless, if the way of duty now called her husband to a less exposed position, Mary's patriotism could not rise to a denunciation of the enemy victory that had caused the alteration. "I congratulate you and the Army that your out of that dirty City," she announced; "let the regulars take your leavings and boast of their acquisition." No long anxiety had marred her general sense of relief, for two days after the battle she had learned of his safety, and on September 19 she had received eyewitness testimony to his well-being from someone who had seen him "sitting on a rock, eating a peice of Beef rosted on the end of a stick by the fire."[44] Not least among her satisfactions, she reported to Silliman that some of the men from his brigade who had

since made their way home to Fairfield were "blessing you
for conducting them safely through," an effective antidote
to the poison earlier spread by the deserters.[45]

A few days later, he and his men removed to the camp
at Harlem Heights, too close to the enemy for Mary to
continue in a comfortable state of mind. "[I]n the Day
Time we can see one another on our Lines very plain, and
in the Night we see each other's Fires very distinct and
clear," Silliman wrote.[46] He had earlier speculated that when
the onset of winter put an end to the campaign he might
obtain a week's leave, a suggestion that Mary applauded.
"These cold nights make me shudder for you (to say no
more); I wish you had you[r] Bed again," she wrote. "O
G[e]orge, what hardships does thy tyrany put thy late sub-
jects to!"[47] Intrigued by the parenthetical phrase, Silliman
tucked into his next letter a small, separate note, not for
sharing with the boys, in which, to judge from her response,
he quizzed her about the more she would not say. She
thanked him for his "sweet whisper" and answered, with
the frankness he admired, *yes I did mean*—and long for
the happy time."[48] The nearness of the British, however,
had put an end to all prospect of enjoying the pleasures of
reunion soon.

Silliman, who was beginning to grow impatient for a
sight of home, now wrote to propose, as the next best
thing to his own return on leave, that his father-in-law,
then making a visit to Mary along with Mrs. Fish, the Darlings, and the Chesters, might ride over with one of the
boys to visit him. He might even persuade Mr. Fish "to
stay as Chaplain," he suggested, "and then Mother will
tarry with you, and you will make each other mutually
happy, and then I imagine there will be another Gentleman in the Army that will write to his Lady pretty near as
often as Col. Silliman."[49] In mid-October Mr. Fish,
accompanied by John, did set out for the camp, but Silliman had no sooner welcomed them than a fierce exchange
of fire with three British men-of-war, which had run up
the river, sent the two visitors scurrying back to Fairfield.

They left behind them a dejected man. Though Silliman still felt more invigorated than fatigued by the rigors of army life (which may in fact have improved his health), a certain disillusionment had set in. Ironically, it was during this period that he consulted Mary on the question of whether or not he should acquiesce in his appointment to the standing army newly ordered by Congress. He had come under considerable pressure from the general officers to agree, "but what says my Dearest?" he asked.[50]

Mary replied that she would like him to postpone a decision until he could come home and talk with her, but she mentioned that in spite of the disenchantment he had recently expressed "Billy thinks you have an inclination for it."[51] Indeed, Silliman's own letters contained hints of mixed feeling on the subject. "Well, my Dearest, what think you of your Husband's coming home over a while in his Gray Locks without any Wig on?" he asked her. "Major Meade Says he knows by my wearing my Hair that I intend to come into the Service again next year."[52] He pointed out that Congress had offered higher wages and land grants to those who did re-enlist, and that as a colonel he might expect to receive twenty-two pounds, two shillings a month, and five hundred acres of land at the end of the war, "very good Encouragements" in his opinion. "By this time methinks I see you turn to our Sons and tell them, well it is all up, I see your Dadda intends to stay in the Army," he went on. "But not to fast my Love; I have to say this, that a Camp Life dont suit me, I had much rather enjoy the Sweets & Delights of Domestick Life at Home, with my Dearly beloved and affectionate Wife, and dutiful Affectionate Children, than to be perpetually in the Noise, Bustle, Hardships & Dangers that are inseperable from a Camp."[53]

Mary, glad to hear it in spite of her dutiful acknowledgment that "the Cause is so important it becomes me at least to be silent,"[54] could not conceal her hope that he would find some honorable way to excuse himself. She was nonetheless taken aback by what followed. The governor and

council, acting on the recommendation of the general officers, named Silliman to a post in the new army without
waiting for his consent; but the lower house of the legislature, citing the complaints of the deserters, rejected the
appointment. "Don't be affronted Love, I *thank them a
thousand times,*" Mary declared. "I hope their *Honours* will
think best you should stay, and regulate those they put
under your command last *May,* that they may if call'd in
some future time behave more in character than in a late
expedition."[55] Her tone, however, betrayed her own
affront. She had wanted him to refuse, not to be refused.

On October 28, 1776, before her letter reached him, Silliman and his men were swept into the Battle of White
Plains. They were among the detachment of light infantry
sent forward to meet the enemy advance beyond the protection of the American lines. They took up their position
behind stone walls, withheld their fire until the enemy had
advanced to within thirty yards, and then fired a concen-
trated volley that temporarily halted the enemy ranks. As
soon as their own flank was threatened, they retreated to
the next stone wall and repeated the maneuver. They man-
aged to keep this up for some time but their last retreat, as
Silliman described it, took place "thro a most furious Fire
from the Enemy, for a half a Mile in length, for so far there
was nothing to cover us from it; I can't compare the constant whizing of the Bullets all round me to any thing more
natural than being in the Middle of a Swarm of Bees."[56]

The Battle of White Plains ended in a draw, leaving the
two armies "exactly like two Cats in a Garret growling at
One another and watching the fitest Season for flying at
Each Other."[57] But Silliman had demonstrated a coolness
under fire that did not fail to gain due recognition. On
November 20 a delegation from the assembly called on him
seeking his pledge that he would accept a commission if
the governor went over the heads of the lower house to
give him one. "[F]or they say that no good Officer must
be allowed to go out of the Service, and they are pleased

to say that the Account they have received of me from the Generals and other Officers places me in that Class," he wrote. "I urge to them that I cant think it my Duty, for a very Respectable Part of my own Country, the Lower House of Assembly, have declared they think me not a proper Person to serve them; they answer, that was owing to the Misrepresentation of the Militia which now begins to be fully understood, and that the Governour & Councill were always unanimously for me; and that the affair of this day fortnight [White Plains] had shown that I was a Man that the Publick wanted & must have."[58] It seemed that Silliman, too, despite his nonchalant words to Mary, had suffered some pique at his rejection and found the delegation's praise a balm to his wounded pride. Even so, he refused the request, and though Generals Spencer and Parsons added their personal pleas for his reconsideration, he continued to refuse.

Apart from his disgust with the militia, concern for the conduct of his professional business prompted Silliman to grasp at the excuse that the lower house had so conveniently provided. He had already asked that Billy attend the court to petition for an adjournment of all his pending cases until January, when he expected to be at home, hoping by this means to forestall the transfer of his business to other lawyers. With obvious anxiety, he went on to assert his confidence "that the Court will not compell any of my Clients to go to Tryal unless they choose it, nor do I think any Gentn. at the Barr will urge it."[59]

He also had a personal reason. Since the British advance toward White Plains had brought the enemy within striking distance of Connecticut he had repeatedly urged Mary to watch out for attack, by land or by sea, and at all costs to avoid being overtaken by the Hessian mercenaries, "the most savage of the Human Race, for they ravish all Women kind wherever they come with as little Shame as the Cattle."[60] She had acted upon his warning at once, engaging a place in a household at North Stratford to which she might go at need, and sending some of her valuables there in advance. Yet Silliman feared for her still, since she might soon be left alone. Jose and Johnny had returned to New Haven, Jemmy had gone to Stonington, and Billy, contrary to his father's command, had received his marching orders. Silliman had attempted to excuse Billy from service on two grounds: first, that poor health made him unfit; and second, that his departure would leave no man at home except for servants. When called upon to gather troops from Fairfield and join Major General Wooster in the defense of the Connecticut frontier, Billy presented his father's orders that he remain. "But the Officers tell him *that* cant excuse him now, since he is now under *one* superior in command, and that it will give great offence if he refuses," Mary explained, "And so he thinks to go."[61]

That summer, Billy had shown signs of restiveness at a confinement to the home front and a close parental supervision that seemed inappropriate to his manhood. Both Sillimans, when speaking of themselves in relation to him, used the terms "Dadda" and "Mamma," suggesting that they tended still to think of him as a boy. In September, evidence of a certain inattention to his father's instructions had forced Mary to explain that business of his own had called him away from home often enough to put him in arrears with other matters. "Pray what may his Business be?" Silliman sharply enquired; "he must not Be so much absent as to neglect takeing proper Care of the Family Business."[62] Billy, who had also begun to resent receiving messages at second hand, made no answer. "Is Billy at Home?" Silliman asked, with rising irritation, in his next letter. "Is he so busy he cant find a Leisure Half Hour to let his Dadda know how he does?"[63] Eventually, Mary made peace by persuading Silliman to write directly to Billy, which put him in a more compliant mood in spite of his father's telltale conclusion. "Billy thanks you for his Letter," Mary teased her husband, "[and] will observe your orders tho you subscribe Your Loving Affectionate Husband GSS."[64]

Billy still hoped, though, that his call to service would provide an opportunity to escape the confines of home and assert his independence.

Once again events conspired to frustrate Billy's martial ambitions. In early November 1776 the British withdrew from White Plains, and Wooster's battalion, raised for the emergency, was allowed to disperse. When Silliman returned to Fairfield in mid-November, his obedient son was there to greet him. Mary had the pleasure of a large family gathering on Thanksgiving Day which included Elizabeth Douglas, little Betsey, and her own two eldest sons, on vacation from Yale for an indefinite period because "provisions were so scarce that the scholars could not be provided for." It was "a happy, I trust a thankfull & delighted little Assembly," Silliman assured Mr. Fish. "Methinks I now hear you tell our Dear Mamma, why my Dear, our Children could hardly have been more happy; Your Pardon Sir; add three more dear Persons, our Hond. Parents at Stonington & our Dear Captain [a playful term for Jemmy] to the happy Circle, and I'll agree you are right."

Mary and Silliman had more reasons than one for wishing the Stonington dwellers at Fairfield. The British had recently seized Newport, Rhode Island, a point close enough to Stonington to wring from Mary the cry "Pray God protect you from their *violence*."[65] This view of the mother country as predator represented a considerable revolution in her thought since the spring. In recent months, the evidence had mounted that the British were capable of meting out punishment so brutal as to dispel all illusion of a mother and child relationship. The harsh treatment of American residents on British-occupied Long Island; the inhumanity shown to prisoners of war at New York; and the unleashing of Hessian soldiers, known for their bestiality, upon defenceless civilians were gratuitous cruelties that could not be excused as the inevitable consequence of war. As reports of these horrors filtered through, they wrought a change

in Mary's feelings, and a curious incident that took place
during Thanksgiving confirmed it. She had written of her
husband's experience at White Plains that "amidst showers
of rolling bullets not one so much as touched his garments," but when she came to mend the coat he had worn
that day she found in the pocket a spent ball "made ragged
so that it might not be easily extracted from the flesh of
the one who was so unhappy as to receive it."[66] This ugly
detail brought the truth home to her, and spurred a whole-
hearted rejection of the old relationship which she had not
been able to make earlier in the year.

At the same time, Mary began to realize that to fight for
the righteous cause of one's native land was not, in this
particular war, so straightforward as it sounded. The line
between friend and enemy was frequently blurred, as was
that between the renegade and the fundamentally patriotic
citizen torn between conflicting claims on his loyalty. The
old, simple pieties could no longer easily resolve the moral
and emotional entanglements of a country at war with its
origins. Mary, seeking to calm the anxieties of her children when they heard that battle was joined in New York,
had offered them the time-honored comfort that this was
a trial of their faith in God. "But, they say, Dadda is as
likely to be killd as any other," she wrote. "I tell them no,
he puts his trust in God, and then read them a part of your
last dear letter wherein you say you doubt not but when
Gods wise purposes are answered you shall be returned
&c—which seem'd to quiet them—Johnne is as stidy as
an old physolopher." Jemmy, however, perceived the flaw
in the argument. He asked, "Mamma, don't the Regulars
trust in God too?", to which Mary, flustered, replied, "I
dont know what they do, but I think their cause is not
good."[67] In fact she did know that the British, no matter
how fallen in her estimation, were not heathens; that many
an English soldier put his trust in God, while many an
English woman prayed for a husband in the field as fervently as Mary prayed for hers. Silliman himself, when close
to the British lines at Harlem Heights, had told her that

he "distinctly heard them sing Psalms" at their daily services.[68] She knew, too, that God-fearing patriots died in battle, whereas many with no claim to sanctity survived.

Mary could not resolve these contradictions, and occasionally they troubled her. For the most part, however, her adherence to the established religion of New England, and her steady contemplation of the heaven it promised, helped her to keep her balance on a shifting earth. Not only her own system of belief, but the social structure that upheld it, encouraged her confidence that her acts, her sacrifices, her thoughts, and her prayers weighed as heavily in the scale of contributions to the war effort as the exertions of the men in the army or at the helm of government. The precept so often uttered by her father and her husband, that prayer and unswerving obedience to God's law would form the only foundation on which a military effort could build with real hope of success, was one to which society in general assented. It meant that a woman like herself, who had faithfully performed her mundane tasks despite fatigue and loneliness, and her spiritual duties despite discouragement, had made a contribution to the cause which she need not regard as inferior. "Most just are your observations on the cause of our ill success. O that I may be enabled to forsake every sin that I have indulged,"[69] she wrote on one occasion. On another, she described herself to Silliman as keeping "a day of fasting and prayer" which she spent "wrestling for you and our bleeding land," her imagery bearing witness to her conviction that, like Jacob when he wrestled with the angel, she had fought a real battle and gained a real victory.[70] "I have the vanity to think I have in some measur acted the *heroine* as well as my dear Husband the Hero," she declared, quoting a favorite verse: " 'The passive Hero who sits down / contented and can smile / under afflictions gauling load / out acts a Cesar's Toil.' " "To apply this to myself has the appearance of vanity, I know," she wrote. "But so far as I can make my bost in the Lord, so far is it giving glory to him."[71]

IV

AS the year 1776 drew to a close, Mary showed no awareness of the momentous place that future generations would
accord it. She derived less satisfaction from having bravely
passed the trials of a year of war than from the belief that
she had almost put them behind her. Though Silliman
returned to his post a few days after Thanksgiving, he had
left Mary rejoicing in the knowledge that he had "deter-
mind not to join the standing army, tho appointed at the
last Sessions of Assembly." His term of service expired on
Christmas Day, and he came home in early January, "I *hope*
to stay," Mary told her parents.[72] But Mr. Fish commented
that the emphasis she placed on "hope" seemed "to imply
a Doubt," and soon afterward Silliman confirmed that in
fact he had "very little Expectation of being allowed to
spend the comeing Summer with my family."[73]

In December 1776 the Connecticut legislature had
restructured the militia with a view to improving its capacity for defending the state. Formerly about 25 percent of
the male population had enjoyed exemption; now all were
liable for service. The newly enlarged force would be orga-
nized into six brigades, and, thanks to Silliman's performance at White Plains, the legislators had named him
brigadier general of the 4th brigade. The appointment
offered him the satisfaction of defending his home state,
together with some degree of control over the ground on
which he fought, whereas his former post had obliged him
to follow the orders of others even when they put him and
his men in an impossible position. It also laid him under a
heavy burden since the territory he must defend included
the southwestern frontier, with its perilous proximity to
the British positions in New York and on western Long
Island. Either this command or his continued responsibility for the Connecticut corps of horse would almost certainly recall him to the field.

Meanwhile, service at home provided no sinecure. Four
months after Silliman's return, Mary told her parents that

he had as yet found no time to do any work about the farm, not so much as to visit the pastures:

> The enemy's frequent attempts and sometimes depredations made on several places about our sea costs has made it necessary for him . . . to place guards all along our sea coasts, and [he] has not only to give dirrections but to visit the Guards from Stratford to New York State. . . . Besides the above, the Governor puts such unbounded confidence in him, he has desird him to officer and fit out two arm'd vessels to cruize along our Shores.[74]

In addition to military responsibilities he had his duties as state's attorney, some of them not only time-consuming but unpopular. The prosecution of local Tories rested in his hands, and also the handling of some highly emotional, occasionally violent, disputes over inoculation.

The trouble arose because, at the time, inoculation for smallpox produced the disease in the persons who took it, seriously enough to make them potential carriers though mildly enough to give them a better chance of recovery than those who became infected in "the natural way." The legislature had delegated to the towns the decision whether or not they would permit the civilian populations to receive inoculation. Only when two-thirds of the inhabitants agreed were the selectmen and justices of the peace authorized to give permits to individuals. Some, more afraid of the disease than of the law, ignored these restrictions; the authorities would then appeal to Silliman to use the militia to suppress violators and isolate the infected. In Stratford feeling ran so high that unauthorized inoculees had dispersed a detachment of militia sent to conduct them into quarantine, and Silliman had responded by threatening them with martial law. His action added to the number of his enemies in Fairfield County, for now many proponents of inoculation joined the disgruntled deserters and the Tories in focusing their discontents upon his person.

Fairfield's proximity to the coast and high concentration of Tories placed all its residents in jeopardy. "Mr. Silliman and his under officers and Soldiers have not gone so much as to the house of God for this great while without their *Arms,* daly expecting an attack," Mary told her parents.[75] In early April she reported that Ebenezer Silliman's widow had packed up and "moved away for fear of the enemy."[76] Two weeks later British raiders tried to land in Middlesex (Darien) and, though driven back, had "anchored off Stamford beyond the Reach of Cannon Shott; they are looking along our Shores to get something or other that is fresh to eat, for they have devoured every Thing that can be eat that is fresh on L. Island."[77] Finally, on April 25, the British landed a large body of troops on the western coast of Fairfield with intent to march across country and destroy the stores and magazine at Danbury.

While Mary and the women of the household retreated inland, Silliman summoned his brigade to Fairfield, which he took to be the enemy's objective. Eighteen hours passed before he realized that they were marching on Danbury, and set off in pursuit with 250 men. By that time the enemy, who had proceeded virtually unopposed, were on the point of carrying out their mission. Major General David Wooster, in command of the militia brigades west of the Connecticut River, had joined Silliman, and along the way they gathered another 250 militiamen and 100 continentals. At Redding, Benedict Arnold caught up with them, and the patriot force divided. Arnold, Silliman, and 400 of the men occupied an advantageous point on the road through Ridgefield in an effort to cut off the enemy's retreat while Wooster attacked them from the rear. After a short but fierce engagement at Ridgefield, Arnold ordered a retreat and took up a new position near the coast from which he made a second attempt to block the British path, but a Tory guide led them around him to Compo Hill. The patriots attacked again, then fell back before a bayonet charge, and the British navy took off the raiders without further ado.

Silliman participated in all these actions, but without distinction. Though he had ample courage, and none questioned his patriotism, he lacked Arnold's gifts for out-guessing his adversary and for inspiring his men to extraordinary heroism. When Wooster died from the wounds he had received, it was upon Silliman's head that the greater share of blame descended for the enemy's success in making a three-day march through a populous part of the state and escaping with an acceptable number of casualties. The fault was not all his, and he had reason for his complaint that anyone in such a situation "must expect to meet with every Obstacle that human Frailty and the malicious & traiterous Designs of our Tory enemies can lay in his Way."[78] Nevertheless, his reputation as field commander suffered as a consequence of the Danbury raid. The local patriots lost confidence in him, and the British made sure to play upon their doubts. Mary reported to her father that everyone at Fairfield remained acutely apprehensive "on account of our enemies which have twice made their appearance by a fleet of 12 or Thirteen sail before our eyes."[79]

In July, Silliman began to think of resigning his command. His personal situation had been complicated by the otherwise welcome news that, ten years after the birth of her last child, and at the age of forty-one, Mary expected a baby. Should he be called away, he would now fear for her safety as she had previously feared for his. There were also more pressing problems. In a letter to his father-in-law, he wrote:

If you will please in the first Place to consider me as a poor frail Mortal liable to Mistakes & Errors; and in the next Place as haveing the Command of a Body of People, from Whom about One Thousand traiterous Tories have gone off to the Enemy; and among whom it is an undoubted Fact, that there are still remaining more fixed and inveterate Tories than there is in the whole State. . . . [In addition,] A great Number of those who are at

Bottom Friends to their Country among us, and who would take it excessively ill to be thought otherwise, have Brothers, Fathers, Sisters, Sons, & in short every kind of Relationship that you can mention among the Enemy . . . when they see vigorous Measures pursued & vigorous Exertions makeing that perhaps may be the Means of taking or slaying a Father, a Son &c, the tender Sensations that they feel on such occasions often times run them into Modes of Behaviour that are altogether inconsistent with the Character of the Patriot.[80]

This plain statement of Silliman's predicament took from Mr. Fish his former happy knack of reducing all questions concerning the war to simple terms of patriotic duty versus Tory disloyalty, each person clearly belonging to one category or the other. He replied:

But I never imagind 'till informed by your Last, tht. the deluded, infatuated, bewitched Tories, gone from you & remaining still among you, were half so numerous & so interwoven with Friends to our Cause, perplexing the Conduct of those, who are zealous & determined to defend it.—Insomuch that, were I to look no further than to things present, and consulted only your apparent safety, personal Ease & Comfort, as well as that of your Family, with which *our own* is inseperably connected, I should, without a moments hesitation, advise you to resign your Office, quit your present Station, attended with incessant Labour, perplexity & Danger, and retire within some sphere of Action, [away] from these consuming Cares. . . . But then—Can this be done at present, with unfeignd Friendship to your bleeding Country . . . Can we find a Man, like minded, that will fill the Station with honor?[81]

Much as he would have liked to return a positive answer, Silliman could not do so. In spite of his detractors, the

governor and council of safety considered him too important to the state's defense to leave his post on any account.
For instance, in August, when ominous indications that
the British were gathering for an attack on Peekskill brought
a desperate call for reinforcements from General Putnam,
Silliman received orders to send his men but not to accompany them. And all the time, as his local responsibilities
increased, so did his vulnerability.

A new possibility now occurred to Mr. Fish, to judge
from an attempt that Silliman made to reassure him. "I
thank you Sir for your kind Solicitude for my personal
Safety; I know the Anxiety of my Friends here on that
Head," he wrote; "But after all Sir I think an Enterprise of
the Kind you mention so extreamly hazardous to the
Enemy that I am fully of opinion they will never venture
it."[82] The letter that prompted this response has not survived, but probably it raised the question that the British
and their Tory friends might mount an assault on Silliman's house, situated as it was three miles distant from the
main settlement at Fairfield. After all, General Prescott of
the British Army, under circumstances much like those of
Silliman, had recently been kidnapped off Aquidneck
Island. Silliman, however, maintained a remarkable seren-
ity in the face of danger. "I have hitherto endeavoured
according to my Ability to consult and adopt the best
Measures for the Defence of my Country so far as it falls
within my Sphere," he wrote. "I begrudge no Pains that I
take for that End; and when the Day of Care & Labour
ends, a most mercifull God has always enabled me through
the last Summer as well as this, when I lay my Head on
my Pillow to cast all the Cares & Anxiety of the Day, into
the Arms of a kind Providence, so that I think I can truly
say that I dont think that the most dangerous Situation
that I have ever been in has ever deprived me of One
Quarter of an hours Rest in any One Night."[83]

Mary too felt that the blessing of her husband's presence
at home had far outweighed the trials of recent months.

"A wish often steals from my heart, O that my dear Parents could be eye witness to our happiness," she told them.[84] September saw her wish partly granted when Mrs. Fish arrived from Stonington to attend her confinement. If the enemy did not stir, Silliman too would be with Mary for the birth of their child, expected in October. On the last day of September, with pride and tenderness, he informed her father that she was "about house yet with the Sprightliness of 18." The next morning he added a post-script that made less pleasant reading:

> Between 10 and 11 Last Night come in another Express from General Putnam with an Account that Sixty Sail of Transports arrived last Thursday at New York; and that they brought [3,000] troops, and that they are but only Part of a larger Fleet, which is Hourly expected. — that the Ships already arrived are brought into the North River. — that their Out Posts are all called in. — that their Troops at Kings Bridge are under marching Orders. — that their Bakers in the City are ordered to work Night & Day to get a sufficient Supply of hard Bread. — that a great Quantity of Ammunition is shiped on the Ships. And everything indicates that they are meditating some important Expedition.[85]

Since it seemed certain that their objective was to take the Highlands and relieve Burgoyne, Putnam had called for reinforcements. The governor and council immediately ordered that the militia go to his aid, and this time, as ill luck would have it, the danger appeared so pressing that they directed Silliman to accompany his men.

It took three days for Silliman's mounted militia to reach Fishkill, partly because, in response to the rumor that a large British force was advancing on Connecticut's southwestern frontier, he ordered his men to rendezvous first at Ridgefield. By the time he did join up with the Continentals, on the evening of October 8, Clinton had captured two forts on the west bank and was in a position to maneuver vessels through the chevaux-de-frise (an under-water barrier of heavy spikes designed to penetrate a ship's hull) in the river. All that saved the Americans from having to race the British north was the news that their army had turned back Burgoyne at Bemis Heights. "On this Occasion the whole Army was drawn up under Arms and formed into a great Square with the Field Pieces placed on an Angle and all the General Officers in the Center mounted on Horseback," Silliman wrote, "when all the Letters were publickly read, which was followed by a Discharge of 13 Cannon and Three loud Huzzas from the whole Army on this joyful Occasion which seemed almost to rend the Air with the Noise."[86]

Though the danger that Clinton would make juncture with Burgoyne had faded, as long as British forces ranged along the river Silliman and his men had to remain in the vicinity in order to parry enemy thrusts. Several times he set out to relieve positions that reported an attack, only to learn that the British had withdrawn before he got there. Then came the "glorious News" that the British Army had surrendered at Saratoga. "I think I never heard nor Read of an Army taken before," Silliman exulted.[87] But he had received no news of his wife since his first arrival at Fish-kill, though she had expected to deliver her child early in the month. On October 25, 1777, he wrote to her express-ing a cautious hope of dismissal within the week. Five days later he reached home just too late to witness the birth of "a fine Baby, a Son who bears his Father's Name."[88]

V

AS soon as he heard that Silliman had returned, Mr. Fish traveled to Fairfield to fetch his partner back. He paused only for a night's rest and to admire his grandson, then he and Mrs. Fish set out for Stonington, where the work that had accumulated in her absence by now required her attention more than did her daughter.

On the very day of their departure, Silliman and Billy received a fresh call to action. General Putnam had conceived a plan to lure the British out of Fort Independence (in the Bronx). Colonel Return Jonathan Meigs would lead a small force toward the fort, and as soon as the enemy emerged, he and his men would feign a retreat, drawing the British after them and into a carefully staged ambush. The plan was carried out, and all went well at first. A messenger reported to the officers and men in hiding that the British had come out of the fort. After that, nothing happened for so long that Silliman and the other officers left their troops concealed while they circled around to take a secret observation of the fort. What they then saw, as Silliman described it, were "two small parties, one of Horse, the other of Foot, of the Enemy, advanced from the Fort on to the high Ground on the other side of the River at about a half a Mile Distance, who were reconnoitring us as we were them."[89]

This, of course, put an end to any likelihood that the British would fall into a trap. On the following morning the officers held a council of war to consider a direct attack on the fort, but they soon abandoned the idea. The enemy far outnumbered them already, and such men as they had would almost certainly depart within a day, when their terms of service expired. As Silliman had observed on a previous occasion, "there is no persuading a Soldier to continue in Service after that period has once come."[90] He also expressed chagrin that of the roughly 2,000 men he had called from his brigade, only 203 had answered. "A Failure totally inexcusable," he wrote, "and yet much may be said in their Excuse as they have been so extremely harassed throughout the whole of this Summer."[91] It was a sympathetic concession he would not have made a few months before. His difficulties, and those that he witnessed among his brother officers, had perhaps made him more perceptive of the common man's lot.

On December 8, 1777, again at Fairfield, Silliman wrote to tell Mr. Fish that, according to a report just received, the British had captured Philadelphia and intended to fortify it for their winter's use. This was bad news; but worse, in his opinion, was that many of Washington's officers had offered their resignations because they could no longer support themselves and their families on their pay, and that Putnam expected the same thing to happen to him at any moment. Silliman commented:

> If the Publick dont and cant provide some Remedy for this threatening Evil, I fear our Army will be wholly broken up.... 'Tis excessively galling to an Officer complaining of these Difficulties to be told by Men of Consequence, Oh, you have great Wages, you must not live so high. I have always felt in Pain whenever I have heard real Want & Distress bantered in this Manner, as I frequently have. May a Most mercifull God preserve us from ourselves: there is now our greatest Danger.[92]

He saw a similar danger in his own sphere of action at home. Throughout the previous year, whenever a commanding officer had called out the militia, both the outright Tories and their "unfriendly, and very cool headed and hearted" fellow travelers had refused to go. While others trudged away, and fell behind with their work as a result, they escaped all loss or inconvenience by remaining safely at home. Those who served began to resent the failure of authority to punish those who did not, and in the past spring a general council of officers had agreed that a file of soldiers should be sent either to fetch any man who ignored his marching orders or to compel his payment of the stipulated fine. Silliman, meeting furious protest that such action would encroach on the sphere of the civil magistrate, had asked the governor for a ruling from the assembly, with the predictable result that while the upper house approved the measure the lower house rejected it. Unwilling to take no action at all, Silliman then returned to the remedy previously prescribed, which was to sue defaulters. He sent Mr. Fish a graphic account of what followed:

> I accordingly sent out between 8 & 900 Writs of which Number perhaps about One half or two Thirds have got served, for I have not taken the Account exactly. You have seen, I doubt not, a Parcell of Boys before now in Consultation to destroy a Hornet's Nest, and that by & by some one more venturesome than the Rest would take up a Stone and, approaching near, would throw it directly into the Nest; and you've observed the Consequences. Just so in the Present Case. Genl. Silliman is going to ruin us all. Why, what is the Matter? Why, he has sued us all. He is the State's Attorney, he & his Son draw all the Writs, and he gets all the Mony for Fees, &c.&c.[93]

Silliman thought rather that all too many of the culprits had escaped him. Not only had four hundred or so of the known offenders yet to receive writs, but a good half of the delinquencies had yet to be reported. Still, he had done enough to increase the clamor of local dissidents against him. Unhappy with the pusillanimity of the government and the disloyalty of so many citizens, disgruntled by what he saw as a general lack of regard for his services and the sacrifice of private advantage they forced him to make, he felt overburdened and unappreciated. More, he felt that many of his fellow countrymen reaped greater rewards from lesser degrees of patriotism. Mary's old neighbor Mr. Cheseborough, approached by Mr. Fish to quote a price for supplying cheese to Mary's family, had named a figure so high as to provoke from Silliman the remark that "I know Mr. Cheseborough is not the only Man that does this, but if he lived in our Part of the Country, he would be in danger of being esteemed a Tory."[94] Mr. Fish agreed, but advised that the Sillimans buy anyway since the cost would certainly increase further, "so insatiable is the Thirst of these Times after high prices for Anything, for Every Thing."[95] Yet while they paid these higher prices, Silliman and Mary had also to adjust to a decline in his income from the law which resulted as much from his various public services as from the depreciation of the currency afflicting all members of society. All these dissatisfactions combined to encourage his decision, in January 1778, to request release from one of his military commands, either the brigade of foot or the corps of horse.

Within the family circle Silliman found the satisfactions that were vanishing from his public life. In March, he and Mary began to make plans for a wedding anniversary visit to Stonington on which the baby, whom they called Sellek, would accompany them, and for a moment a shadow from the past fell across her mind. "Next month I hope to bless my dear Parents with the sight of this dear little Sprout of theirs," she wrote. "But don't let us depend too much on such a pleasant scene, but remember the Pass'd wormwood and gaul, and rejoice with trembling."[96] These fears proved groundless. Sellek not only survived the journey but displayed a positive genius for traveling, and his father found him "a very facetious and merry Companion . . . never so well suited as when on the Road."[97]

Indeed, Sellek had wholly captivated his father, and whenever Silliman wrote to the child's grandparents, on whose tolerance he could rely, he let his pen run to such long, loving descriptions as fond parents will ever indulge in. That July, he sent them this vignette of their precocious "little sprout":

> Our Dear little Sellek has got a Go-Cart (as they are called) in which he runs about the House out of one Room into another like a little Spirit, and . . . [just now] he came running out of the Kitchen to his Mamma; & looking and seeing papa writeing at the Desk, nothing would do but that he must have his little high Great

Chair (in which he commonly sits up at Table & Break-
fasts with us, with as much Decency as most People do)
and sit up at the Desk with Papa and have some Papers
to play with. ... Yesterday he went out in the Field
with us to help us rake Hay soon after Breakfast, &
when he got tired lay down on his Blanket, spread on a
Bundle of Hay in the Shade, & took his Nap (some of
us sitting by to watch him all the Time); & waked again,
& kept with us till we came in to Dinner. By his Good
Will he would be always out with us.[98]

If Silliman took a special joy in the child of his middle
age, it was not to the exclusion of the other boys. They
had their own place in his descriptions of home life, surrounding him while he wrote, "paying their Duty to their
Hond. Grand Parents, and my Dear partner in the Center,
pleased & delighted with our employ." Yet they could not
give their parents the uncomplicated pleasure afforded by
the sight of a healthy infant. Silliman and Mary worried a
good deal at this juncture about the future of her elder
sons. In January, Jose had returned to Yale for the remainder of the academic year, at the end of which he expected
to receive his degree. Johnny, in a lower class at Glaston-
bury, would not go back until March. Before that time
arrived, Jose had come home for good. Caught between
rising expenses and dwindling funds, the college had suddenly decided to dismiss the senior class in order to save
the cost of their board. Mary thought that Jose should seek
employment, but no suitable post immediately presented
itself. She feared that Johnny's class, too, would be dismissed, and wondered what he would then do for an education. She also feared that Jemmy, busy for some time
past with preparations for his entrance to college that
autumn, would find the door forever closed.

The Noyes estate did not provide the security for John's
sons that Mary might have expected, for the depreciation
of the currency had caused the rents to decline in value at
an alarming rate. Indeed, the uncertainty of the times ren-

dered the future of all three boys more precarious than she could possibly have foreseen, and the character of the step-father she had set over them would weigh even more heavily than she had thought in tilting the balance of their lives. Silliman did not disappoint her, and she might well have blessed her own sound judgment as fervently as she blessed the "kind providence. . . . [which] has put us into generous hands always open to their need; an own Father could not be more attentive."[99]

The summer of 1778 was a season of comparative calm for the Sillimans. "The scene of action as to war seems now to be nearer you than us," Mary observed in a letter to her parents, a reference to the allied operations at Rhode Island.[100] She herself was enjoying a respite from care. Her husband was at home. Her concern for Johnny and Jemmy turned out to have been premature, since Yale would remain open to them at least for the coming year. Jose had no prospect of work, but he had passed his final examination for bachelor of arts, and though there was to be no public commencement that year he would receive his degree at New Haven on September 9. Jemmy would accompany him there in order to take an entrance examination that his tutor said he would easily pass, then he and Johnny would return together for the fall term.

Heavy snow and bitter cold ushered in the year 1779. Mr. Fish sorrowed over "the most pinching want of Bread, among many, that ever I knew," though he added quickly that he and his wife would have enough to eat.[101] He was set back, however, when the members of his church refused to vote him an increase in salary that he had requested. Like other members of the clergy, he was hard hit by the combination of inflated prices and devalued currency. At seventy-one years of age, he had begun to feel taxed by the work of parish and farm; his wife had been so ill throughout the winter that her duties, too, had fallen upon his shoulders, and now he had to bear an additional weight of anxiety about his finances.

Yale College also found itself in difficulties again, and

one morning in January Mary looked out of the window to see Johnny and Jemmy returning home on foot, the steward having dismissed the scholars for lack of provisions. Mary had for some time felt uneasy about Jose's idleness, and the return of her other grown sons now impelled her to make the decision that he should go to Stonington. This would serve a double purpose: he could continue his studies under his grandfather's tutelage, and in return provide a badly needed helping hand. After his departure, the household settled into a steadier routine than the war had permitted for some time. Silliman still received occasional calls to action but always in response to some local alarm. They rarely took him from home for long, and Mary, who was to bear him another child in August, fully expected that this time she would have him at her side.

Six

GRIEVOUS TRIAL

AT one o'clock on the morning of May 2, 1779, Mary and Silliman were startled awake by a heavy pounding on the door. Silliman knew at once what was upon him. For some time he had kept two loaded guns ready at the head of the bed; now he caught one up and ran to a window shouting, "Who's there?" *"God damn you,"* came the reply, "let us in or you're a dead man."[1] In the moonlight Silliman saw the space in front of the house filled with men, some armed with huge stones which they were using as battering rams. He thrust the gun through the pane and fired, but fortunately the powder flashed in the pan; fortunately, because the enraged attackers shouted that if he should kill one of them they would murder all in the house. The next moment they abandoned the door, broke in a window, rushed in, and seized him.

Silliman asked leave to dress before they took him away, which they gave, but they followed him into the bedroom where Mary lay trembling with Sellek beside her. The appearance of these ruffians, carrying their guns with bayonets fixed, increased her terror, and Silliman, pointing out her pregnancy, asked them to wait outside. Realizing that his first attempt to meet force with force had almost brought disaster on his family, he took care to address the raiders henceforth in polite, submissive terms. In response they withdrew, though they remained just beyond the bedroom door. Silliman dressed quickly, embraced his wife, and went out to them. They demanded his money but he told them he had only Continental bills, which were no use to them. They demanded his correspondence, but he said he kept only his private correspondence at home. Then, while some of them set about smashing every window in the house with the stocks of their guns, others began to hunt for plunder. When Silliman quietly observed that he took them to be gentlemen, and that plundering was ungentlemanly work, they desisted, though they kept the valuables they had already snatched up. They did not discover that all the communion silver belonging to the church was stored in a basket beside the bed, Silliman having hastily draped the folds of Mary's bedgown over it. Nor did they find the large bundle of public papers that he had contrived to drop on a bedside table.

Mary, listening intently, heard them leave the house, and sprang into action. She flew to Billy's room, but he was gone. She found the servants hiding in an upper room, and sent Peter running to rouse Deodate Silliman's household. Deodate immediately set off in pursuit, on horseback, firing a gun as he went in order to alarm others in the neighborhood. Meanwhile, from the top of the house, Mary could plainly see the raiders driving their prisoners across country toward the whaleboat on which they had come. As answering gunshots began to sound from other houses round about, she saw them increase their pace, pulling the two men along by their arms to make them go faster, and using poor Billy, at the time weak and shaky from fever and ague, with a harshness born of panic. They had moored the boat a good two miles from the house at the head of Black Rock Harbor, but they reached it before

Deodate could overtake them and moved briskly off in the direction of Long Island.

I

MARY heard nothing of the kidnapped men for three weeks, weeks of terrible uncertainty about their fate and constant fear of another night attack. Johnny and Jemmy had been about to leave New Haven for the vacation when the news reached them, and they came at once. Two schoolboys were not the comfort that her grown son would have been, but when she wrote to Jose at Stonington it was to urge that he stay there. "I . . . fear you should come as we have so many Tory *Enemies* and we expect to be plundered," she told him. "I have sent away some of our valuable things and intend to send more. We have a guard every night, [but] I fear if you was at home the enemy would be for carrying you off too." In the next sentence, with a change of subject that seems both incongruous and eminently reasonable she added, "I am concerned about shirts for you, am getting along my cloth as fast as I can, have cloth in the Loom for jackets and breeches for you, and some linnens for a summer coat; will get it wove as soon as possible."[2]

Once again, indeed, the daily round served Mary as an anchor. She had the work of house and farm, increased by the absence of the two most able men; she had Sellek, who, in the way of small children, had let the memory of that dreadful night slip from his mind, but who needed comfort for the absence of his beloved Papa; and at night, when sleep would not come, she had letters to write. She wrote to give family, friends, and acquaintances an account of the kidnapping, and she wrote to certain highly placed men appealing for their help in securing an exchange for the captives.

She wrote, of course, to Governor Trumbull. So did Mr. Fish, whose letter survives only in a draft in which the dashed-off phrases vividly convey the tumult of his feelings:

> 'Tis needless for me to offer anything in Favour of Mrs.
> Silliman, To *One* so well acquainted with her as your
> Excellency is ... left with three orphan sons (by Mr.
> Noyes) all of vertuous characters, & promising fair to
> be usefull Members of Community, could their Educa-
> tion at College be compleated, which (by reason of the
> Times, lightning the Rents of their Patrimony) Depends,
> Chiefly, on the Fatherly & Generous Exertions of Mr.
> Silliman whose liberal hand is open wide to supply all
> Deficiencys of their own Resources—the tender cir-
> cumstance of an Unborn Infant whose expected hour is
> near approaching: In which Situation the shock of a
> sudden nightly assault by the enemy came nigh to the
> dissolving of her frame—the Issue of which Impres-
> sion, remains yet doubtful: And if Mischief should fol-
> low, there is danger of quenching our coal that is left,
> the support of our old age.[3]

Jose carried this letter to Trumbull, stopping on the way
at Colonel Chester's in order to enlist his support, then
riding on to Fairfield. Mr. Fish did not intend Jose to stay
more than a night or two, for he needed to have the horse
returned to Stonington. But he thought that, danger or
no, Mary would soon have to call the one remaining man
of the family home. "Dear Child, what will you do alone,
when sons return to college?" he remonstrated. " 'Twill be
next to impossible for you to get along, without somebody
to do errands & necessary chores: What if you should, with
the President's leave, keep *Jimme* at home till Johnne's time
is up at N. Haven?"[4]

As it happened, when Jose rode up to the door on May
24, he found that Billy had unexpectedly arrived the day
before, paroled by the British because of his illness. Dead,
he would be worthless to them; sick and in need of nursing, he would be an expense. So they had sent him back

where the burden of care would fall on others, while retaining their right to use him as a pawn in the game of prisoner exchange. From a letter that he brought, and from his own lips, Mary pieced together an account of what had been happening to him and his father since her last sight of them.

Their kidnapping had been allegedly planned and ordered by General Clinton, British commander at New York. The whaleboat was manned mostly by Tory defectors who had formerly lived at or near Fairfield. A man named Glover who had built a cider mill at the farm, and a man named Bunnell who had made shoes for the family, led the expedition. Heavy seas made the return to Long Island difficult and dangerous, but the kidnappers, elated by their success, passed the time gloating over their plunder and their captives. Though they had shown moderation compared to what they might have done, they had taken some of the household's most prized possessions including "a beautiful fuzee," "a pair of pistols inlaid with silver all over," and "an elegant sword" which Bunnell flourished about over the head of his erstwhile employer.

When they arrived at Oyster Bay, Colonel Simcoe (a notorious British officer) hailed the boat.

"Have you got him?"

"Yes!"

"Have you lost any men?"

"No!"

"That's well," Simcoe rejoined. "Your *Sillimans* and your *Washingtons* are not worth a man."

He ordered the prisoners to the guardhouse, over Silliman's protests that his rank entitled him to a better disposition. At the guardhouse he protested again to the officer in charge, who answered that a general in the militia had a lower standing than a general in the Continental army. "But how will you view me when my exchange is talked of?" Silliman asked. The officer then withdrew to consult his commanding officer, and shortly afterward the two men were carried to a neighboring house, given breakfast, then removed to a carriage in which they rode to New York escorted by a troop of dragoons. "When their arrival in the city was known, there was a great flocking to see a rebel general," Mary wrote. "But by and by a gentleman came and whispered him to go with him, for fear he would be insulted by the rabble."[5] Before the day was out, Silliman and his son had been transferred to decent lodgings under guard.

None of these details appeared in the letter from Silliman that Billy had brought with him, perhaps because it was the second he had written. The first, sent by a flag a few days after his capture, never arrived. It is more likely, however, that Silliman could find no way to tell the story without offending the British censors under whose eyes all his letters, including those he received, must henceforth pass. An account that he had sent to Mr. Fish, which did arrive, discreetly referred to the kidnappers as "Refugees" and "Foreigners" rather than "Tories" and "enemies."[6] The letter that Mary received at Billy's hands also began and ended with pointed praise for the "Genteel and humane Behaviour" of Mr. Loring, the British commissary of prisoners, who would read it before it passed. There were other signs of the constraint that resulted from his awareness of censorship. Though he addressed Mary as "My Dearest Love," and closed with a tender prayer that "Heaven [may] enable us to make a right use of this grievous Trial, and preserve us to see one another again when its own wise Purposes are answered," his letter was otherwise emotionless.[7] When a man given to express his love and longing freely through his pen whenever parted from his wife has almost nothing to say on the subject at a time so fraught with anguish, his very silence may express his feelings as eloquently as any outpouring of words.

Silliman wrote that he had tried not to lapse into inertia. He was working to negotiate exchanges for some of the Connecticut rank and file imprisoned in the Sugar House and investigating ways and means to promote his own exchange. His fellow captives of rank, Brigadier Generals

Thompson and Irvine of Pennsylvania, and David Waterbury of Connecticut, hoped to be paroled at any moment
in order to meet with Washington and seek exchanges for
themselves, an endeavor in which they had reason to expect
success. Silliman saw no prospect of his own or his son's
release "unless his Excellency Governor Trumbull will be
so kind as to use his Intrest with Congress to permit him
to have the Disposal of One of the British Brigadiers
belonging to Gen. Burgoyne's Army that are Prisoners . . .
and one Brigade Major, to offer to General Clinton in
Exchange for me and Billy," he wrote. "If the Governor is
willing to take this Trouble and succeeds with Congress, I
make no Doubt but that our Exchange will be easily
effected, but if not, I do not see any other Method that has
any Air of Probability in it."[8] He had written to Trumbull
but realized that, whatever the response, he must expect to
remain a prisoner for some weeks. Therefore, he had asked
and received permission to remove to Long Island and there
take the smallpox by inoculation, which he expected to do
as soon as Billy had departed.

II

THE unwonted formality of her husband's manner of
writing, his unmistakable warning not to set her heart on
his early return, and the news that he might even now be
in the throes of a deadly disease with none but strangers to
nurse him caused Mary great unhappiness. Yet she had the
comfort of knowing for certain where he was and of
receiving Billy's unforced corroboration of the statement
that his British guards showed more humanity than his
Tory captors. And though, as she told her parents, "we
have so many Tories about us I am still afraid we shall be
plundered,"[9] the combined presence of Billy, Jose, Johnny,
and Jemmy offered some protection from local marauders,
while the government had posted enough extra guards

along the shore to relieve her immediate fear of another attack from that quarter.

Silliman, on the other hand, had begun to grasp the full bleakness of his position. He could obtain no word from home for almost four weeks after his capture and Billy's release. In the absence of any regular channel for communication between Connecticut and British-occupied New York, his family and friends could write only when they knew of some person traveling from one place to the other, not a frequent occurrence. Even then, the messenger was rarely able to carry letters directly to Silliman. More than once letters brought to New York and passed to a third party for transmission to his place of imprisonment waited weeks before the last part of the journey was accomplished. Sometimes they never arrived. Mary's first opportunity to send to him came sixteen days after his disappearance. Miss Betsy Moore, sister to General Huntington's wife, who was making a journey to New York, undertook to carry a letter; but she could take it only part of the way, and almost two weeks more elapsed before it reached Silliman. Since he had left Mary shocked, frightened almost out of her wits, and six months along in her pregnancy, it is understandable that his inability to find out what had happened to her since rendered him nearly frantic.

By the time he received reassurance on that score, other problems had arisen. He had left home without money and with only the clothes he stood up in. At first he had assumed that the Continental army would supply him with necessaries, as it did the other captive officers. On May 21, the Continental agent for the prisoners informed him that, by order of General Washington, officers captured while not on active service would receive no assistance. Penniless, he appealed to Governor Trumbull. "I therefore must beg of your Excellency to take some Method in which I may be supplied with money to answer my Necessary expenses," he wrote, "for the little I have recd is expended, and I cant suppose that however the Continent may treat

Militia Officers when Prisonners that my own State will permit me to suffer."[10] He resented the shabby treatment he had received and felt mortified that the sending of this message would put his British overseers in possession of the knowledge that the Continent had disowned him. Nevertheless, knowing that his personal finances would inevitably suffer from his abrupt departure and indefinite absence, he did not want to ask for money from home.

Soon he lost face again, through a cause that embarrassed him still more. "When I was brought into New York, I was soon informed that Ensign Russell Bissell of Hartford had been a Prisoner in the Sugar House for about 8 or 9 months," he told Mary; "of this Young Man I had heard an extraordinary Caracter long before I was taken, and haveing an Opportunity with Mr. Loring I made such a Representation of the Matter that Mr. Bissell was taken out of the Sugar House and was allowed to come out on to [Long] Island on his Parole. And two or three Days ago he forfeited his Honor, broke his Parole & ran away."[11]

On June 12, when he wrote that letter, he had received no communication from anyone since Mary's letter of May 18. He did not know if Billy had arrived safely, or even if any of his previous letters had reached her. To crown his frustration, it had taken him six weeks to find a household on Long Island that would accommodate him while he took the smallpox inoculation. He now expected to go within a day or two to the house of Mr. John Dyne at Flatbush and to be inoculated there by Colonel Ely. On June 16, he had at least the satisfaction of achieving that objective. If there were any virtue to his lack of news from home, it was his happy ignorance of Mary's having already received three separate reports that he had taken or was about to take the disease, one by his own letter and two by rumor, which had kept her apprehensive ever since Billy's return. Not until July 26 would she receive the letter that told her the correct date of his inoculation; not for many weeks more would she hear from his own pen that he had come through.

On July 17, having "cleaned up and laid by my small Pox clothing," Silliman sent Mary the news that he was out of danger although the disease had run a full course. "I had so many Pocks on my Face they will mark me," he told her, "but just enough for a Stranger to find out that I have had it without asking." At the height of his illness, he had received "a Cordial to revive my Spirits" in the form of a second letter from Mary. A few days later, he heard that the British had mounted a full-scale attack on Fairfield, bombarding the town with their ships' cannon and land-ing troops who had sowed death and destruction at large before them. "But even here, whilst I deplore & lament the desolated and ruined Circumstances of so many Dear Friends," he wrote, "I have abundant Reason for the most ardent & Devout Thanksgiving to the great Governour & Preserver of all Things, that I am informed and think that I have Reason to beleive that my beloved Wife and Dear Children and Family were all well [at] the Begining of last Week; and that the destructive Horrors of Warr did not reach either our Habitation or Property."[12]

Silliman's informant, probably one of the many Fairfield men captured in the raid and carried to the Sugar House, had rendered a true account. Mary and her family had escaped, and the house had received no damage thanks to its distance from Fairfield proper. The raid had fulfilled a fear that had risen steadily in Mary's heart ever since the kidnapping, much as she tried to suppress it. "The dreadful fright that I had . . . made me feel like the timorous roe and I started at every noise," she wrote in her Reminiscences.[13] A raid at nearby Green Farms on June 16, though the intruders did no more than plunder and smash a few win-dows and looking-glasses before they were driven off, had heightened her nervousness. Yet when she received word that Jemmy had fallen ill at New Haven, much as she doubted his safety at Fairfield, she saw nothing for it but to have Jose fetch him home, with all possible speed. Thanks to this apparent misfortune, both young men were well clear of New Haven when the enemy attacked the town on

July 6. Among those who turned out to fight, and among the dead too, were students known to Jemmy. Word of events traveled so swiftly that it reached Fairfield on the same day, and Jose immediately rode back to find out what had become of Johnny. That evening the fleet withdrew from New Haven, destination unknown. The following morning it appeared off Fairfield.

Mary met the emergency calmly. She did not allow the first appearance of the ships, which she saw from her roof-top, to panic her into a flight that would leave the house vulnerable to the depredations of local Tories even if the British withdrew. She ordered up the horses, had the servants load a carriage with valuables and household effects, and returned to the roof to see what was happening. Only when the roar of the cannon and the movements she observed convinced her that the enemy would land did she decide that the family must evacuate, all except Billy and Esther. They had chosen to remain in the hope that they could save the house from total destruction should the raiders penetrate that far. Billy relied on his value to the British as a live prisoner to protect him; Esther perhaps thought that her age and sex would grant her immunity from harm (though she might have found her mistake had she come face to face with the foe). The rest of the household were to go to Mr. Eliakim Beach at North Stratford (later Huntington), the retreat that Mary had arranged some months before.

At the moment when Mary gave the order to depart, Jemmy had what she described as "a hard fit on him," probably chills and fever, but she had no time to lose. She got him up and into the carriage with herself and Sellek, while Amelia and Peter rode horseback. A short distance from the house Mary stopped the carriage and sent Peter back for something she had forgotten. The party traveled three miles more, then stopped again when Jose appeared on the horizon, riding at full gallop. He reported Johnny safe, then asked Mary's permission to keep on to Fairfield so as to swell the ranks of the defenders. "I gave him my

consent," she afterward recorded, "for I thought I ought
not to withhold my son, where others were jeopardizing
their lives." Again the carriage moved forward, and again
it halted when the tackling broke. "By this time the Cannon began to roar, which pleased Selleck, and he would
mimic them by saying *bang, bang,*" wrote Mary, "But they
were doleful sounds in our ears." She and Amelia were
endeavoring to repair the damage when Peter overtook
them, and soon set them on their way once more.

The rest of the journey and its aftermath are recalled in
her Reminiscences:

> The firing grew heavier, and as we travelled many ran
> out of their houses to speak with us, women distressed
> for their husbands, sons and brothers, fearing that they
> would fall in battle. . . . But oh that dreadful night! We
> could see at seven miles distant, the light of the devour-
> ing flames by which the town was reduced to ashes. The
> night was spent in dreadful expectation, and sleep
> departed from my eyes. . . . But how it was with *the
> young man Joseph* I could not hear, until the next morn-
> ing, when I had great reason to bless God for his pres-
> ervation, for he had been where the bullets flew, and a
> cannon ball killed a man that was not far from him.

Three days later Mary ventured back to find her house "full
of distressed people who had lost their habitations."[14]
Seeing that Billy and Esther were ministering ably both to
them and to the estate, she decided to return to her refuge
at North Stratford, leaving Holland Hill to those who had
no other shelter.

Despite the kind attentions of Mr. and Mrs. Beach, not
to mention the lively company of her two younger sons,
Jemmy and Sellek, Mary felt forlorn. As the time of her
confinement drew near, hope faded that Silliman would
obtain a short parole in order to be with her, and for the
first time not even her mother, who was unwell and unable
to travel, would attend her delivery. But on Saturday, July

24, Mr. Fish unexpectedly appeared at Mr. Beach's door, and though he could stay only three days, his visit put fresh heart into her.

Knowing that a flag would leave Stonington for New York within a few days of his return, Mr. Fish suggested to Mary that he carry back a letter from her for transmission to Silliman. She seized the occasion, the first to present itself in some time, to give her husband the family news in full, including the information, perhaps worded with an eye to the British censor, that Billy was "better than when he left you, but is not well yet." Jose had taken a temporary post as a schoolteacher, while Johnny had undertaken the role of liaison between Mary at North Stratford and the household at Fairfield. Jemmy, now well enough to travel, had returned to Stonington with Mr. Fish, to study under his grandfather's eye until college reopened. Sellek, "very well and fat as a little seal," had not forgotten him. "When I took out your Coat in order to send it, he ran, got hold of the Buttons, and called Pappa, Pappa; this both pleases and affects me," she wrote. She feared that Silliman had probably suffered for the want of his summer clothes but had had no opportunity to send them until now, and still could not send the shoes he had ordered since the shoemaker had not begun to work on them. With manpower so depleted by the demand for militia to defend the coast, it was hard to get anything done. She had received no letter from him since the one that he had written just after his inoculation. "I comfort myself that you are now well of that dreadful disorder; it is wise to hope for the best," she wrote. "But how rejoicing it would be to hear from your own hand that you are well through."[15]

III

SILLIMAN received this letter four months later. On August 20 he had written Mary a graphic account of the

obstacle course that letters to him ran. Eight weeks had
gone by without a word from anyone and, knowing that
her confinement was past due, he was desperate for news.
A recent visitor from New York had mentioned that he
knew a man in the city who had letters for General Silliman and only awaited an opportunity to send them on
(why they were not sent with the speaker was not
explained). Since then, Silliman had twice paid for a messenger to fetch the letters. On the first occasion the gentleman was not home; on the second he said that he had
already dispatched them by another hand. They never
arrived, and as Silliman could not find out the carrier's name
he could pursue his inquiries no further. On August 21, by
then almost mad with frustration, he received a letter from
Mr. Fish, but since it had been written on June 14 it gave
him no information on the subject that concerned him
most.

On August 22, several letters reached him at once. The
first one he opened came from the local minister, Mr.
Beebe. Dated August 9, it read:

> Dear General,
> I heartily Congratulate you on the prosperity and
> Increase of your Family by the Birth of a fine Son of
> which your lady was delivered Yesterday Morning
> between the Hours of Six & Seven. . . . I wish & pray
> that for her Sake you might be permitted to make her a
> Visit, and sure I am that if there is any Remains in the
> British Officers of that Generous Noble Spirit that
> Breathed through the whole of General Amherst's Army
> in the Year Fifty-Nine, under whose command I had
> the Honour to serve the whole of that agreable & Suc-
> cessful Campaign, they will not deny you a short parole
> at least.[16]

How it came about that this and other announcements of
the birth reached Silliman within three weeks, while other
letters took months or disappeared entirely, is not clear,

though the event was merciful. If, however, Mr. Beebe's closing words aimed to flatter the British into still greater mercies, they missed their mark. Silliman had written to Mr. Loring on July 20 and 30 and again on August 19, pressing his request for parole. On August 27 he told Mary sadly that "the Matter is at an End now, at least for the present . . . he [Mr. Loring] has not been able to obtain Leave for me to go out."[17] As for an exchange, he saw no hope of that.

The prospect before him would have looked blacker still had he known that the spate of letters announcing his new son marked not so much the end as the beginning of a drought. A note from Johnny written on Mary's behalf asking what he wished to call the child drew the cheerful reply that "I had got an Opinion somehow or other that *Polly* would be a pretty Name for it, but these last Letters have made that altogether improper," and that she should name it whatever she pleased.[18] Two months would pass before he knew her choice or received any answer to a tentative request for reassurance that the baby was "perfect."[19] None of his kind correspondents had thought it necessary to specify the child's normality, and the omission had raised a faint flicker of doubt in his mind, a sign that four months in captivity with no end in sight had begun to leave its mark.

Now it was Mary who had the distractions of excitement, action, and change, while Silliman strove against a sameness and a narrowness in his days beyond anything she had ever experienced in her domestic routine. Neither she nor her baby showed ill effects from the harrowing night of the attack on the house, the strenuous exertions of the recent evacuation, or the lonely, fearful days and nights that had passed between the two. On the contrary, Mary told her parents that she had never enjoyed better health and had found her seventh confinement, at the age of forty-four, the easiest of all. She had awakened in labor at daybreak on August 8. Mrs. Beach summoned the midwife, who arrived soon afterward with several other women including Mrs. Beebe. By six o'clock that morning all was over; Mr. Beebe came in, gave thanks at Mary's bedside, went down to breakfast with the women, "and all got away time enough to go to meeting (as it was Lord's day)." Johnny took the news to Fairfield, where Esther immediately surrendered the loom and the important task of weaving the winter's wool cloth to the younger women servants and went to Stratford to nurse both mother and child. Five weeks later, Mary presented the baby for baptism in Mr. Beebe's church. She named him Benjamin, partly for a brother of her mother's, but more in memory of her beloved and unforgotten brother-in-law, Benjamin Douglas.

The time had come for Mary to return to Fairfield, where many matters awaited her attention. One of the least pleasant was the necessity to write to Jemmy at Stonington and prepare him for the possibility that she could not afford to send him back to college that fall. "Johnne took his degree and had to pay the Steward ninety pounds, only for about 2 months Board and Tuition, (only for himself)," she explained. "If your dear Dadda was at home, believe he would send you, but then he could get of our Tennants perhaps an equivalent, but that I cant do at present. Don't let this sink your spirits, my dear." To her parents, she added that, rather than send John to his grandfather for further studies, she had decided to recommend that he keep school at Fairfield. People wanted the young man to undertake the task, and "considering the good he may do to the little flock here, who want schooling extreamly, as well as the consideration of getting something for himself in these expensive times," she thought he should comply.[20] This proved a fortunate decision in another respect, too, since it gave John an opportunity to demonstrate his capability as an administrator of his father's estate. When Mary proved able to send Jemmy back to college after all, John accompanied the boy "instead of a father . . . [to] see what he can do for his support at Bethany," presumably by pressing the tenants there to pay the rent.[21] Whatever the precise nature of his business he accomplished it "to good purpose," Mary said,[22] and Jemmy was assured of his continuance at college for at least another year.

Jose, though older than John, had not played the father's role himself because a bad bout of jaundice kept him confined to bed, while Billy had enough to do in managing the Silliman farm and continuing to press for an exchange. During October he spent time with Governor Trumbull at Hartford, then rode to Horseneck on business apparently connected with that interview. When Mary wrote of it to Silliman, however, she merely stated the fact, and neither commented on the purpose of his journey nor enlarged upon her hopes for its outcome.

Meanwhile she wanted to share with her husband some of the details about the new baby that he could not now acquire through the usual, pleasant means of daily observation. They were such little matters that it pained her to think of a stranger reading what she wrote, "but some of my full heart will out." Benny "lives almost Intirely on the Breast and is a fine little fat fellow," she wrote; "His little brother Selleck is very fond of him. They both sleep with me; they both wake before sunrise, when I get up and leave them to play together, a sweet sight to a fond parent."[23] The additional information that Sellek entertained everyone who would listen to him with the statement that "the Regulars have got his Pappa, and they are naughty Boys," she prudently reserved for correspondents whose letters from her did not have to pass British inspection.[24] "Love and harmony reign throughout my family, which is a great comfort to me, but I am full of domestick care, perhaps wisely ordered that I may not pore too much on the absence and situation of my beloved Companion and Head," she told her husband; "Johnne sends his duty to his dear father, says he believes he should cry for joy if he should come home."[25]

Silliman had ceased to torment himself with any such hopeful imaginings, and had begun instead to plan for a winter passed in prison. He thought it certain that Billy too would have to submit to that necessity. "I have been informed that Orders are sent out to all the American Pris-oners, that are at Home on their Parole, immediately to return to their captivity," he wrote on November 13. "Whenever Billy gets his Orders to come in . . . I should be glad to have him bring in a Bed with proper Linin. . . . A Pair of Mittens and a Pair or two of Winter Stockens . . . would be very agreeable by the Time that I get them."[26] Yet even as he wrote, events were in motion that raised fresh hope of his release.

IV

UNTIL recently, the efforts to set him free had focused on the question of what enemy officer or officers already in American hands, to whose release General Washington would consent, would be acceptable to the British in exchange for Silliman. When it became clear that no such prisoner existed, some of Silliman's friends decided that they would have to take one, "and Judge Thomas Jones, on Long Island was thought a proper person as he was a great tory and . . . the Chief Justice of their Superior Court." Furthermore, since he was already on parole to Governor Trumbull, having been taken from his home in August 1776, held captive in Connecticut, and then released pending an exchange that had still not taken place, he would hardly be expecting another visitation.

With the governor's blessing, Captain David Hawley of Stratford and Captain Samuel Lockwood of Norwalk gathered together a whaleboat and a crew of twenty-five men. On the evening of November 4 they embarked for Long Island; on reaching the shore, they "drew their boat up and hid it in the woods, and they lay concealed all the day & travelled in the night." They had many miles of enemy country to traverse. When they arrived at Judge

Jones's house, which looked to their unsophisticated eyes "like a castle," it was about nine o'clock on the night of Saturday November 6 and they could hear sounds of music and dancing. Captain Hawley rapped on the door. No one answered. He broke in a panel, entered, and by a piece of remarkable good luck found the judge himself just entering the hall with a guest, a young man named Willett. Hawley's crew jumped in behind him, seized both men, and hurried them out into the night.

They knew that they would have to pass a point where Judge Jones kept a guard on duty. As they drew near the place, the judge began clearing his throat loudly and repeatedly; warned to stop, he persisted until Hawley threatened to run him through. After that, the Americans continued without further incident, marched as far and fast as they could that night, and at daybreak retired with their prisoners under cover of the woods. It was on the third night of the expedition that they reached the whaleboat, and, as Hawley told Mary, "glad they were to find it, for had it been taken in their absence they would have been in a woeful plight."[27] Next morning she received the welcome news that, though the raiders had lost six men who were captured when they lagged behind, those who had returned brought with them not one prisoner, but two, the second of whom they hoped to exchange for Billy.

Deodate Silliman immediately started out for Hartford, where he obtained a flag under which to travel to New York and a letter from Governor Trumbull to General Clinton offering to exchange Judge Jones for General Silliman. He carried a letter for his brother, too, in which, for the first time in many weeks, Mary allowed herself to speak of her loneliness, her longing, and her renewed hope. She also told Silliman that "the Judge was so good as to Breakfast with us the morning after he was brought over; he appears to be an agreeable Gentleman."[28] But to compare this with the account of the same occasion that she entrusted to her private journal is to appreciate the con-

stant care she took not to offend those who might either
alleviate or augment her husband's trials as a prisoner:

> After being mutually introduced, I observed to him that
> the fortunes of war had brought him here under dis-
> agreeable circumstances, and as I could so well sympa-
> thize with him and his family, I wished to do everything
> in my power for his accommodation, until the purpose
> of his capture was effected, when I hoped that Mrs.
> Jones, myself, and our partners, would be made happy
> in seeing each other again. But to my disappointment,
> I found him insensible and void of complaisance, and
> sullen discontent sat on his brow. He made me no reply,
> but asked this question: did they plunder when they
> took your husband? I replied, not much. He said, they
> have plundered my house—I don't believe they have
> left my wife a second sheet. This I was sorry to hear,
> and afterwards enquiring of Capt. Hawley, he told me
> that he had held up the idea that there should be no
> plundering, but when they had landed on the other side,
> the men said, what are we to get by it if we take Judge
> Jones? We run a great risk and we don't know but we
> may be killed. Unless you give us leave to plunder we
> will go no farther. He then saw that the expedition
> would be frustrated and he was obliged to tell them
> they might plunder.*

Though Mary entertained Judge Jones as her guest for two
or three days more, time enough for him to recover from
his first chagrin, he continued "very unsociable" and she
was glad when the authorities removed him to safer quarters at Middletown. His wife showed a better grace, for
she wrote to Mary "expressing her great thankfulness for

---

* Benjamin, when he read and copied the Reminiscences, wrote in the
margin the logical question, "How could they plunder when Judge Jones
was hurried off secretly?" They may have snatched up an item or two
from the hall, but with the house full of company it is hard to see how
they could plunder on the scale that Judge Jones implied.

(to use her own words) my politeness to her dear Mr. Jones, and begged me to accept a pound of green tea."[29]

Mr. Willett had not accompanied the judge to Holland Hill since he had been almost immediately paroled so that he might help in working toward the exchange. He acted as emissary, not only between Trumbull and Clinton but between husband and wife, which vastly improved their communication from that time forward. Obligingly, he also carried clothes and blankets to the prisoner, which improved Silliman's creature comforts, too.

"Liberty! The Prospect is so charming, so delicious, that I hardly dare indulge my Hopes for Fear of Disappointment," Silliman wrote on December 1.[30] Though he warned Mary that such exchanges were as often refused as accepted, it is easier to preach than to practice the wisdom of moderating one's hope, and when four weeks passed without word, Silliman showed the strain. "I long to see you all and yet I dare not indulge my Hopes for fear of a Disappointment," he told her, and in the next sentence burst out fretfully, "What can be the Reason that Governour Trumbull takes so long a Time to determine upon the Matter?"[31]

His impatience was understandable but misguided. The decision did not rest with Trumbull alone. The proposals that he had received, drawn up by Isaac Bunnell and others of the so-called Loyal Refugees, had complicated the question of trading Jones and Willett for the two Sillimans by making that exchange contingent upon another. They wanted to get back Captain Glover, a participant in the raid on Silliman's house and now a prisoner himself on a capital charge, along with three other Loyalists then resting under sentence of death, in return for four American prisoners from the Sugar House. They also demanded that the Americans make up weight on the exchange for Billy Silliman by adding the release of one John Pickett to that of Mr. Willett. Trumbull could hardly set himself up as sole adjudicator in a case that raised the question of whether the state should admit any circumstances as justifying the release of men condemned as traitors. He had therefore laid the matter before the assembly, where it received prompt but lengthy consideration. "Some say it will by no means do to give up those under sentence of death for high Treason," Mary told her parents, "But *I think* if we can get back some of our good Folks for some of their bad ones, it will be good trading."³² Eventually, the legislators agreed. By February 21, 1780, all of the British prisoners named in the exchange were on their way to New York— with the exception of Judge Jones.

A few days earlier, the judge had sustained an injury in a fall from a sleigh that rendered him unfit to travel on the day appointed. Since Connecticut had guaranteed his return the moment he recovered, everyone had expected that Silliman would nevertheless come home with the rest of the American prisoners. "But alass, our Flag returns, and no news from you! and soon after, those that were exchang'd, without any intelligence!" Mary exclaimed. "What can be the reason we can't imagine. Sometimes I fear you are sick, but hope for the best."³³

Not sick in body, but sick at heart, Silliman forced himself to sit still for some days after the other prisoners had gone home. Still no summons came for him, and on March 6 he appealed to William Franklin, who was, in the eyes of the British, still governor of New Jersey, and for that reason the most influential American Loyalist at New York. "I had the strongest Expectations that I should before this Time have received the same Permission which Mr. Jones has," Silliman wrote, "and that I should before this Time have been on my Return to my Family and Friends. What the reason of my Detention can be I am at a loss to conceive."³⁴ Franklin showed both courtesy and compassion in his reply. He too had expected Silliman to leave with the others, but had since been informed that "Sir Henry Clinton had omitted mentioning anything concerning the Proposals to General Knyphausen, and that the Exchange of an Officer of Your Rank militated with his Instructions, at least till the Result of the intended Meeting of Commissioners for settling a General Cartel [for the exchange of prisoners] was known." He had written to Knyphausen certifying that Clinton had agreed to the exchange in full and recommending that, since "the Rebels" had carried out their part of the bargain except where accident had forced a delay, Silliman be immediately released.[35] Furthermore, he had followed up the letter with a visit to headquarters, where he had made a personal appeal for action.

Though Silliman recognized Franklin's good will, he was dismayed by the suggestion that he might have to wait for the settlement of a general cartel. He wrote again to Franklin, submitting a copy of Clinton's order and asking that it be laid before General Knyphausen "which it appears to me must be sufficient to remove any Difficulty that may remain."[36] Silence ensued. On March 14 Silliman wrote Mary a letter that came closer to despair than any he had written since the kidnapping, and closer to reproach. He had heard nothing from her since December 22. Though Billy had recently sent word that she was well, and did not write only because she expected to see him at any moment, he had found it hard to bear that the flag which arrived from Connecticut to escort his fellow prisoners home had carried no letter from her to assuage his own disappointment. "It would have been a great Satisfaction, to have received a Letter from under your own Hand (My Love) if it had been only two Lines to have told me yourself that you and our Dear Family were well," he wrote. He told her how eagerly he had waited since the departure of the others "with strong Expectations of being called into New York, in order to return to you again My Dearest." And he told her of his appeal to Franklin, which now appeared fruitless. "I am myself as far from guessing when the happy Day of my Deliverance will arrive as I have ever been at any time," he concluded. "I am of Opinion that there is at present no Prospect that I shall see you very soon."[37]

Silliman never sent this letter or one of similar tone that

he had addressed to Billy on the same day. He told Mary later that he had withheld both because "on Reviewing them, I thought there was more in them that would give you Pain, than would afford you Pleasure."[38] He was glad that he had exercised restraint when he received a letter from Mary, dated March 12, which explained her earlier silence. "My dearest Mr. Silliman," she began, "With a heart full of tenderness and concern I sit down once more to write after flattering myself that our epistolatory correspondence was at an end for the present." Expectation alone had not kept her from writing; Billy had given that excuse in order to spare him anxiety. Since then, despite the suppression of his own letters, she had somehow heard that her omission had grieved him, and thought it better in that case to tell the truth. "The evening before he set out for Horse Neck in order to meet you, as I was setting by the Fire, with the Babe in my arms, I was seiz'd with a strange turn in which I was almost deprived of my senses, and quite of articulate speech," she wrote. "I was supported . . . to the Bed, where after lieing a little while I in a measure recovered, but was so confused on the morning Bille set out, I dare not attempt to write . . . thank a good God, I can now tell you I am very well."[39]

Almost a month went by; then, on April 6, Silliman informed Mary that General Knyphausen had recently sent a letter to Governor Trumbull in which he promised that, the moment Judge Jones could travel as far as Kings Bridge, Silliman would begin his journey home. He hoped to be with her within the week. On April 13, he was still in New York. "It is now Nineteen Days since General Knyphausen's Letter to Governor Trumbull went out," he wrote, "which is a Length of Time sufficient to allow that to get there, and for Mr. Jones to have received his Orders and to have got in, provided Mr. Jones is well enough to travel; but I have not yet heard a Word more about it. I scarcely dare indulge my fond Hopes and anxious Wishes and yet it seems as though I might; it seems as though every Obstacle was now removed, and that the time is very near

that will again restore to me all that is most Dear to me.
. . . In patient Hope of that Happy Event I endeavour, and
think I do keep myself calm and quiet."[40]

Another ten days passed.

V

IN the eight weeks since Silliman had seen his fellow prisoners go rejoicing home without him, he and Mary had
suffered more than at any previous time. Yet it was a fact,
an appalling one, that neither had experienced more than
a minor irritation compared to the nonranking prisoners
and their families.

Silliman lived in comfortable quarters; he could write
and receive letters; he could obtain books, received the
newspapers daily, and had the leisure to read both; he could
ride and walk within very generous limits; and he had access
to the congenial company of other officers in detention.
Were it not for Mary's pregnancy at the time of his capture, and the care of two babies that had since rested on
her, he could have invited her to visit him in New York.
Such were the privileges accorded prisoners of his standing. For the men in the Sugar House, captivity had a cru-
eler meaning. In summer they suffered from close
confinement in the heat; in winter, lacking warm clothes
or blankets, they perished from the cold; at all times, they
starved. Like their physical sufferings, their distress of mind
was also greater. Once in the Sugar House, a man had
almost no opportunity to send or receive news of home
unless a new prisoner arrived from his old neighborhood
or a captive officer was kind enough to send a message for
him. From beginning to end of his imprisonment Silliman
had exerted himself generously to do everything he could
for these unfortunate men, and his own trials should not
be underestimated. Nevertheless, there can be no doubt
who suffered the greater hardship.

On April 27, Judge Jones boarded a boat at Black Rock Harbor, the point from which Silliman and Billy had unwillingly sailed nearly a year before. Mary had hired the vessel, which was appointed also to bring Silliman back, "and we agreed that if they obtained him two flags should be hoisted when they returned, that we might know for certain that he was coming," she wrote. That small precaution against disappointment says much about the preceding months when hope was raised and dashed, raised and dashed, over and over again. She went on:

> The vessel sailed with Judge Jones about 8.OC in the morning. . . . We hoped that in two or three days, we should receive him who had been so long separated from us. But about one OC (meridean) we saw the same vessel returning, and to our surprise we saw two flags: this we could not understand as we knew that [she] had not had time to go to New York. . . . The fact was that, the same day we were sending the judge off, they at New York were sending off [Mr. Silliman]. Their flag of truce hailed ours and asked if they had Judge Jones on board—Yes! Well, we have General Silliman too, was their answer, and they soon boarded each other; and as I had sent a fine fat turkey for [Mr. Silliman's] comfort on the voyage home, they hasted to dress it, that the Judge might dine with him before he went on, which he did. And after taking leave each vessel went on its way. When our vessel came within call of our fort and battery on Grover's Hill near Black Rock, one called to know if they had Genl. Silliman on board. He then leapt on deck and waved his hat, when there was so loud a shout that we heard them plainly at our house (at the distance of two miles), and then all the cannon were fired off.[41]

Deodate and Jose had served as escorts to Judge Jones and were therefore among the first to welcome Silliman as he boarded the boat. When she docked, Billy, John, and a large number of friends thronged the wharf and claimed the right to greet him next. He made his way up to the house attended by a crowd of jubilant well-wishers, and there he was "received at the Gate, by the Dearest and most affectionate of Women," he wrote. "Erect on a Seat in the Stoop, the Dear Little Selleck stood looking & Expecting a Papa he had been taught to expect; but, poor little Fellow! he could not find a Feature that he could own in me. I soon gave him a little Hat, that a Lady in New York had sent him as a Present, hopeing to ingratiate Myself with him; he was mightily pleased, and walked off to one of the Family to show it, and was askt who gave it to him: —he turned and pointed to me, & said *that Man* gave it to me."[42]

If he experienced a pang at the discovery that Sellek had after all forgotten him, Silliman had joys enough that day to outweigh it. As he walked into the house he found Amelia waiting for him in the hall with Benny in her arms. "Here is your little boy, Uncle," she said, and held the baby out to be "embraced . . . with heartfelt delight."[43] Benny, just eight months old, corresponded more closely to Silliman's memories of Sellek than Sellek himself, though, as Silliman said, that young man soon grew "mightily pleased with and fond of" his father.[44]

On the following evening Silliman sat down to write to his parents-in-law. The paper before him was covered with smudges and crossings out, which he excused with the best of excuses. "If you please to observe, you will think something extraordinary is the Matter, that my Writing is so incorrect," he wrote. " 'Tis so: encircled by a Company of Friends, one of whom is going immediately to Lebanon, I snatch the Opportunity while talking with them to write a Line to our Hond. parents to let them know how happy we are. . . . I hope that we shall wait on our hond. parents next Month, and shall hope to celebrate our happy Anniversary with you. My Company talk so much that I must take my Leave of you for the present, and with my own & Mrs. Silliman's Duty to our Hond. Parents."[45]

III

The New Age

Seven

TRIFLES

THE wave of happiness that rushed over Silliman when he rejoined his family, and the stream of friends and neighbors who came to share his gladness, did much to wash away the marks of his ordeal. When he addressed himself to family and other business, however, a sobering array of problems met his eyes. Though Mary had done her best, the farm had suffered. On May 13 he wrote to tell Mr. and Mrs. Fish that he and his wife could not after all make an anniversary pilgrimage to Stonington. "I . . . found on viewing them that I had not a Horse fit to ride a Journey upon . . . till they gain flesh by Grass," he explained. "Our Hay has been a long time gone." More serious, "the total Stop put to all my Business for so long a Time; the very great Expences that have attended my own Situation abroad—the inevitable Expences of Family at Home—but above all the amazing Depreciation of our Mony, which diminished what Cash I left behind faster than all the other Matters did," had left him with little reserve. "But these are Trifles," he declared. "My Dear Mrs. Silliman, our Dear

Children & Family, our Habitation and the Residue of our Substance are all safe; 'tis enough, I complain not, but desire to rejoice & give Thanks to our great Preserver."[1]

I

THE public business had also suffered during his absence. Because the state could no longer keep the men supplied with food, the coastal defenses maintained by his brigade had begun to crumble, and disloyal elements of the population had lost no time in seizing the opportunity thus presented for illegal trading with the British on Long Island. Colonel John Mead of Greenwich informed Silliman that the state was losing control of her western frontier; that he could not ride about Greenwich with any assurance of safety; and that he had either to remain in hiding or to move his habitation constantly in order to avoid kidnapping. The last revelation touched a raw nerve in Silliman. He had not told Mary, but during the voyage from New York to Fairfield a gang of roughs in a whaleboat had followed his vessel shouting taunts and vowing to recapture him. He lost no time in relaying Mead's testimony to the governor, in taking such measures as he could to shore up the defenses of the western frontier, and in representing his personal danger before the Fairfield authorities to such good effect that they granted him a guard for his house at the town's expense. This relieved his mind of anxiety, if not of regret, when business obliged him to leave home again within a few days of his return.

Silliman had decided to present a memorial before the assembly at Hartford requesting that the state redress at least a part of the loss he had sustained through his imprisonment "since all my Trouble came by means of my being an Officer in their Service."[2] Both Houses debated his petition for nine days, with the same result as on a previous occasion. The upper house voted in his favor, the lower house against him. As Mary recorded the decision, the lower house claimed that "if they allowed him his wages and expenses, then others would apply, and there would be no end of it."[3] The upper house, perhaps suspecting a certain disingenuousness in this argument, appointed a committee to examine "the Reason of the different Votes." Silliman thought it wise to remain at Hartford until the committee made its report, although, as he warned Mary, he saw "very little Probability that any thing will be done for me." He went on:

> What shall I do my Love?—My late expensive Absence has cost me a great Deal of Mony.—should I again fall into the Enemy's Hands it would hurt me irreparably almost.—To reduce myself to a private Character would be my best Means of Safety, . . . were it not for the advice of some great Characters, and for Fear that the People of my own County would be disgusted at it, I should most certainly do this.—What shall I do my Dearest? I wish I had Your Advice.—I am at a great Loss how to conduct.[4]

It was not the first time he had asked his wife's advice, but the plaintive irresolution of this passage strikes a new note. Silliman had made an abrupt transition from the limitations of captivity to freedom at large in a world of complex choices; a world, furthermore, in which his own place had changed. In his bewilderment he seemed less to consult Mary's opinion than to ask that she set his course. She appeared to him the one fixed point from which he could take his bearings, and in recent months, after all, she had grown more accustomed than he to make decisions.

Silliman's cause failed, as he had feared it would. He was not present when the general assembly rendered its decision, having been ordered by the council of safety to Stratford, where a suspicious character calling himself Van Dyke had appeared. Silliman found no trace of the man, but while he was there the still more alarming intelligence reached him that, in the wake of a raid on Horseneck by Delancey's corps of Loyalists, the frontier guards had abandoned their posts, and the flight of all of Greenwich's patriot inhabitants might soon follow. The council of safety proposed to raise a new state regiment for the frontier and ordered Silliman to draw three hundred recruits for it from his brigade. Unfortunately, his men had grown tired of such calls, and most of them answered by paying the five-pound fine for refusal to march. As Silliman wearily girded himself for an assault on this latest addition to his military problems, the council of safety called on him to resume his role as state's attorney. A spy in the council's pay had collected pro-British statements from a number of residents in Fairfield County, and Silliman was expected to prosecute them. The government that had no use for his appeal still had plenty of use for his services.

As a consequence, when Mary left for her first visit to Stonington in over a year, she went without her husband. In early July Silliman escorted her, along with John, Sellek, and Benny, across the Housatonic River and watched them out of sight. Jose had stayed behind to help his stepfather catch up on the farm work. The two men set themselves a grueling pace, working from morning to night to bring in the hay with "scarcely Time to eat our Victuals," Silliman told Mary. But on July 10 the arrival at Newport of Rochambeau's expeditionary force, sent by the French government to bolster the faltering resolve of the revolutionaries, obliged him once more to sacrifice private advantage to public need. The haying must wait while he recruited and equipped his brigade's share of the fifteen hundred militia and one thousand additional Continentals required from Connecticut for combined operations with the French. "If Col. Whiteing had half so much on his Hands when I was a Prisoner," Silliman wrote, "I don't wonder that he should tell me that he was tired of having the Chief Command, and that he rejoiced that I had got back again to rid him of it."[5]

Since Esther kept "the Family Business in its proper Channels," Mary's absence did not add housekeeping to Silliman's tasks. He missed her, though, and missed his infant sons, almost unendurably. Less than two months had passed since his triumphant and joyful return. In that brief time he had found himself even poorer than he had feared, denied assistance from the state whose service had cost him his prosperity, and yet all but overwhelmed by its demands upon his time. Though he had tried to conceal his depression, Mary knew that this was in every way a bad moment to leave him bereft of the solace of family. She had arrived, however, to find her father ill, and he had since grown worse. In mid-July, herself torn between the need of her parents and the need of her husband, Mary wrote to Silliman suggesting that she remain at Stonington for two or three weeks more.

Silliman agreed at once that she must stay, but his cheerfulness gave way for a moment. "What shall I do my Love so long without you?" he asked. "Your vacant Chair at Table looks melancholly,—Your Bed Room lonely and unsociable." He clung to the hope that a rapid concentration of allied forces around New York would lift the immediate threat to Fairfield County and so release him from his post long enough to allow a quick visit to Stonington. On July 24th, about to review the entire guard along Connecticut's borders and coastline, he wrote that "[if] I find all in the order that I expect, I shall on Munday next set out to wait on my dear Sweet Heart home." Later that evening he added a postscript: he had just heard that the British had embarked the greater part of their troops on transport ships and brought them together below Kings Bridge, while nine large ships of the line had gone to block up the French at Newport. A British assault on Newport would relieve the pressure on the western frontier almost as effectively as a gathering of strength at New York, in which case "I shall be at Liberty to indulge myself," he wrote.[6]

Toward the end of the month Silliman sent Jose and Jemmy, on vacation from Yale, to Stonington ahead of him, in case he could not come after all; "and that I could not," he wrote on August 1, "was thoroughly determined by the Arrival of the British Fleet in Huntington Harbour" four days before. "You well know the Constant Recourse that is had to me almost every Hour of the Day," he reminded Mary. "You know the Reluctance & Unwillingness of the People to my taking the proposed Journey with my Dearest. . . . Youll therefore not think it strange that the same Disposition should again prevail, when only by going on to almost any Hill, they could see such a formidable Armament of the Enemy within two or Three Hours Sail of them." To compound his difficulties, of the 338 men detached from his brigade for combined operations against New York, only 104 had come in, and the attempt to remedy the default required his "most incessant Attention." He could not leave, and would not ask Mary to return. "I wish most ardently your Dear, Dear company and Society again my Dearest best beloved," he confessed. "But I cannot wish you to come away while Things are in the Situation they were in when you wrote last."[7]

On August 4 Silliman addressed a long letter to the governor and council of safety describing the many difficulties besetting his command, particularly that of keeping men under arms without adequate provisions, and asking to be relieved of it. A few days later, the fleet at Huntington retreated to New York and one of the Connecticut state regiments previously sent to reinforce the Highlands received orders to return to Greenwich. Soon afterward, Silliman left his post long enough for a visit to Mary at Stonington. His four-day return journey included visits to friends and a pause at Lebanon, where he conferred with the governor and council of safety and learned of two communications that were awaiting him at Fairfield. One announced that the council had issued "new Orders for my going on in my Military Command without limitation of

Time."[8] The other, dated August 16, ordered that he immediately detach 150 men from his brigade to fill vacancies in the regiment on guard at the western frontier, a circumstance which raises the suspicion that the council had not known of his absence from home.

The loss of a few days made little difference to the security of the state, and Silliman had come back in time to attend the Superior Court at Danbury where he duly prosecuted those who had signed declarations of loyalty to the Crown. Nevertheless, the evidence suggests that he had taken a kind of French leave, and had done so knowing that his second in command, Samuel Whiting, had come under suspicion of pro-British sympathies. If so, there were extenuating circumstances. Silliman had been separated from his family for all but a few days since his return; he had reason to fear that if he did not go to Stonington that summer he might forever lose the chance to see his loved and honored father-in-law alive; and he had never before skimped on his duty to the state although, in his view, the state had evaded her responsibility to him. He had, however, absented himself from his command for personal reasons, and his absence during this uneasy period could not have pleased the local populace.

II

ON the first evening of his return to Holland Hill Silliman wrote to Mary comparing himself to "the lonely Turtle waiting for his Mate."[9] Mary arrived so soon afterward that she must barely have received the letter before she started out for home, although, to judge from a note in which she bewailed her inability to send Mr. Fish some claret for his health, her father had not recovered. Perhaps what she had seen when Silliman came to Stonington had hastened her return. Certainly she found him tired, unhappy, and almost as ill as her father.

Silliman had taken a heavy cold that had not yielded to
treatment some three weeks later when he left to attend
the assembly at Hartford as deputy for the town. Though
his indisposition began to cost him the quiet rest that
nothing had formerly disturbed, he took his seat every day,
except when military emergencies sent him riding out "to
one Place & another on our exposed Sea Coast & western
Frontier, through a good many Storms, and sundry Times
wet to the Skin."[10] By October 25, when a messenger called
him out of the assembly to tell him that Mr. Fish lay on
the point of death at Stonington, Silliman felt so debili-
tated that for once he could not rise to the demands of
duty and affection. He left Mary free to go if she wished,
but she too chose to remain. She may have considered that
an early onset of winter could cut her off for weeks from
Fairfield and her little boys, or she may have hesitated to
leave her husband alone again, sick in body and weary in
spirit as she perceived him to be.

Two weeks later the assembly rose. After an illness of
seven weeks' duration Silliman had begun to feel better,
and he included a visit to Jemmy at New Haven on his
homeward ride. He arrived at Fairfield late that night to
receive the good news that Mr. Fish, against all odds,
appeared likely to recover. It was a happy homecoming, in
no way spoiled for Silliman by the manner in which his
youngest son received him. "In the Morning before it was
light little Benny awaked,—heard a Man's Voice talking
with his Mamma," Silliman told the Fishes. "He raised
himself on one Elbow, and spatted one Hand full in my
Face, and cried & quarrelled with me and would not be
reconciled to me till the Negro Girl came & took him up."
Amused and unruffled, Silliman rejoiced in his restoration
to the daily sight of his two "fine active Boyes, sprightly as
Hawks, every Day mounted on their Sticks (for Horses)
with their Whips in hand riding and pranching round the
House."[11] Yet the incident illustrated the extent to which
his inability to accompany the family to Stonington, and
his long absences at Hartford both before and since their

expedition, had kept him a stranger to the children more than five months after his release from captivity.

Mary too had known little of the companionship for which she had pined in their year apart and, with her husband so weighed down by work, she had continued to carry the dual responsibility for household and farm except during her six weeks away. "Poor Woman! I often think that on some Accounts, and under some Circumstances, that she is now much worse off than when she was a Widow," Silliman ruefully admitted to her parents. "A Great Part of the Time since our Marriage, she has had all the Cares & Troubles of Widowhood, with Anxieties & Distresses of mind that Widowhood is a Stranger to."[12] Mary herself, looking back in later years on her life at this time, wrote that "what of the revolutionary war that still remained caused me much trouble in various respects in my domestic matters, and I had each day as much care and anxiety as I could well get along with."[13] She did not regret her marriage to Silliman, however, only the circumstances that gave them so little time together.

The whole family assembled for Thanksgiving, and on December 7, 1780, Silliman and Mary witnessed the marriage of his eldest son to Phoebe Jennings. Billy had gone into mercantile business for himself in the town of Fairfield, and in recent months his name had all but disappeared from Silliman's and Mary's correspondence. Though there is no evidence of a serious breach, or any reason to suspect one, it is possible that Billy had made a quiet personal declaration of independence, a move perhaps facilitated by his year-long freedom from paternal surveillance and direction. Silliman was impressive in physique and authoritative in manner; in contrast, the picture of Billy that emerges from the correspondence is of a man prone to poor health and markedly deferential in his demeanor. Even as the victim of a dramatic kidnapping he had played the role of accidental adjunct to the prize represented by the older man. Now, in his twenty-fourth year, Billy showed no sign of any ability or ambition to assume the mantle of public office that his father had inherited from his grandfather, and wore with pride in spite of the trouble it caused him.

Silliman's principal problem during the first four months after his return from captivity was a shortage of food for his troops. By the autumn he was grappling with a short-age of ammunition as well. And as Connecticut's capacity to maintain an adequate coast guard declined, her shore-line towns witnessed a veritable orgy of plundering and kidnapping. To give just one example from Silliman's cor-respondence, during July an entire guardhouse comple-ment of men was captured and carried off by the enemy along with twenty-three head of cattle, a coup by no means unusual in its daring. In December the organization of Tory refugees as a group called The Associated Loyalists, adver-tised in a proclamation issued at New York as licensed to plunder all those outside the King's protection, threatened to make a bad situation worse. One way and another, the coastal population seemed to stand in almost as much dan-ger as those who lived close to enemy lines. As a result, when the government of Connecticut mounted a fresh effort in 1781 to recruit a force for combined operations with the French against New York, few of the men were willing to withdraw their protection from their own homes and families in order to bestow it elsewhere.

In response to the shortage of recruits, the government called an emergency session of the legislature for mid-Feb-ruary. Though both Silliman and Mary were unwell at the time, he answered the summons believing that "the Busi-ness now lying before the Assembly, is of a Nature so important to our Country, that I think no Man who has a Voice in her Councills, ought to leave them . . . without the Most urgent Necessity calls him off."[14] He also took the opportunity to put forward some business of his own.

Again he requested his release from all military duties, and this time the assembly agreed. They gave no reason for their change of heart, but very likely they saw that Sil-

liman's declining health made him physically incapable of
the work. In any case, Mary welcomed the decision. In the
nine months following his return her husband had been
more often away than at home; now she might see that
situation reversed. From her point of view the one drawback to his resumption of private citizenship was that it
would entail the withdrawal of their official protection.
"Our Guard is to continue until he returns, when they will
be discharg'd," she wrote. "And now our only confidence
must be in him who never slumbers nor sleeps."[15] Though
Silliman's altered status would make him less liable to
another kidnapping, it would not preclude the possibility.
Other private citizens had been carried off, some of them
more than once. For Silliman and Mary a repetition would
have meant not only emotional distress but worldly ruin
beyond hope of recovery. The immediate effect of his new
freedom, however, was that for the first time in three years
they could indulge in the simple pleasure of a wedding
anniversary celebration at Stonington.

Silliman planned the occasion with almost ceremonial
care. Determined that the old people should "see all their
posterity once more together,"[16] he arranged that Jose,
John, and Jemmy, as well as Benny and Sellek, would join
himself and Mary at the parsonage. He knew that Mr. Fish
had passed a sickly winter that had left him in low spirits.
On May 5, 1781, he had written the Sillimans an unusually
gloomy letter, pessimistic about the outcome of the war
and pathetically anxious for a visit since his health would
not permit him to come to them. Yet in spite of his sev-
enty-six years and growing infirmity he continued to serve
his parishioners. In a letter that reached Fairfield just as the
Sillimans were about to set out, he mentioned that he had
caught a cold from riding seven miles out and seven miles
back through inclement weather in order to perform a
marriage service.

On the road, the family heard that Mr. Fish was recovering; on arrival, they saw that he was dying. The ceremony

for which Silliman had unconsciously prepared now began
to unfold. Over the next few days a procession of people
made its way to their pastor's bedside, where he prayed
with them, preached to them, and took his leave of them.
Last of all, on the morning of May 29, an aged Indian
woman sought admission. Mary, who knew that her father
was near his end, tried to discourage her, but she insisted.
Mr. Fish greeted her warmly, smiling, taking her hand,
and saying, "Farewell Esther, I hope we shall meet in
heaven." He then called for his grandsons. The Noyes children came in and knelt to receive his blessing. His last
words to them were that they should never forget their
descent from "a long Train of worthy Ancestors," John
wrote, and "what a blot & Reproach we would bring upon
them, & upon ourselves if we should not walk in their
Steps."[17] As they rose, weeping, Silliman carried in his two
little boys and placed their grandfather's hands on their
heads. "Why, you make me as good as old Jacob," said Mr.
Fish, "I am not worthy to be named with him."

Exhausted, he sank back on his pillows, and Mary
attempted to place his head in a more comfortable position. "Let my weary head rest where it inclines," he told
her. He had just fallen asleep, and Mary had gone into the
other room to drink tea with her mother and Silliman,
when Jose, who had stayed with his grandfather, ran in to
report a change. They reached the old man's side just in
time to see him take a last breath or two and die "without
a struggle," his features composed in a peaceful, pleasant
expression. Two days later his remains were carried to the
church he had served for forty-nine years, its unpainted
wood now blackened with age, though local legend held
that the change had come about overnight, at the time of
the separations. There, from the desk where he had
preached, and where James Davenport had once denounced
him, his old classmate, colleague, and friend, Nathaniel
Eels, delivered his funeral sermon.

Looking back, Mary wrote of her father as he lay dying
that "all who saw him had reason to say 'let me die the

death of the righteous & let my last end be like his.' " Sellek, then not quite four years old, in his seventy-ninth
year told Benjamin that he distinctly remembered "the
death scene, and the laying on, upon our infant heads of
the good man's hands, & his parting prayer & blessing."[18]
In these recollections there was no shadow of sorrow. The
Sillimans had much to fret and grieve them at that time:
their financial losses; their disillusionment with the state
government, which they felt had repaid loyal service with
injustice; and Silliman's ill health. The death of the man
whom they had all honored and loved, and who in truth,
in their eyes, had acquired the stature of a biblical patri-
arch, might have been expected to deal them a crushing
blow. Instead, the perfection of it; the serene and stately
manner of his movement toward the grave; the attendance
of all his children, including those to whom he had represented the fatherhood of God; the steady faith and hope
that he maintained; and the unbroken peacefulness of his
passage through the gates of death seemed to them the
apotheosis of a Christian life. As such it conferred on them,
aspiring Christians all, a blessing and a promise.

The whole family remained at Stonington for a few more
days to help Mrs. Fish set the house to rights; then, Mary
recorded, "she went home with us (to Fairfield) and spent
the rest of her days there, to the comfort of us all." Mrs.
Fish, who (though perfectly literate) rarely wrote letters,
appeared a somewhat shadowy figure in the early records
of the family, but in these later years emerged briefly into
the light. Devoted to Sellek and Benny, "she would always
give them their meals," Mary wrote, "dress and undress
them, and learn them good lessons, and sit by them until
they went to sleep, as they were her delight."[19] Benjamin's
remembrance corroborated his mother's:

> Our grandma took almost the entire charge of us . . .
> She knit our stockings—she went into the kitchen gar-
> den & gathered green corn and roasted it for our repasts.
> She taught us prayers and verses, combed our heads &

put us in to good order for each day, & won our
young hearts.[20]

III

NOT until June 1781 did Silliman find the time to address
his financial problems, and then he moved cautiously. Since
the new state currency continued its rapid depreciation, he
saw little point in suing for debts that antedated his captivity. Besides, he still cherished a hope of obtaining compensation for his losses from the legislature, a hope that would
to some extent depend upon his gaining re-election as deputy to the general assembly. To bear down hard on his
Fairfield debtors might disturb the delicate balance of the
entire local credit structure, thereby jeopardizing his chance
of election and with it his chance to bring a new petition
for redress from the vantage point of an official representative. Silliman did not figure in the town's delegation to
the legislature elected that April, but this was probably
because he let it be known that his wish to accompany
Mary to Stonington would make the appointment unwelcome. His fellow townsmen had not lost their regard for
him: in June they named him moderator of the town meeting, and in September they re-elected him as their deputy.
It is to be hoped that he appreciated the honor of the
appointment, for he gained little else by it. The October
journal of the general assembly shows that, after all, he
made no further appeal.

For the next five months his public duties so engrossed
his time that he felt little benefit from his return to civilian
life. The assembly, having failed to complete its business
during the autumn, had met by adjournment on January
10, 1782. Almost a month later Silliman told Mary that "the
great Publick Affairs which brought us together are but a
few of them done." The affairs in question were the perennial problems of raising men and supplies for both the
Continental army and the state's defense, and the impedi-

ment to their resolution was lack of money. "To tax the People further at this Time seemed impracticable as they are now loaded with Taxes," Silliman allowed. "But if we do not, the Army must, and we doubt not will, disband, for it is impossible for them to live without Provisions."[21] Three days later he reported that, though he and his fellow delegates often sat until eight o'clock at night, they could not possibly finish their business in less than another ten days. By that time he would be due at the Superior Court in Danbury, "so that I don't expect any thing more than just to call & see you a Day or two as I go along," he lamented. "Such a Course of Life,—Such Absences from Dearest Connexions is exceedingly disagreeable.—I dont at all like it."[22] On the following Sunday, however, he added a happier postscript. A fellow member had carried him off for what had proved a pleasant day at Middletown, and a Dr. Dickinson, at whose house it ended, had cordially volunteered to deliver the letter to Mary in person.

When the general assembly of 1782 at last adjourned, Silliman began to pick up the threads of his professional life, commencing with his role as state's attorney. When the Fairfield County Court opened on March 2, 1783, he took an aggressive tack, proceeding without the sanction of a grand jury in six actions. In the April court he initiated two suits for the recovery of personal debts, which were successful, though in each case the court awarded him slightly less than he claimed. By the August term of the Fairfield Superior Court, he was acting as attorney in ten litigations. In December, at the Superior Court, he served as counsel in seven private cases, while at the county court he proceeded by the usual course of grand jury presentment against more than twenty suspected inimicals, illegal traders, and libelers of the government, himself prosecuting all those who answered the summons. Thus, he seemed to be recovering his position as one of the leading attorneys in the country.

Yet all his efforts were insufficient to recoup his losses, and his professional resurgence was brief. His work as state's attorney would naturally diminish when the war ended in April 1783, but the records show that his private practice also fell off, and this at a time when the state's efforts to restore solvency had increased the business of many lawyers by driving creditors to sue for their debts. If ill health played any part in Silliman's decline it was a small part, for during this period he continued active in Fairfield town government and as a deacon of the church. It is more likely that his professional losses followed from the same cause as his financial losses: the three years during which his career had come almost to a standstill. Not only his twelve months in captivity, but the military demands upon his time both before and after had kept him from carrying more than a very few clients.

Now he found that the private cost of public spiritedness ran high. From a membership in the inner circle of prominent lawyers he had moved into the position of an aging outsider. In 1782, his fifty years made him conspicuously older than most of the leading attorneys of the county. His age, combined with his inability to keep up with current changes in the law, lessened his effectiveness as counsel. Nor did it help that, unfair as it may seem, his war service had left him with a tarnished reputation. He had acquired a name as a man who had failed to defend the coast (no matter that the coast was indefensible), and who had resigned his command at a bad time. Furthermore, the inadequacy of his response to the Danbury raid, the tardiness of his brigade in reinforcing the Highlands, and his association with the abortive raid on Fort Independence had given rise to retrospective rumors that his own poor judgment, rather than the carelessness of others, had led to the near capture of his brigade in New York. Some measure of his fall may be gained from the decision of the general assembly in 1787 to pay him 20 percent less than the compensation he had claimed for services rendered while on active duty, on the grounds that he had asked for more than he deserved.

Clearly, Silliman's labors had won him no laurels at

home. Perhaps that is why victory, when it came in April 1783, received no mention in his or Mary's correspondence. Though the war had ended, their troubles continued; though their belief in the fight for independence remained firm, the immediate aftermath of its achievement inspired no jubilation.

IV

DURING these years, important changes were taking place in Mary's life. In 1782 she and Silliman became grandparents when Phoebe Silliman gave birth to a daughter, baptized Martha Ann, but called Patty. At the same time her Noyes sons began to choose their careers and to form their families.

In 1782 John and James, following in the footsteps of their father and grandfather, chose the ministry as their path in life. The act affirmed their sense of belonging to the time and place where birth had set them: the pre-revolutionary America in which, more often than not, children expected to pattern their lives on those of their forebears. To Jose, who had yet to commit himself, their calm acceptance of a destiny ordained by both nature and nurture contained a promise of peace and security that the opportunities of the present restless time did not hold. Soon after his younger brothers had declared their intentions, he announced that he would allow their example to direct his own course.

Nothing could have pleased Mary more than to see all three of John Noyes's children enter the church. Though she knew that, as ministers, they were unlikely to grow rich, she believed that they would gain a spiritual reward sufficient to outweigh worldly considerations. The knowledge that, from here on, they would spend less and less time at home likewise gave her no pang, since it would cause no violent disjunction in her accustomed course. She had her two little boys, who had only recently begun their first lessons at the schoolhouse, about a quarter of a mile from Holland Hill, and would not leave home for years to come. And she had her mother, whose presence carried the continuity of Mary's days backward in time to her own childhood.

In November 1783 that long, loving relationship ended. Mrs. Fish, who had enjoyed excellent health since moving to Fairfield, fell ill with what Mary called "the bilious colic." She suffered excruciating pain for ten days, during which Mary said that she never lost her patience or ceased to show "love, tenderness and gratitude" toward those around her. "Only when she was a little deranged she would call for my father to lay her pillow, and said, nobody could lay it so well as he," Mary wrote. Sellek and Benny went every day "to bid her goodnight, and also to bid her good morning which she affectionately returned," Benjamin recalled in after years. "One morning, however, she was silent & took no notice of us, & when we enquired why grandma did not speak we were told that an angel had come down from heaven in the night and taken her soul through the window."[23]

Rebecca Fish died on November 27, 1783, within a few weeks of her eightieth birthday. Fully resigned and truly "thankful that I had her so long," Mary nevertheless felt the earth turn when she buried her mother. She had lost a husband, yet been a wife again; she had lost children, yet been a mother; but with both her parents gone she would never again be someone's beloved child. A solemn rite of passage in every life, it held a special poignancy for Mary, who had so long and happily occupied the place of daughter. "I believe there never was a more ardent affection between parents and children than between us, nor time nor distance ever abated it," she declared, in a last tribute to her upbringing. Yet her mother "came to her grave like a shock of corn that was fully ripe," and a new crop soon burgeoned. It also happened in that year that Jose Noyes married Silliman's niece Amelia Burr, a doubly joyous occasion for Mary and Silliman since both bride and groom had grown up as children to them. The couple settled in Fairfield, and in October 1784, just as Mary supervised the shipment to Stonington of a stone monument to be raised over her father's grave, she held in her arms a grandson baptized Joseph Fish Noyes.

Jose had continued to vacillate on the subject of a career. Since his graduation from Yale he had dabbled in law, and then in theology, but his decision to become a clergyman had not held firm. He now turned back to the law, and his stepfather probably helped him to complete his training. During 1784, when illness incapacitated Silliman, he employed Jose as his secretary and may have introduced him to future clients. Jose soon acquired a small practice of his own, mostly in the collection of debts, and repaid Silliman's generosity by helping in the continuous task of managing John Noyes's estate. He did reasonably well, and became prosperous enough to purchase a house and lot together with four additional acres of land, but he gave no promise of distinction in his profession.

In that year, true to his prenuptial promise, Silliman persuaded Jose, John, and James to divide the Noyes estate among them, exclusive of the third set off for Mary, as a precaution against possible seizure of their inheritance for their stepfather's debts. To the surprise and distress of both parents, Jose refused his consent to an equal division and claimed his right as eldest son to take one-half of the property, leaving John and James with one-quarter each. Mary and Silliman urged him strongly to consider that legal right did not always coincide with moral right, which in their opinion demanded that he take no more than his brothers. Emboldened, perhaps, by the secular tone of the times, Jose rejected this line of argument and insisted that the division take place according to the letter of the law.

Though Jose had consigned them to lesser portions, John and James held a steadier course than he. By 1784 both were licensed and, like their grandfather Fish, had begun their lives in the church as itinerant preachers. Over the next two years John received invitations from several church

committees, and on one occasion preached at Stonington
from *"that venerable Desk"*²⁴ once occupied by his grandfather, a powerfully evocative experience, though it did not
lead him to settle there.

James traveled less and settled first. He had been the
most academically distinguished of the Noyes brothers.
During his sophomore year at Yale he gave the English
oration at commencement, and at his graduation in 1782
he made the Latin response, honors achieved by neither
Jose nor John. In 1784 he became assistant to James Dana,
minister of the First Church in Wallingford, whose health
was degenerating. Less than two years later Dana persuaded his congregation to induct James, then only twenty-
one years old, as colleague-pastor with himself, generously
renouncing his own salary in order to make the arrangement affordable.

Dana had achieved notoriety at the time of his ordination in 1757 when a New Light minority, objecting to his
theology, had invoked the power of the local consociation
of churches, together with a special council representing
the New Haven and Hartford consociations, to block his
installation. In a classic reversal of roles, the Old Light
majority had defied the authorities and ordained him. This
act of disobedience had led to the severance of fellowship
between the Wallingford church and the consociating
churches.

The breach had never been formally repaired, but James's
ordination became the occasion for a symbolic reconciliation. Eight neighboring churches sent delegates, including
the First Church of New Haven, where James's grandfather Noyes had served; the Wethersfield church, which
sent James's cousin, Colonel John Chester; the Fairfield
church, which sent Silliman, Billy, and the Reverend
Andrew Eliot, who had prepared James for college and
who preached the ordination sermon; and the Woodbridge church, which sent James's uncle Thomas Darling.
Though the Yale College church had not lifted its ban on
fellowship with Wallingford, President Ezra Stiles took part

in the solemn procession of dignitaries from Dana's house to the church, as well as in the ceremony that followed, an elaborate, three-hour service that included a sermon lasting one hour and thirteen minutes. Mary's feelings on the occasion can only be imagined, since no account of them has survived. The scale of the proceedings conferred extraordinary honor on James, the youngest of her children until only six years before. The representation among the delegates of both the Noyes and Silliman families and family friends showed that her second marriage had extended and enriched the lives of herself and her sons without incurring any loss of earlier ties. And that the son of John Noyes, a peacemaker himself, should become the center of an attempt to mend an old quarrel between church brethren would surely have pleased her most of all.

The wounds had not completely healed. In the December following James's splendid ordination, the family was shocked and mortified to hear a report that, accused of having drunk too much at a wedding, James had been required by Mr. Dana to confess his error before the whole congregation. Since the Wallingford church records contain no mention of the incident, which would certainly have created a sensation in the parish, it is quite possible that the report originated not in fact but in the vestiges of the old animosity. By 1789, in any case, when Mr. Dana, unexpectedly recovered, accepted a position in New Haven, James had brought many of the dissidents of the 1750s back to the parent church, and took sole charge of the pulpit by general consent.

John continued as an itinerant preacher for a year after James's ordination. In that time he was offered, and declined, two handsome settlements, one from Derby's Great Hill Society, the other from Little Compton in Rhode Island where his Grandmother Fish had grown up. The call he accepted came from the less affluent parish of Norfield (present-day Weston), where he was ordained on June 5, 1786, with James and Mr. Dana in attendance, though with much less fanfare than his brother. John's reasons for choosing Norfield, as Mary explained them, showed the influence of his grandfather Fish. "The people there are not wealthy people, except two or three, and give him but a small support," she wrote, "but they are very fond of him and united to a man."[25] John apparently was also very fond of one of the parishioners, for, still pursuing the path trodden out by his forebears, shortly before his ordination he married Eunice Sherwood, the daughter of his predecessor Samuel Sherwood.

The Sillimans thought themselves fortunate to have all their grown sons living near them: Billy with Phoebe, and Jose with Amelia, at Fairfield; John with Eunice at Norfield, only ten miles away; and even James, the farthest off at Wallingford, within a day's ride. In 1786 Jose and Amelia added a second son, John, to their family, and two years later a third whom they named James, thus reproducing exactly the pattern that Mary had followed in naming her sons. In 1787 Eunice Sherwood Noyes gave birth to her first child, Samuel, followed a year later by a girl named Mary. In 1788 James married Anna Holbrook, and in the following year they became the parents of Catherine. Together with Billy's daughter, Mary's grandchildren now numbered seven, all living and thriving.

Meanwhile, at the parental home on Holland Hill, Sellek and Benjamin recorded that Mary supplemented the education they received at the local school with lessons in "the elements of English reading." And in a charming reverse image of Mary's early lessons with Becca in their father's study, Benjamin described how his mother began each day with a period of religious instruction for Sellek and himself.

She taught us prayers and hymns, and every morning heard us read in the Bible and other religious books adapted to our age. In mild weather we usually resorted to the parlor-chamber, the best chamber in the house, which was also reserved for our guests. Here, while our mother combed the hair and adjusted the dress of one, the other read or recited passages of Scripture or hymns of sacred poetry.

These pleasant, informal sessions culminated less pleasantly, in a stiff, uncomfortable ceremony on Sunday afternoons when the Silliman boys together with the young blacks of the household were required to recite as much of the catechism as they could remember, "and all were glad when this exercise was finished."

Mary also taught her sons manners, which she regarded not as merely social adornment but as a ritual whose practice would encourage and assist the development of inner grace. Politeness to all persons, in particular the elderly, was the foundation of her teaching, and she set a high value on courtesy between parents and children. "If we received a book or anything else from her hand," Benjamin wrote, "a look of acknowledgment was expected, with a slight inclination of the head, which she returned." The "blunt reply to a parent, without the addition of *sir* or *ma'am* to *yes* or *no*" was never heard in her household. Mary taught as much by example as by precept. "I do not remember to have seen a finer example of dignity and self-respect," Benjamin wrote of her, "combining a kind and winning manner and a graceful courtesy with the charms of a cheerful temper and a cultivated mind." The beauty of her character "attracted the wise and the good, and won the thoughtless to consideration," and her sons thought it "a great blessing to have had such a mother."

Silliman himself contributed almost nothing to these lessons. As a "decidedly religious man, [though] without austerity" he "shed a holy influence over the family," but Benjamin supposed that he was too much "engrossed by public and private duties" to do more.[26] Young as he was, Benjamin perhaps did not realize that personal factors may also have detracted from his ability to bear as active a part in educating his sons as Mr. Fish had borne toward his daughters. It is a tribute to Silliman's determination to protect his children from unchildlike cares that neither was aware of his failing health and deepening anxiety about his finances.

The memories that Benjamin and Sellek recorded of their early youth portray a happy home. The Sillimans were renowned for their hospitality, their house was "rarely without visiting or lodging friends," and conviviality reigned. The children were proud of the fine figure that their father made among his company. Strongly built and habitually erect "as if he were at the head of his brigade," he dressed fashionably and sported silver knee and shoe buckles. His complexion was dark, his eyes hazel, and he wore his brown but graying hair in the current style "short and curled in the neck—without powder and descending a little below the collar of his coat." His mouth was the strongest feature of his face, the lips "rather thick with a marked expression of friendliness & tenderness and some- times of pleasantry." He smoked his long-stemmed pipe quite heavily, but in drink he was temperate, though on festive occasions "a rich brandy sling—in a quart tumbler, well sugared and nutmeged, was passed around just before dinner; all partook in moderation & we (the little boys, as we were called) . . . were allowed the bits of sugar & the drainings at the bottom of the glass." A courteous, atten- tive listener, Silliman also loved to tell stories, and told them well, with "brevity, spirit & point."[27] He took partic- ular pleasure in the society of educated women, but the boys noticed that he was at his best and most sparkling when old soldiers of the Revolution were among his guests. Nevertheless, he did not confine his hospitality to mem- bers of his own social circle. He sometimes brought home an indigent guest to share the pleasures of his table, though always taking care to avoid any offensive appearance of patronizing them.

Among his family, he was no less pleasant. In his chil- dren's eyes, Silliman appeared "a bright, cheerful man . . . [whose] principal source of happiness was in doing his duty and making others happy."[28] He made their mother very happy indeed. Even now, his love for her was "like that of a youthful husband." He liked to have her at his side whenever possible, and she often accompanied him when he rode out on business, sometimes in a carriage, sometimes riding together with him "on the same horse, she on a pillion sidewise and sustained both by a stirrup and by holding on upon her husband." The continued strength of their physical attachment may be inferred from Silliman's comment to his sons, delivered as advice on the subject of their own future marriages, that he never took his worldly affairs to bed with him because "the bedroom of a happy pair should be the sanctum consecrated to conjugal endearment and to communications with ones maker."[29] By 1788 he was far gone in illness and worry, but he concealed it so well that, when Mary and the boys were simultaneously inoculated, a sudden decision necessitated by the discovery that they had exposed themselves to smallpox, his "smiles and cheerful deportment" as he nursed them through the aftermath "had the benign influence to scatter every cloud."[30]

Yet Mary suspected that money worried him more than he would say. There were many signs of trouble, but none more suggestive than his approach to provision for the future of his adored younger sons. Mary wondered why he did not have them taught Latin, but when she questioned him he would only answer that he thought a sound knowledge of reading, writing, and arithmetic more practical. Once Mr. Eliot asked him bluntly if he did not intend to send Sellek and Benjamin to college, and he replied that he did not know. For a man of his background and standing to express any doubt that he would give his sons an education for the professions indicated something very wrong; still, Mary clung to the hope that time would set it right. She knew that he had many debts, but she also knew that no single creditor had a claim against him that he could not meet. Although he would have been in trouble if all of them had pressed him simultaneously, this was not likely to happen. Nor did any of his creditors sue him, perhaps deterred by his positions as state's attorney and justice of the peace, though a man's place in society did not always protect him. Whether by luck or by management, Silliman had so far contrived to keep his head above water, and had his problems consisted solely of his private debts he might have continued to do so. Unfortunately they did not.

As commanding officer of the 4th brigade, Silliman had handled a large amount of public money which he disbursed to the colonels of the regiments for recruitment purposes and for payment of soldiers' wages. Overwork had made him careless about taking receipts, and he had not always followed correct procedure in making allowances to his officers for raising men. Such was the confusion of the early postwar period that not until 1784 did Silliman receive a summons from the Committee of the Pay Table to settle his accounts. At that time Jose wrote to excuse Silliman from an immediate appearance on the grounds of illness and to say that he would present himself as soon as possible. In fact, Silliman put off the day of reckoning until 1787. A letter he wrote on April 12 of that year to Andrew Adams shows that he was attempting to track down the missing receipts, but with little success. The state comptroller, Oliver Wolcott, Jr., who chose to take an uncompromising stance, presented a claim against Silliman in the staggering amount of eighteen hundred pounds. From that day on Silliman ceased to hope that he could pay his debts, let alone restore his old prosperity.

V

IN 1789 Silliman kept the Fourth of July with friends at Fairfield. He returned home in acute distress and continued so for several days, "his disease baffling the skill of the physicians." Eventually they diagnosed his ailment as the "stranguary," a painful disorder of the bladder and urethra. The treatment they administered did little good; complications developed, and Mary, with a knowledge born of sorrowful experience, saw "death's harbinger in his face" long before Silliman himself understood the finality of his illness.

Yet death did not come so soon as to spare Silliman the knowledge of Billy's ruin. In 1784 he had formed an ambitious partnership in the retail business with a man named Wright White. By 1787 the partners were unable to pay their bills; all attempts to reach a compromise with their creditors failed, and Billy went into hiding to avoid arrest. In October 1789 he was apprehended and committed to Fairfield jail, whence he might emerge only for exercise within the limits of the town square. He could not obtain leave to visit his father, whose sickness kept him confined to the house for most of that winter, or to accompany him the following May on a voyage to Long Island that the doctor had advised on therapeutic grounds.

Mary, though she felt "a great aversion to going on the water," mastered her fear for her husband's sake and went with him.[31] The venture began unpropitiously and finished in disaster. Silliman arrived so exhausted by the journey, yet so unable to sleep that night, that Mary thought it best to return on the next boat to the mainland. The second voyage, alas, was worse than the first. It ended in shipwreck just off Fairfield, from which the passengers barely escaped with their lives after a terrifying passage through heavy seas in a longboat.

After that, though Silliman endeavored to behave as usual among his family and friends, Mary saw that he deteriorated daily. It had been the custom for Mr. Eliot, when he finished writing his Sunday sermon, to take Saturday afternoon tea with the Sillimans. On July 17 he came as usual, Silliman joined him at the table, and the two friends were talking animatedly when Silliman gave a sudden convulsive jerk that caused him to drop his cane. He recovered himself at once, dismissed the incident as nothing, and passed the rest of the evening pleasantly. On the following morning Mary had just combed his hair and was about to arrange his cravat, small tasks that had become hard for him to perform, when he gave the same convulsive motion again. In another moment, an apoplectic fit struck with full force.

Mary attempted to hold her husband up while she cried out for the servants and turned the key in the bedroom door to give them access, but since the door had been already undone she had in fact locked them out. Before they could break in Silliman crashed heavily to the floor. When they did gain entrance, they helped her to place Silliman on the bed. The noise had brought Sellek and Benjamin running, and they bore agonized witness to the scene that followed. When Silliman regained consciousness he seemed confused to find the room full of people, including neighbors who had hurried over to lend their assistance. He rose and began to pace up and down, loudly declaiming his intention to quit the house. "His strength was great and he strode around the room not in a defiant manner but like one accustomed to command and who did not expect to be opposed," Benjamin wrote. It took several neighbors and a powerful manservant to restrain him. "When the paroxysm subsided, he became mild and calm and resumed his usual amiable and winning manners," in which mood he tried to reassure the frightened boys. Sellek expressed great reluctance to leave him in order to attend church, but his father gently told him, "Go to the meeting my son, I do not know when I can go again."[32] The doctor arrived, and Silliman sat down to describe the events of the morning. In the middle of a sentence he had another seizure, from which he once more recovered.

The next two days passed without incident. Many friends and neighbors called, and he conversed normally with them except that, as Mary noted, he "sometimes . . . appeared a little lost." The one missing face in the procession of visitors was that of his eldest son. "One day when he was a little delirious he said, 'I should like to see Billy but—ah— I forget he cannot come,' " Mary wrote.[33] An occasional parole to visit a dying father would have seemed a small enough mercy, but the creditors, to whom the jailer was personally responsible, probably opposed it because they hoped that Silliman's danger would drive him to pay Billy's debts in order to bring him home.

In the end, Billy came only once, at night, in secret and in disguise. Jose came every day, James and John as often as distance and professional responsibilities allowed. In the early afternoon of Wednesday, July 21, when John Noyes arrived with his mother-in-law, Mrs. Sherwood, Silliman insisted on rising from his bed and walking, with support, into the parlor where he entertained them with his customary cordiality. On his return to the bedroom he sat for a moment in the armchair contemplating the bright, summer scene beyond the window, then turned, took Sellek and Benjamin each by the hand, and said to Mary, "My dear, I believe I am going the way of all the earth. Take good care of our dear children." Those were the last words he spoke to her as husband to wife. After she had helped him back into bed he repeated the phrase "the morning of the resurrection, the morning of the resurrection," over and over again.[34] Mr. Eliot came to take her place, and after a while Silliman fell into a doze. Mary, Sellek, and Benjamin had just re-entered the room when the sleeping man made a terrible sound and went into convulsions. Jose and John hurried in, and all six looked helplessly on as the last agonies ensued, mercifully ended by death a little before sunset.

The burial took place two days later in the churchyard at Fairfield. Billy joined the mourners when they reached the town square, but even then no latitude was shown him, and at the eastern limit he was forced to take his leave of the cortege. Benjamin remembered all his life the sorrowful sounds of that hour: his mother's low weeping as they passed on to the meetinghouse, and the rattle of stones and earth on the coffin lid at the moment of farewell. From the graveside the family went straight to poor Billy's lodgings at the jail, where they comforted him with shared memories and shared tears. Silliman had fathered three sons, but six wept for him. The Noyes children mourned

their stepfather no less bitterly than his own offspring, and
in the midst of her grief Mary thanked God that time had
justified her in the risk that she had taken, with their lives
as well as with her own, some fifteen years before.

The passion that had fired Mary then intensified her sorrow now, yet she resigned herself more easily to Silliman's
death than to the suspicion that public ingratitude had
rendered his last years unjustly and unnecessarily miserable. When she came to write an account of his problems
for his sons, in case she should die before they were old
enough to understand a verbal explanation, she rehearsed
again the loss of his legal business during his years of army
service, the loss of both lawyer's and officer's pay during
his year as a captive, and the melting away of what money
there was through the combined evils of depreciating currency and inflation. But "worse than all the rest," she said,
was the demand that he repay the state the sum of eighteen
hundred pounds, which had "sunk his spirits and discouraged him about settling his other debts."

Characteristically, he had striven to keep the peace of the
home, which he valued above all else, unbroken by the
despair he felt:

> He got along with his family as he could under these
> embarrassments, keeping up a cheerful countenance
> before me even when in a low state of health, as if all
> were well and prosperous. He saw no way to extricate
> himself, and he feared it would make me unhappy—
> therefore he remained silent, and I believe it was a means
> of shortening his days.[35]

In other words, the losses and disappointments that Silliman had dismissed as trifles when set against the blessings
of family, added to the effort entailed in keeping the family
atmosphere unspoiled by worry over money, had mounted
a pressure that hastened his death.

Eight

UP THE
HILL

SILLIMAN'S death completed the cycle of change in Mary's life that had begun with the death of her father. With her mother and her husband gone, too, she stood alone as the center and support of a spreading new family circle. As her sons moved outward into the world, their ties to her secured them; as their independence grew, so did their love and respect for her as family matriarch. And as the generation of her grandchildren increased, they too looked on Mary as one having authority.

I

WHEN Mary took stock of her circumstances she saw that her second widowhood was to differ sharply from her first. John Noyes and his parents had left her with ample assets and few debts; Gold Selleck Silliman had done precisely the reverse. Only after his death did Mary find out how large a sum the state claimed back from him: not a pleasant discovery, it proved to be the first of many.

In 1775, a few days after their wedding, Silliman had retired all his debts with Mary as his witness. His troubles had begun shortly afterward, when he agreed to act as co-executor of his father's will together with his brother Ebenezer. Silliman's disappearance into the army a few months later had prevented his immediate attention to the matter, and the demands of military business had kept him inactive until the closing years of the war. In 1788, when the two brothers at last exhibited their accounts to the probate court, it emerged that Silliman had neglected to pay off several notes of hand, given by his father, on which huge interest charges had accumulated. Shortly after Silliman's death this error became the subject of a family controversy, and in addition to other problems Mary had to confront the possibility that the estate would be found as heavily in debt to his father's other heirs as it was to the government.

When Mary turned for advice to Andrew Rowland, the local judge of probate and a family friend, he suggested that she declare the estate insolvent. Mary had nothing to lose by that procedure since her widow's third would take precedence over all other claims and, together with her life interest in what remained of the Noyes and Fish lands, would support her. Her husband's creditors would have been wronged, however, and her two younger sons would have lost their inheritance. For both reasons she approached the task of administration as if the estate were solvent, though rumors to the contrary precipitated an avalanche of claims, many of them highly questionable. To just claimants, Mary gave their due; with the others she did battle, and frequently emerged victorious. "I desire heartily to sympathize with Mr. Nathaniel Wilson," Benjamin jeered, when the first pretender went down to defeat, and "likewise with all that numerous class of respectable Gentlemen who, since the death of our *Hond. Father,* have exhibited claims against our estate, which had he survived would never have made their appearance.[1]

When Mary turned claimant herself, she more often met with failure. A first examination of Silliman's books had suggested that if she could call in all the money owed him a decent estate would remain. On the strength of that expectation she took the step that Silliman had hesitated over: she arranged for Mr. Eliot to begin preparing Sellek and Benjamin for admission to Yale. She soon found, however, that the tendency of the judicial system to favor local interests impeded her efforts to collect. For example, when she sued for a debt long owed to Silliman by the town of Norwalk, and for which he had obtained an execution in 1786, the county court found in behalf of the defendants. Though Mary then entered an appeal in Superior Court, her creditors would not necessarily await the results of such lengthy procedures. Attempts to recover money out of court fared little better. "Many debtors were dead or left nothing," she explained, "and many that were living were unable to pay, and some were gone into distant countries." Several times during these years, desperate circumstances drove Mary to petition the probate court for permission to sell real estate, and in the end about one-third of the Silliman lands disappeared in this way.

The statement in Mary's Reminiscences that, among her problems when Silliman died, she counted "a great family" to support surprises the reader at first since all but two of her children had by then attained financial independence. The explanation casts an odd sidelight on a peculiar institution. Mary referred here to her domestics, "eleven of whom were negroes, and all small but three, and of those two were women." The census of 1790 contradicts her slightly, settling the total number of her household at eleven, seven of them slaves. It is possible that memory failed her and that she had conflated the number of her slaves with the number of her household. More likely, since two of the women were married "and had children very fast," perhaps at one point she owned eleven slaves counting the newborn children.

Whatever the case, Mary found that because the care of

their children left the women "little time to spin," she had
in effect fewer servants to work for her than to feed and
clothe. During the 1780s, it appeared, her husband had even
increased his debts by hiring "a man and one or two women
to manufacture for this great family."[2] In the first year of
her widowhood the cost of continuing to maintain it
amounted to the staggering sum of £182.8.0. But for a cod-
icil to Silliman's will, which allowed her "one years Provisions for Herself, my two sons, G Selleck, and Benjamin,
and such Servants as she may have," Mary could not possibly have paid these bills.[3] She saw that from then on she
would have to economize, and that the first step toward
reducing the expenses of her household was to reduce its
size or, in other words, to dispose of slaves.

There were three ways to do this. There was emancipation. Her father's will had provided for the freeing of a
slave in 1790 (nine years after Mr. Fish's death), while Job,
a slave at Holland Hill when Mary first married Silliman,
had since received his freedom and now lived nearby as
head of a family of six free nonwhites. There was also the
possibility of giving slaves to other members of the family.
And there was sale.

Since the end of the war, Connecticut's laws had come
by degrees to encourage emancipation. Before that time,
an owner who freed a slave remained liable for his support
should he become indigent. In 1784 the legislature revised
the code so that any child born to slave parents after March
1 in that year would automatically gain freedom at age
twenty-five, a first step toward abolition. The second step
came in 1788 with the passage of a law requiring that the
owners of slaves in this category register them, and forbidding their transportation out of state. In March 1792 it
became unlawful to transport any slave out of the state for
the purpose of sale, while masters who freed slaves between
the ages of twenty-five and forty-five were thenceforth
absolved from responsibility for them. In 1793 the lower
house even passed a bill forbidding the sale of blacks within

Connecticut, though the upper house immediately struck it down.

Thus, it was in the context of a legal environment increasingly favorable to emancipation that Mary sold two of her slaves. The evidence is fragmentary, but what there is leaves little room for doubt. In Mary's account book an entry dated February 7, 1792, records the receipt for forty pounds "for Negroes sold" one "Jas. Blackman," and another dated January 1793 acknowledges a further payment from him of twenty pounds.[4] The timing of the sale is disturbing. First, it took place before Mary felt the full pressure of the claims against the estate. She was not obliged to settle them until the commissioners appointed by the probate court had made their report, which would take another year or more. Second, it took place immediately before the passage of a law diminishing the cash value of blacks, a fact which raises the suspicion that Mary had prior knowledge, purveyed to her by influential friends, that she used in timing the transaction so as to maximize her gains. Even if this were not the case, that she sold her slaves at all, given the growing distaste for the trade, strikes a discordant note.

It is necessary to remind ourselves that Mary had grown up accustomed to the enslavement of blacks, in circumstances as benign as a barbarous institution would allow. Her father had owned slaves, and had used his power so humanely as to give her no more reason to question his mastership over them than she had to rebel against his authority over herself. It is true that Joseph Fish once described corporal punishment as fit only for "vassals, negroes and other sordid slaves, when nothing else will do,"[5] a statement which, though it exists as an isolated example, shows that the kindly parson was capable of consigning certain persons (though, notably, not blacks alone) to an inferior category of human being. There is no reason to think, however, that Mr. Fish himself meted out such treatment, and some evidence to the contrary. Becca

had once written of a certain "Jack," sold by her father at
a time of financial duress, that on a subsequent visit to the
family "the poor creature cryd heartily when he went away.
He longs to live with us again."[6] Since Jack's freedom to
go visiting suggests a reasonable decency in his new owners, his tears presumably did attest to his affection for the
Fishes. That affection, while it does not prove the point,
militates against the notion that Mr. Fish was given to
beating him.

In the Elm Street house of the Noyes family it was the
same: there were slaves, yet no abuse of their condition.
Benjamin, in later life an abolitionist, would one day defend
his mother's ownership of Peter, which dated back to her
first marriage, on the grounds that slavery "was then the
custom" and that Peter was "held by a light tenure."[7] We
have no reason to doubt the statement or to conjecture any
difference in the treatment of the slaves at Holland Hill. In
the context of the times, Mary behaved with propriety
toward the black members of her household both before
and after her husband's death. For though she complained
that the support of "this great family" cost her both time
and money, and that as a result she "got along but poorly,"
she strove for two years to keep and care for them.[8] When
at last she did resort to sale, she might fairly claim to have
acted under pressure, even though it was not pressure from
creditors.

By other accounts than her own, the Silliman slaves consumed more than they produced, and one of them, a man
named "Tego," became "bold and sometimes insolent" to
Mary after Silliman's death, perhaps on the assumption that
a solitary white woman was even more powerless than a
male slave. It was this man, and with him his wife Sue,
that Mary sold. The evidence, though inconclusive, indicates that the decision to part with Tego was prompted as
much by the difficulty of dealing with him as by the need
to retrench. The sale of his wife, a valued member of the
household, described, in contrast to her husband, as "kind
and faithful," probably reflected Mary's unwillingness to

sunder what God had joined. If any of the children were theirs, however, they remained for the moment at Holland Hill. There is a puzzling entry in Mary's accounts of two years later crediting Billy with sums owed him "on acct. of Sue," sums roughly equivalent to her former appraised value, which suggests that the family bought her back.[9] Perhaps her new owner was removing from the neighborhood, and Mary redeemed her so as to keep mother and children close. We cannot be sure of this. We do know that during the smallpox epidemic of 1793, when the authorities removed all restrictions on inoculation, Mary paid for the slaves (including old Peter) to undergo the process, and herself nursed them through the disease. Then, over the next few years, she freed the remainder of the adults and put the children out as indentured servants until they reached the age at which the law declared them free.

For years to come, Mary would suffer the consequences of having owned slaves. On at least two occasions, families to which children had been sent attempted to break the indenture and return them to the Sillimans because of their unruly behavior. One discontented master even demanded financial compensation for trouble and loss caused him by the girl that he had taken. Furthermore, from time to time claims were made upon the family because former slaves had become indigent. Mary and her sons honored these claims. But they did so grudgingly, with evident condescension toward the black race, and altogether this chapter of Mary's life story only reinforces the now-accepted fact that ultimately slavery benefited no one. The slaves had learned habits of dependence that left them ill-qualified for freedom, while Mary acquired little from her ownership of them besides recurrent problems and moral dilemmas imperfectly resolved.

II

WITH every means that she employed either to raise or to save money, Mary remained poor. Her power with the family was not the power of the purse. Billy's letters to her from prison in the months following his father's death show as clearly as anything the nature of her authority.

Though now in his thirties, Billy reverted from the customary salutation of "Honored Mother" to the juvenility of "Dear Mamma," and consistently portrayed himself as helpless without Mary's guidance. "I am Distressed, I know not what to do, I want Counsel & Direction," he told her.[10] His quarters were dirty and scantily furnished; the jailer chivied him from morning till night and harassed his visitors, driving his wife and child away when they attempted to bring him a few creature comforts. He praised Mary's answers to these plaints for their "very affectionate & Instructive & comforting" properties and their "tender & Melting Language"; yet affection and tenderness were not all that he sought from her.[11]

In his wretchedness, Billy seemed to look back on the days when he had enjoyed a degree of local prestige as the son of a prominent man and to seek from Mary the authoritative direction that he had received (and sometimes resented) from his father. In December 1790, when certain well-qualified friends advised him to petition for an act of insolvency, he would not take the first step without her approval. He submitted a draft for correction according to the dictates of her "better judgement," assuring her that "it is the first wish of my Broken Heart to obey you my Dear & Hond. Madam & act in conformity to your inclination as near as I can."[12] Not until she approved would he dispatch the petition, which the legislature then granted, though not without requiring a partial payment of his debts that he could make only by borrowing from Jose.

All of Mary's children displayed the same disposition as Billy to regard her as the source of a moral authority whose power derived not solely from her piety but also from her ability to translate piety into action. She had shown that ability in overcoming the despondency and fear she felt when she suffered a succession of bereavements. She had shown it when she allowed faith and hope to lead her beyond the safe confines of a known and mastered solitude to confront the risks of second marriage. She was to show it in her second widowhood as well, and never more plainly than when she refused to despair of giving her younger sons an education equal to that which the other males of the family had received. All the men that Mary had loved had attended college; with the exception of her father, all had attended Yale. She associated the qualities that she had admired in them and taken to herself, particularly those of discipline and probity, with their learning, and she was determined to pass that inheritance on to Sellek and Benjamin.

The price of a Yale education in the 1790s seems minuscule to us. Tuition and lodging cost less than eight pounds a year, board from six to seven shillings a week. The basic expense of keeping two boys there for four years thus amounted to roughly one hundred fifty pounds. Mary's accounts, however, show that in fact she spent almost twice as much. The difference is ascribable to the various extras she had to supply, such as spending money, certain mandatory items of clothing beyond the scope of home manufacture (for instance, velvet breeches for formal occasions), and special charges levied to cover the expense of matriculation and graduation ceremonies. Furthermore, the money represented only one side of the cost to Mary of sending Sellek and Benjamin away. The loss of their labor, added to the sale of her one field hand and the death or migration of all but one of her brothers-in-law, made her even less able to support her household on the produce of the farm than she had been during Silliman's captivity. Her account book suggests that she turned her female servants into a cottage industry for the manufacture of textiles and exchanged their surplus production, together with wood cut from the home lot and the use of her team of oxen, for the manual labor she could not afford to hire. When Esther's death in December 1794 and Peter's decrepitude, ending in his death in 1796, reduced her ability to offer even these exchanges, she had to make do with the occasional help of either Jose and Billy or visiting grandchildren; neither substituted for the daily assistance of two strong sons.

Mary did not entirely lack assets in the struggle to support herself and educate the boys. She had inherited her father's properties in Farmington and Stonington, as well as a life interest in a third of the Noyes and Silliman lands. Upon her marriage to Silliman, both the Fish and Noyes properties had come under his power of disposal subject to her consent. He had left the Noyes lands intact; the Fish properties he had sold and applied the money to investments from which Mary still derived income. Yet all her monetary resources yielded no more than fifty to sixty pounds a year, a sum insufficient to cover her day-to-day expenses, let alone the bills from Yale. Meanwhile there were obstacles to capitalizing on her interest in the Noyes lands.

As a general rule, dower lands not occupied by the family would be leased during the widow's lifetime, passing to the male heirs at her death. Because the widow was responsible for wastage on such lands, leasing entailed a risk. Sale would bring in cash without that risk, but sale required the consent of the male heir. Where there was more than one male heir, it often required the prior division among them of the widow's dower right. Even then she was entitled to receive no more of the proceeds than the annual interest on the principal sum. Though the children could buy out her life interest, when the assets were jointly owned it might be difficult to reach agreement on terms. Silliman had never used the Noyes property to provide for his own children, and Mary would not do so. That was properly a burden to be borne by his estate. But John and James contributed indirectly to the support of their half-brothers by doing all they could to ease their mother's circumstances. The division of her Noyes dower lands had made them, together with Jose, equal proprietors in two parcels which they sold for buyer's notes. Payment fell due upon Mary's death, but in the meantime she would receive the interest. Jose also sold lands in which, while his brothers had no rights, his mother possessed a life interest. He seems to have bought her out, though not for cash but for services rendered in helping to settle his stepfather's estate. Billy certainly pursued that course, purchasing Mary's dower right in a house that Silliman had left him with a waiver of payment for services he had performed.

These transactions took too much time to be of any assistance in resolving the immediate problem of educating Sellek and Benjamin. For that, Mary still had to depend upon their father's estate, which placed her in a quandary. If she postponed their entrance into Yale until the estate were settled, the boys would lose time and the benefit of the preparation they had already received. On the other hand, if she took money from the Silliman estate before its solvency had been established she might forfeit her bond for its proper administration. In the end, Mary decided that the object in view was worth a risk. In taking that risk, she displayed a capacity for bold action that contrasted strongly with the nervous indecision of her former widowhood. She arranged with the college to finance the boys' education by deferring the principal payments until the year 1795. By then, she expected to know whether or not the Silliman estate would cover the expense. If not, one recourse remained: to use her personal income in "hiring" (borrowing) money with which to repay the college. Thanks to her willingness thus to place herself in jeopardy, in 1792, Sellek and Benjamin, aged thirteen and fourteen, entered Yale College as candidates for the bachelor's degree.

Among the reasons for Mary's determination to give her

younger sons the same opportunity that their elder brothers had received was her desire to preserve the principle of
equity. Upon that principle, to a large extent, would depend
the family harmony that she held, literally, sacred. She was
unpleasantly surprised, therefore, when a dispute arose that
threatened to disrupt that harmony, and arose, after all her
care to prevent such feelings in the Silliman boys, over an
inequality between the Noyes brothers. John and James
had long kept silent concerning the division eight years
before of their father's estate, in which they had obtained
only a quarter share each while Jose took one-half. In early
1793 they were reminded of it when the division of Mary's
dower lands took place with Jose again receiving a double
portion, and one of them wrote to Sellek and Benjamin
making a rare critical reference to Jose's unbending atti-
tude. During a general family visit to the boys at Yale that
summer, Jose chanced to pick the letter up and read it. A
"disagreeable scene" ensued, followed by an angry parting.

Back in his peaceful household at Wallingford, James
experienced remorse. The affair "continues to lie with
weight upon my mind," he admitted to John. He still
believed that Jose had wronged them both, but feared that
they stood to lose something more valuable than property
if they kept up a quarrel with a brother. "God forbid that
I should bear hatred against him," he wrote, "or be indis-
posed to do him a kindness when it is in my power. . . .
Tho you and I inherit comparatively a pittance of our
Hond. Father's estate, yet the smiles of providence have
hitherto attended us, & I trust will continue to do so, if
we are found faithful in the service of our great Lord &
Master." He concluded with an eloquent appeal for John
to join him in proffering the olive branch. "Thus far in life
we have lived like brothers, sharing in each other's joys &
sorrows," he wrote. "Soaring above the spirit of avarice,
let us show to our Brother that our happiness arises more
from the testimony of a good conscience than from the
possession of those things which perish in the using."[13]

Mary, at Norfield when this letter arrived there, copied

and transmitted it to Jose together with a letter of her own. She wrote:

> Not to tell a dear child of things a Parent sees that wants correcting, for fear of hurting his feelings, is a false tenderness. . . . I am determined for the future if I see my Children, any of them, doing wrong or in danger, not to spare, as their present peace as well as eternal is concerned. When the harmony of a family is broken we should search for the cause: for it is our Savrs. Legacy, My pece I give unto you—and so far as we don't study what belongs to that peace, so far we do wrong: and in a measure despise that unspeakable gift—This I know you would not do for the world did you see.

Not for the first time she asked him, "Did you do right to take a double portion. . . . You were all children of one father equally beloved by both your parents and why should one have more than the other?" Though the civil law allowed it, God's law required that we do unto others as we would have them do unto us. "These were my thoughts & such my words to you about the time of distribution," she reminded him. "But you was fixed having the law on your side; not equity." His brothers, she knew, had at first reacted against his decision with disappointment and resentment, but had since transcended these unworthy feelings. "And I believe," she wrote, "they have ever treated you as tho you had shared equally." The letter that he had recently seen did not detract from their forbearance because it had never been intended for his eyes.

Mary had also kept silent for the sake of peace, but the time had come when she felt that silence no longer served that purpose. She wrote:

> Now my dear Son I suppose you see how this matter has wore. You have been industrious & oeconomized I know: but how straiten'd have you been at times—Sold one piece of land after another & obliged to live on it & could not pay your debts which are now heavy on

you. And it appears to me that your estate is moulder-
ing away & that by & by you'll run thro' all.—Search
& see why it is so. Is there not a cause.—And now my
dear son lay the matter before God, beg direction, ask
him to open your eyes to see everything that belongs to
your peace. . . . If you have done wrong in taking a
double portion, resign & make over now, and God will
bless you in your going out & coming in, in your basket
& in your store.[14]

Mary seemed also to suggest that Jose was shielding himself from the recognition of his decline by concentrating
instead upon the apparent promise of his public career. In
May 1792 he had succeeded to his deceased stepfather's
position as justice of the peace, and he was receiving rapid
promotion in the militia, soon to culminate in his designation as major of the 4th regiment. Yet his advance had
not proceeded without opposition, and Mary hinted that
the reason might lie with the known dishevelment of his
private affairs. Remove the cause of that, and more than
his finances would be restored. "Then shall you support
the dignity of the important offices you sustain," she told
him, "and you be more & more furnished to do good to
your fellowmen & to conduct in all points so as that your
enemies shall be ashamed having no evil thing to say of
you."
   For Mary, so direct a statement of disapproval constituted a departure from her usual mode of conduct toward
her sons. The strength she had acquired in maturity was
always tempered by the gentleness and humility she had
learned in girlhood from parents who, like herself, taught
by example as well as by precept. Mr. Fish had thought the
text "Fathers, provoke not your children to anger, lest they
be discouraged" (Colossians 3.21) one that all parents should
keep in mind, and Mary seems to have done so. She wielded
authority with a light hand, and her command of respectful attention from grown sons undoubtedly derived much
of its forcefulness, paradoxically, from her ability to rec-

ognize and observe a time to refrain from speaking. In her letter to Jose, the statement that "for the future" she will speak more promptly indicates a feeling that on this occasion she had held her tongue longer than she should. Goaded to speak at last, she had spoken powerfully: too powerfully, perhaps, for the good of the wavering man who received her words. Conscious that his younger brothers, despite the modesty of their ambitions, had so far achieved a greater worldly success than himself, he did not need to be reminded that they had also excelled him in spiritual terms. And the suggestion that financial reparation was an essential step on the road to return would have discouraged him profoundly, for all the evidence suggests that he had already sunk so deeply into debt as to lack the means to repay his brothers even had he felt the inclination.

After Mary's letter to Jose, the subject of the half share disappears from the correspondence. So sudden and complete a silence cries out for explanation, and one which suggests itself is that Jose replied confessing his inability to restore the disputed extra portion; that Mary passed his letter on to John and James by way of extenuation; that upon her recommendation all members of the family agreed to expunge the episode as far as possible from memory; and that, as a necessary preliminary to this effort, they allowed it to fade even from mention. This would explain the absence of any answer from Jose in Mary's papers. It is not likely that he ignored so powerful an appeal from his mother, or that it failed to touch him. It is very likely, on the other hand, that if Mary found Jose honestly unable to respond as she had hoped, she would redirect her energies to making peace.

III

THAT summer, perhaps eager to reinstate himself as a respected member of the family, Jose performed an important service for Mary. On the advice of the commissioners appointed by the probate court she reopened the question of her husband's debt to the government, and Jose undertook to act on her behalf.

Mary had chosen her moment well. Since the federal government had assumed responsibility for much of the state's war debt, Connecticut's finances had improved considerably. The new state comptroller, under less pressure to be rigorous, credited Silliman's account with almost one thousand pounds more than his predecessor had allowed. Since in the meantime Silliman had accounted for some of the money he had received during the war, the debt was thus reduced to less than four hundred pounds. Soon afterward Mary retired it with a cache of state securities that she had recently uncovered in the house, for, in Benjamin's caustic words, it seemed "entirely right to pay the ungrateful state in its own money."[15] So ended a bad business that had broken the health and darkened the last days of a faithful servant of the Republic.

In the same year another weight of anxiety was lifted from Mary's shoulders when the arbitrators in the dispute over Ebenezer Silliman's estate reached a decision favorable to her. She had won two significant victories, but she had not won the war. The estate was still mired in litigation, and apparently as far from settlement as ever, when in 1795 she faced the necessity of increasing the payments on the debt she owed to Yale. Though she had reason to feel more assured than before of the estate's ultimate solvency, most of the income from it still had to be reserved for legal costs. She did divert forty-one pounds toward the college bills, knowing that even if the worst happened, and the estate were forced into bankruptcy, she would nevertheless receive a third of what remained and so be able to repay what she had borrowed. She dared not abstract more, however, and though John made her an interest-free, unlimited loan toward the boys' educational costs, she was obliged to pledge her own small income as surety in borrowing the rest.

In the short term, this meant even more stringent economy at home. In the long term, should the residue of the Silliman estate prove insufficient to redeem her personal debts, it could have meant her imprisonment. Many a father faced with these alternatives would have withdrawn his sons from Yale. Few would have felt it necessary, given the circumstances, to send more than one of the children there in the first place. Mary accepted both the hardships and the risks of continuing on the course that she had set herself without complaint, compromise, or self-pity. The only portrait of her that exists, commissioned by Jose during this period, shows a woman of formidable strength and determination, but also a woman able to greet the world with a delicate, playful smile. Benjamin wrote of the likeness, a copy of which he owned in later years, "it is herself."[16]

The boys themselves found it harder to make the sacrifices that their continuing education, under the circumstances, required of them. The letters that Sellek and Benjamin wrote home show that, as students, they led far different lives from their brothers before them, paring all expenses to the bone and living in cheap lodgings at some distance from the classrooms. Benjamin made the best of things, assuring Mary that their long walk to and from classes provided the exercise necessary to offset long hours of study; but a wry reference to commons (the college dining hall) as a place "where we must all do pennance, without distinction" betrayed his awareness that a distinction did exist between the Silliman boys and their fellow students.[17] Knowing how their mother also stinted herself, they were sometimes tempted to abandon the whole enterprise and find some way to make a better living for themselves and for her. The wisdom of completing their education prevailed, however, and in 1796, aged sixteen and seventeen, both boys were graduated from Yale.

Together "from the cradle to manhood," as Benjamin put it, they now experienced their first separation. Sellek accepted a tutorship that would take him to South Caro-

lina; a deep cut Benjamin had sustained on one foot that
became infected forced him to spend the next few months
at home. Finding himself for the first time in four years at
close quarters with the difficulties that Mary had faced
continuously since his father's death, Benjamin missed the
outlet of conversation with Sellek, whose sanguine disposition balanced his own tendency to melancholia. "O my
brother, I wish I could at once lay open my heart to you,
without the trouble of writing," he lamented. "My mind
is racked & torn by a thousand anxious cares, half of them
perhaps imaginary, but real or imaginary, they have the
effect of sinking my spirits." One cause of his discomfort,
not imaginary, was "the embarrassed situation of our
affairs."[18] He had exerted himself to improve the situation
and predicted that as a result "the productions of the farm
will, this year at least, support the family, which you know
was far from being the case last year."[19]

Physical work improved Benjamin's health as well, and
within a few months he was able to accept a teaching post
at a small private school for girls in Wethersfield. Now it
was Mary's turn to sigh for a sympathetic ear. Though she
knew that both her younger sons had long borne a heavier
weight of care than belonged to their time of life, she had
slipped into the habit of confiding her problems and anxieties to Benjamin while he was at home, and she found it
hard to break. "I want to be continuelly conversing with
you, and as I have so long leaned on you, when you was
with me, I am apt to reach out to you even where you now
are," she confessed. "But my dear son let not any thing
that I have communicated, or shall communicate trouble
you. . . . I trust that by and by we shall owe no man anything but love."[20]

IV

IN 1798, after eight years of often cruel struggle, Mary's
affairs at last took a turn for the better. Her personal

finances remained precarious, and one day that spring she broke off a letter to Benjamin with the words, "this moment comes in Capt. Wakeman, and says his sone wants the moneys we borrowed of him. And now which way shall I turn?"[21] By then, the struggle against insolvency had become so much a way of life for Mary that, when a session passed without a suit against her, she not only found it worthy of remark but considered that only "pure lenity, in the creditors" could account for it.[22] In fact, the worst was over. The pressure exerted through the courts had begun to relent. The danger that Silliman's estate would prove insolvent had passed. This left Mary free to sell off her share of it in order to reduce her debts.

Mary's domestic circumstances had also changed. In 1798 Sellek returned from South Carolina, and that autumn he and Benjamin decided to make their father's profession their own. Together they entered upon the study of law with an attorney at New Haven, and Benjamin obtained a tutorship at Yale College as a source of extra income. They would remain dependent on Mary for some of their living expenses until they gained admission to the bar, but she need no longer feel obliged to provide a home for them. If they should need shelter, a brother's door would be open. John and James therefore urged Mary to consider that the time had come to "break up house keeping" and henceforth divide her time between the households of her married children.[23]

Since the "little boys" had gone away, the Fairfield grandchildren had surged in to fill their place. The children of John and James came to stay as often as their parents would send them, but the children of Jose and Billy ran in and out all through the year. By 1798, they numbered seven. Amelia had given birth in 1791 to a fourth child, Samuel, and in 1794 to a fifth, Rebecca, and the Sillimans had a second daughter, Mary Ann, born in 1797. If Mary gave up Holland Hill she would see these children only on periodic visits. She would also lose the ability to gather all her children and grandchildren together under one roof, as she had done (except for two occasions during Sellek's absence) on every Thanksgiving Day since her husband's death. These were the reasons for staying. In the end, the reasons for selling outweighed them.

At sixty-two, though strong and active, Mary could no longer manage Holland Hill. She admitted that "things are going to rack about the house and farm . . . and by [next] spring, it will be worth less than it is now."[24] To sell while she could obtain a decent price would at one stroke bring in sufficient money to clear most of her debts and set her at liberty to reduce her future living expenses by merging with her children's households. It would also relieve her loneliness, which persisted in spite of the frequent presence of one grandchild or another. Long after they had retired to bed Mary would sit reading and writing, the silence and solitude around her accentuated by the sounds she recorded of "the wind and our old faithfull clock, that by every vibration tells me my minits are flying, and that I ought to be in constant readyness to obey the summons when called."[25] Soberly, but not sadly, Mary came to the conclusion that her small means and her advancing age both urged that she surrender the independence which, though it had come to her later than to most, she had learned to use and value rightly.

Though Mary began to sell off personal property in the spring of 1798, she did not immediately succeed in selling the house and land. More than one prospective buyer withdrew on the very verge of closing. It is on record that one such withdrawal occurred because the interested party had received private information from a friend at Fairfield that had prejudiced the sale, and a clue to the nature of that information may be found in the comments of a grandson of Silliman's who visited the homes of his grandfather, and of his great-grandfather, Judge Ebenezer Silliman, some ninety years later. They were "neither of them calculated to wed their occupants to this life," he wrote. It is true that the nineteenth-century taste for comfort and ornamentation which probably informed this judgment did not apply in the 1790s. But his observation that the cellar of Silliman's house lay under a foot of water, with stepping stones attesting to the permanence of its presence there, would explain Mary's difficulty in selling the house, while his remembrance that his own father had described the farmland as soggy and "sour" might account for both the reluctance of buyers and the difficulty of running a profitable farm there even during Silliman's lifetime.[26]

It appeared that Holland Hill had more potential as the residence of a professional man than as a farm. In October 1798 Jose offered to purchase it for the appraised value of seven hundred pounds (about twenty-three hundred dollars) provided he could sell his other house. Though his debts had mounted steadily, he still saw himself as up and coming, and the legislature continued each year to extend his commissions as justice of the peace and major in the militia. A month later he renewed his offer, and, no other purchaser having appeared, the Silliman brothers, who held the residual interest, consented to its acceptance. On January 21, 1799, they conveyed the home lot to Jose for £704.0.0, less than half of which he paid in cash. Ownership reverted to the seller if Jose failed to pay the remainder within two years, but he did not fail, and Mary's share of the transaction (which apparently included a generous purchase of her life interest by Sellek and Benjamin), together with the sale of household goods and other sources of income, enabled her to repay most of the loans she had taken out in order to put the boys through college. The end of the century found her living within her means for the first time in years, and by the middle of 1800 she had consolidated her interests into seventeen hundred dollars' worth of U.S. stock, two-thirds of it yielding a 6 percent return.

V

IN February 1799 Jose moved his family to Holland Hill, and Mary departed for the first of her sojourns in a child's house, that of James at Wallingford.

Mary regarded this season of her time on earth not as a harbinger of decline and loss, but as an opportunity. In Benjamin's words, she seemed "to be travailing *up* instead of *down* the hill of life."[27] Her letters and journal entries show that she possessed a confident opinion of herself as a valuable contributor to a household rather than a burden. In deciding when and for how long to reside with each child she gave the preference always to the house of sickness, or the house where a new baby would add to the duties that she expected and desired to assume. "I would not wish to be a drone to suck the honey that my busy bees make," she wrote. By the end of the year 1800, the marriages of her three Noyes children had borne fruit in the birth of twenty grandchildren, nineteen of them living. Only James had lost a child, a two-year-old son who bore his name, in 1794. In addition to these offspring of her blood, there were two more grandchildren in Billy's family, and a third on the way. For the period, this represented a high rate of survival.

In her travels from household to household Mary shaped a unique role for herself, a role she had rehearsed during the childhood of Sellek and Benjamin. She took the practical work of child care as far as possible into her hands, just as her mother had done during her years as resident grandparent; but Mary also assumed the educational tasks more often performed by a father, including the teaching of the scriptures. At the same time, having shed her responsibilities as head of a household, she found herself with "more leisure than ever I have had since I was a young girl at my father's home," leisure that she employed in reading, writing, and meditation.[28] Thus, she made of her new situation a heightened opportunity to serve God in both the active and the contemplative life.

The hours that Mary gave to writing were still the night hours when the day's work was done and the rest of the family asleep. "Among other mercys that I have to be thankful for," she observed, "is that I need but little sleep compared to what man[y] do. And I wish not to sleep a moment more of the time away than is needful."[29] She continued to keep her journal, while increasing the volume and scope of her correspondence. In a season when scattered places of residence and the demands of different occupations and circumstances tended to drive the boys apart, she drew them together by relaying the news and circulating the letters of each one to all the rest. In her own letters, she did not confine herself to the details of daily life, but also engaged her correspondents in a continuous spiritual conversation. In her journal, too, although she did set down events, she gave more time and space to the record of her meditations, tending in the movement of her mind to turn outward to God and eternity rather than inward upon the private and particular. Some of these meditations she copied for dissemination among her children in the hope of influencing them to give their lives the same grand ultimate direction.

In form and content, Mary's religious discourse with her sons bears comparison to that of her father's correspondence with herself, her sister, and Gold Selleck Silliman during his wartime absence from home. Yet there was considerably more of it, particularly in her letters to Sellek and Benjamin. Mr. Fish, notwithstanding occasional diatribes on the vices of the age, had been able to assume that society in general would reinforce his beliefs; Mary could no longer do so.

John and James gave her little reason for concern despite the times. It was not just that they had chosen the church as their profession: they also practiced its teaching. For example, they had turned the other cheek to Jose to the full extent required in the command that "if any man will . . . take away thy coat, let him have thy cloak also." In recent years, though their growing families made increasing demands upon their resources, both of them had lent money to the brother whose grasp of the greater share had cut down their own. As for Jose himself, he appeared sincere enough in his profession of Christianity to give Mary hope that, if he could not make pecuniary restitution to his brothers, he would in time restore his soul. All three of the Noyes children had formed their characters in a period little changed since Mary's youth and even that of her parents. Sellek and Benjamin had not had that advantage. She saw them, "just coming on the stage in this age of infidelity and irreligion," as less firmly anchored in the past than their brothers, and correspondingly less secure with respect to the most vital aspect of their futures, "the infinite importance of our precious souls!"[30]

In worldly terms, both boys appeared likely to do well. The youthful age at which they had surrendered all illusions of a future laid out before them and guaranteed by their father's position in society had left them better prepared than their brothers to meet the challenge of post-revolutionary social change. But in Mary's eyes their chosen field of law, though she had known at least one good man to follow it, had the potential to seduce those not yet confirmed in their faith into expediency, inattention to religious duty, and possibly unbelief. "I hope the early instruction you have had," she wrote, "and your own acquirements in knowledge and the divine spirit's aid have caused you to stand the test of all the ridicule that has been levell'd at our excellent religious system." To keep them strong in faith she recommended regular spiritual exercise in the form of devotional reading and prayer, and strict observance of the Sabbath as a day given wholly to God no matter how strongly ambition tempted them to work. Only thus would they obtain "an inheritance that no-one can deprive you of, and without [which] you would be poor had you millions at your command."[31]

No stronger proof of Mary's priorities could be desired than her response when Sellek had the good fortune to obtain a post as attorney in the wealthy community of

Newport. Sellek had found his future wife in the person of a young woman named Hepsa Ely, daughter of the Reverend David Ely at Huntington, Connecticut, and his eagerness to marry her had accelerated his pursuit of advancement. At Newport he plunged into work, and into the building of a social reputation to enhance his professional opportunities, with a zeal that produced almost immediate results. Mary wholeheartedly approved his choice of bride and rejoiced in his progress toward the prosperity that would make their marriage possible. Nevertheless, she saw danger in the means he must employ to gain that end. "While on the one hand I have reason to be thankfull that he is treated with so much politeness by so many persons of respectability," she confided to Benjamin, "yet I fear that his desire of popularity so essential to his future emolument, will lead him into snares that will be injurious to his better part." She recounted the story of a man, now an eminent clergyman but originally trained for the law, who had turned his back on that profession when ordered to draft an instrument on the Sabbath "as he could not do violence to his conscience." And she reiterated the gospel question, "what shall it profit a man, if he shall gain the whole world and lose his own soul?"[32]

These were not abstract exhortations. Mary was responding directly to her perception that the secular impulses released by the American Revolution had led the new generation to change the main focus of their outlook on life from a hopeful gaze toward eternity to a sharp eye for worldly gain. The young often questioned the necessity for strict adherence to the precepts that Mary had called on her sons to observe. Sellek and Benjamin, as it happened, thought their mother's views well worthy of consideration. As her father's constancy in a time of upheaval had impressed itself upon Mary's character, so her ability to strive and sacrifice for principle compelled the admiration of the young Sillimans. Of her early struggles they knew only what they had heard from older family members, such as their grandmother Fish during her last years

with them. It was Mary's bravery in recent times that had
formed their image of her. Benjamin, when he began to
write his own reminiscences, reproduced that image clearly:

> She was a heroic woman and encountered with firmness
> the trials and terrors of the American Revolution in
> which my father was largely concerned. . . . In her wid-
> owhood, after my father's death in 1790, she struggled
> on in embarrassed circumstances & gave my brother &
> myself a public education, forming our minds at home
> to purity & piety. Whatever I have of good in me I owe
> under God mainly to her.[33]

On the eve of his coming of age, Benjamin addressed a
paean of praise to Mary for "that kind parental wing which
for 21 years has been constantly extended for my protection."[34] Sellek, too, in an echo of her own words years
before, saluted her as "the best of parents," and assured
her that, though he had sometimes departed from her
teachings, he had always come in time to reconsider.[35] Yet,
of the two brothers, it was Benjamin whose life showed
the strongest marks of Mary's influence.

In 1801 Benjamin received a proposal that he take charge
of an "important and flourishing academy . . . not far from
Savannah [Georgia]." The position paid well, and within
a few years he might gather enough capital to set himself
up in the practice of law there, "where the profession commanded more ample rewards than at the North."[36] The
offer tempted him all the more because his lack of means
had long forced him to suppress a strong romantic urge
toward marriage. As boys, both Benjamin and Sellek had
spent many an evening listening while their mother read
aloud their father's eloquent love letters; as a young man,
Benjamin had often confided in Mary his longing to find a
woman for whom he could care so deeply. "What I ardently
wish for you both is that your hearts may mingle with
generous souls like your own," she had returned, but with
a reminder that they must first "lay a foundation for a sub-

sistence."[37] Sellek had made that beginning; Benjamin had not. In a letter to his mother on June 14, 1801, he wrote:

> I am happy to hear you my dear mother, bear such honourable testimony to 'the sweet domestick enjoyments' of wedlock.—I have always eyed them with a fondness perhaps too great—since I have no rational prospect of enjoying them these many years—business must precede matrimony, for I have no idea that this corporeal tabernacle, will so far condescend to the more refined character of its celestial inhabitant, as to dispense with its *bill* of *fare* & take up with such light & pungent food as *refined ideas & exquisite feelings.*[38]

The post in Georgia, though it would mean going far from home, appealed to him very much because it might reduce "these many years" to one or two.

In July, however, a chance meeting under the elms at Yale with its president, Timothy Dwight, an old friend of both his parents, presented Benjamin with an alternative. When he told Dwight of the opening at Savannah and his inclination to accept it, Dwight countered with the astonishing proposal that instead he apply for the newly instituted professorship of chemistry at Yale. To the reasonable objection that the candidate would lack all but a slight acquaintance with the subject, Dwight replied in words that Benjamin summarized thus:

> Time will be allowed to make every necessary preparation; and when you enter upon your duties, you will speak to those to whom the subject will be new;—you will advance in the knowledge of your profession more rapidly than your pupils can follow you, and will be always ahead of your audience.

Benjamin, both elated and alarmed by Dwight's confidence in his abilities, asked for time in which to consult certain trusted advisers before he answered. As one might expect, "pre-eminent among them was a wise and good mother"[39] whose voice is clearly audible in his later account of the reasoning that led him to his choice.

Benjamin had for some time shared Mary's reservations about the profession of law. With a bow to his father and his brother, he allowed that "right may sometimes be vindicated against wrong and injured innocence protected" and that "with requisite talent and learning, & the impulses of a generous temperament, a career at the bar might be truly noble."[40] His exposure to the law at work, on the other hand, had convinced him that "the temptation would often be strong—especially when backed by wealth, to contend against justice and by the force of talent and address to make the worse appear the better cause, and to screen the guilty from punishment, the fraudulent from the payment that is justly due."

How did the study of nature compare? Mary had recently written a letter to Benjamin and Sellek in which, though she was not addressing this question, she had nonetheless suggested an answer to it. Nature, she wrote, served God's purpose in that it showed man his own fallen state and need for grace in contrast to the original purity of God's other creatures:

> They answer the end of their creation; and I suppose are the same as when first made, every kind after his kin, and as it is said that God takes pleasure in all his works, so he views them all as the effects of his wisdom and benevolence, and can now as when they were first created pronounce them all very good, and in this view nothing is made in vain, although it may appear [so] to us, as it did to the Poet, when he said, "Full many a flower is born to blush unseen/And waste its sweetness on the desert air."[41]

When Benjamin came to explain his eventual decision to exchange the law for chemistry, he did so in words that echoed hers. "In her [Nature's] works there is no falsehood, although there are mysteries, to unveil which is a very interesting achievement," he declared. "Everything in nature is straitforward and consistent; there are no polluting influences; all the associations with this pursuits are elevated and virtuous and point towards the jnfinite creator."[42] Thus, guided by Mary, he made his approach to a new science along an old-established path.

Proud as she was of the distinguished career that followed, it is doubtful that Mary ever fully understood Benjamin's contribution to the development and popularization of the sciences in America. She had a keener appreciation of another decision he reached a year later, in which she had also played a part. It had long troubled her that neither of the Silliman boys felt able to make the profession of faith that would have admitted them to full membership in the church and allowed them to receive the sacrament. Though she was careful to restrain herself from exerting undue pressure, the smallpox epidemic of 1793 prompted her to a rare exhortation. While they were no longer in danger from that quarter themselves, the mortality she saw all around her reminded Mary that death could take many forms and strike where least expected, and that, as matters now stood, her sons were spiritually unprepared to meet it.

She invited them to suppose that their mother had on her deathbed bid them spend an hour a month in some act of homage to her memory. "Would you not at once promise that you would?" she asked. "And it would be very odd in you to say, I am *afraid,* I *cannot,* I am not worthy." She went on to draw the parallel:

> Now consider God is the father of your spirit, you are fallen creatures by nature. Christ Jesus comes to restore God's lost image on the Soul . . . and he with his dying breath as it were has told us to do this in remembrance of him, and how stupid it is in us to say I cannot do it, I am not worthy . . . he will make you propper subjects for his church here and at that trium-

phant, not for works of righteousness that we have done, but for his own sake who will make us comely by the comeliness he shall put upon us.[43]

Still they hesitated. In 1797 Sellek reopened the subject of his doubts with his brother John, and Mary, who held the authority of her clergyman sons in high respect, had great hopes that John would succeed where she had apparently failed. Again she was disappointed, and in the summer of 1801 she decided to take Sellek's approaching nuptials as the occasion to address another letter to him and his younger brother. She had prefaced her own first marriage with a profession of faith, probably in response to her parents' wish, and she clearly hoped to draw the like response from Sellek. "Superior helps I am very sensible you meet with in the works of eminent divines, with which the present day is replete, stemming the tide of practical atheism, infidelity and vain philosophy," she acknowledged modestly. "Yet perhaps a word from a tender mother may contribute a mite to the all-important purpose of furthering you in the way to eternal life."[44]

Sellek did not pursue the subject, but Benjamin over the next few months conducted an examination of his thoughts and feelings very much in the manner of his grandfather Fish. Sometimes he inadvertently revealed the perils of that course, as in a morbid meditation written on his birthday in which he questioned God's reasons for continuing his worthless existence. To his mother, by contrast, he addressed a simpler, strikingly candid statement of his difficulty in acceding to her request:

> When I read that one of our frigates has fought a severe battle with a ship of superior force, I feel it at once. I trace every circumstance in my mind, and fancy that I hear the roaring cannon, the shouts of victory, and the groans of the dying. But . . . when the awful truths of Christianity are announced from the desk, I do not

always feel the interest which the subject ought to command.[45]

Mary too had passed through a period in which she might have said, as did Benjamin in this same letter, "not that I doubt, but that I do not feel." Time had opened her heart as well as her mind, and perhaps her example did as much as her words to persuade her son that he need not perfect his faith in order to take the sacrament. In September 1802, at Newport for the birth of Hepsa's child, a daughter named Mary Amelia, she received with equal joy the news that Benjamin had made his profession and received his first communion in the Yale chapel. Characteristically, however, she did not use the event to bring any further influence to bear upon Sellek.

VI

THE settlement of the two younger boys left Mary satisfied with the disposition in life of all her children except for Jose. During the spring of 1800, little more than a year after he had taken proud possession of Holland Hill, he greeted Mary on her arrival for a visit with the announcement that he had resolved to leave it.

Jose had heard of great opportunities awaiting men of enterprise and energy in the lands to the west, then known as New Connecticut, now as the Western Reserve of Ohio, and had begun to dream the emigrant's dream of achieving in alien fields the success that eluded him at home. The move that he proposed would place a son, a daughter, and the five children who had been, Mary said, "the most with me of any of my grandchildren, and were all dandled on my knee and caressed in my arms," at a distance from her of more than five hundred miles.[46] In May, when Jose left on a journey of reconnaissance, she cherished a hope that the contrast between the comforts of home and the rigors of the frontier would weaken his resolution. By the time he returned, she knew that necessity, not choice, dictated that he go. During the five months of his absence the family had begun to discover what Jose would not openly admit, that he had sunk into debt almost to the point of insolvency. Once Mary understood the extent of his embarrassments she resigned herself, though painfully, to his emigration.

In March 1801 Jose advertised his house, lands, and possessions. A quick sale followed, at a higher price than the family had thought possible: a good omen for the enterprise. The new owner moved in promptly, but allowed Jose and his family to occupy the parlor while they completed their preparations, and also accommodated Mary when she came to help them. She found Amelia, lately troubled with a persistent cough, "in high spirits about going and the more so as some doctors told her that she would probably recover her health by the journey and the change of climate."[47] Still, the sight of the house in the hands of strangers, however hospitable, and the impending departure of her "dear ones," led Mary to exclaim, "many changes have I seen in this dwelling! a checkered scene indeed! *exquisite delight,* and *poignant anguish* has been experienced here, and I cannot say what yet awaits me."[48]

On June 3, at nine o'clock in the morning, Jose, Amelia, and four of their five children (James having remained behind to study with his uncle at Wallingford) took their leave. Mary afterward described the scene to Benjamin:

> We all sustained the parting pang with as much fortitude as could be expected, and it was almost up to what we had previously resolved, so that by standers gave us much credit for our firmness. I walked with your sister as far as the schoolhouse: she mounted the carage, I took a lonely seat on the schoolhouse, and looked after

them untill the objects by which they past hid them from
my sight, when I commended them to the care of a kind
providence, and returned to the vacant mansion.

There she gathered her few things together, then withdrew to Billy's house, where she would spend the next several weeks.

Mary had gone to Fairfield prepared to encounter a
change in local attitudes toward her and her children. The
period of Silliman family influence, which in happier days
had embraced the Noyes sons too, was ended. Like Billy
at the time of his imprisonment, Jose and Amelia had
experienced such hostility during their last months at Holland Hill that "a lonely cottage in the wilderness is much
to be prefered."[49] Yet his retreat had not ended the attacks
upon him, as Mary soon discovered. Ten days after he left
she informed Benjamin that she was about to "go on the
hill . . . to secure by attachment yr. Brs. sleigh and harness
left there, as we are informed by a friend that Abijah Morehouse threatened to attach it for what he pretends yr.
Brother owed him, which in reallity is nothing at all."[50]

Morehouse had also laid claim to the sword that had
belonged to Silliman, a piece of effrontery that enraged
Benjamin. Never should "a sword which has been drawn
by a brave and good man in more than one battle," he
wrote, "be prostituted to grace the side of some poltroon,
who struts in uniform, on a review day, but has no more
of worth or of the soldier, than his wearing a sword can
convey." Child of a new age, Benjamin had yet enough of
the old school in him to set his back up against an upstart's
attempt to acquire a piece of his family's history. The same
conservatism dictated his politics. He viewed the rise of
the Democratic party with more than repugnance: with a
fear as of the apocalypse. He greeted the election of Jeffer-
son with the comment that "It may be true that the Lord
reigneth, but I think it is also true that the devil has come
down having great wrath." He asked Mary to give his

father's sword to him because "I think it not improbable if this atrocious spirit of Jacobinism continues to spread I may be called upon to use it."[51]

In a subsequent oration given at Hartford to the Connecticut chapter of the Cincinnati,* Benjamin delivered himself of still more violent expressions of opinion, comparing the new politics to a second deluge that raged across the land, and picturing his home state as one of the few remaining sanctuaries raised above its path of destruction. Many of his auditors criticized his intemperance, but more approved. Those who, like Benjamin, were critical of the social and political changes that had accompanied the Revolution, voted to publish the oration. Mary joined in their approbation, for in this as in many respects Benjamin's views mirrored her own. She deplored the postwar rejection of traditional values in the great world and saw the petty spite that Morehouse and others at Fairfield showed toward the remnant of a once-respected family as a local manifestation of the general decline. Except for Billy's family, nothing remained at Fairfield to remind her of the good years there; even her old friends the Eliots had moved away. She relinquished Holland Hill, if not without a sigh, with no backward glance of longing to return.

By the end of July Mary received word that the emigrants had arrived at their destination, a settlement named Warren, thirteen miles to the northwest of Youngstown, "in fine spirits."[52] Jose wrote glowingly of his first impressions, while Amelia, though she said that she would not repeat the journey if they sent a coach and four to fetch her, seemed nonetheless to have grown the stronger for it. But that winter her cough returned, accompanied by a persistent fever. All the signs pointed to consumption, and on May 7, 1802, less than a year after Mary had said farewell to her, she died. Hers was the first grave in the settlement, so that, in Mary's words, she "began to people

---

*A society formed by revolutionary war officers in which membership passed from father to eldest son.

the mansion of the dead in that part of the new world." For twenty-seven years Mary had cherished Amelia as her only daughter, and her grief was great. What then must Jose feel, she asked herself, left "by the beloved wife of his youth in a howling wilderness, with four motherless children, each with aching heart pouring their full souls into his afflicted bosom!"[53]

At first, indeed, the thought of attempting to pioneer without Amelia daunted Jose, and he considered returning home, or at least sending back the two younger children. When he recovered the courage to stay, keep his family together, and again set his hand to the plough, he acknowledged God as the source of his renewal, but in words that gave his mother more alarm than reassurance. God, he declared,

> has graciously given me supernatural Tokens that he has received the Soul of my dear departed Wife to himself . . . [He] has actually (seeing that my circumstances required it) spoken to me by Day, & by night . . . shewed me the path of wisdom . . . & where mine enemies have plotted my destruction he has shown me the secrets of their hearts, so far as it was important for me to know them.

Jose recognized that these assertions "may expose me to the Charge of enthusiasm," and in this, at least, he did not err.[54] Nor was it the first time that he had incurred the charge. An earlier letter in which he told Benjamin that he had dreamed of death impending, either for Hepsa or for the child she carried, had already drawn from Mary a stern injunction against repeating the story to the family at Newport lest it frighten its subject into the disaster allegedly foreseen. To Benjamin she added, with some asperity, that she thought Jose "in danger of being a little inthusiastical with respect to dreams."[55] Since, however, both wisdom and compassion urged that she refrain from direct criticism of a son in circumstances whose pains and temp-

tations she remembered well, she said nothing to Jose but
suffered in silence through these and more descriptions in
his letters of "God's preternatural manifestation of himself."[56]

Certainly she could not quarrel with the cheerfulness and
hopefulness he maintained in the face of misfortune. "Perhaps there is no Country on the American Continent where
the people can live more independent and more easy than
here," he wrote, "the Country will well bear a Panegyrick."
The children were "all happy & contented, not one of them
willing to go back to Connecticut." His farm was thought
to occupy "the pleasantest situation in the Town; it is also
supposed there is no better land on the reserve." The mantle of failure had fallen from his shoulders "& a Gracious
God has filled me with Corrage & perseverance so that
mountains of difficulties have prostrated themselves as Mole
Hills before me." Hearing that Billy Silliman had also begun
to think of emigration, Jose urged that he come to New
Connecticut, where "Two Days Labour in a Week will
afford as good a support as Six in New England." He knew
that his encomiums on the rich soil and lavish crops would
"sound like a great story with you," he wrote, "but if you
will take the trouble to visit us, we can cure your unbelief."[57]

Mary nevertheless retained a certain skepticism. Despite
Jose's paradisial rhapsodies she persisted in referring to
Ohio as "the wilderness," and not without reason. The letters his children sent her suggested that they lived at
present a harder life by far than they had known before.
They had no woman to help, not even eight-year-old Becca,
who had gone to live with a family at Youngstown. There
was no mention of schooling for any of them. John did the
cooking, while the washing and mending were sent out.
All the boys worked in the fields, and Mary noted that the
labor had apparently so stiffened young Joseph's hands as
to produce an alteration in his script. Still, the children had
"not intirely lost their handwriting or their gift of compo-
sition,"[58] and it seemed to bear out Jose's claim of prosper-

ity that by February 1803 he owned a second farm at Burton, about twenty-three miles to the east of present-day Cleveland.

Since this acquisition would add considerably to Jose's work in the coming season, it was with some surprise that in May, without prior notice, Mary received a brief note announcing that he had started out for Connecticut and would look to see her either there or at Newport. A letter he wrote to Benjamin en route provided more detail. He had engaged a housekeeper and enough field laborers "to harvest & do all other necessary work, & so have told the Boys when they feel like work they can work, & when like play they may play." Becca, now back home, was "as happy as one of the Royal Princesses at St. James." He himself was traveling in style, "mounted on an elegant horse which I bought from a Gentleman from Baltimore, where the horse was bred," while at night he stayed in the best accommodations to be had. "I have got to be so much a Citizen of the World," he wrote, "I seem to be at home wherever I go." As he retraced his path, his reflections gave him only satisfaction:

> How changing the Scenes of Life, of pleasure & of pain. This Month 2 years I was passing thro this place with my family, going I hardly knew whither, only I knew I had to encounter the hardships of the wilderness. . . . Tho Providence has bereaved me of my beloved Wife, yet by his Blessing I have obtained a noble Inheritance for my Children which with their Industry will make them forever independent. Am now in easy circumstances, with good prospects before me.[59]

Yet still he gave no reason for his sudden decision to return.

Mary, impatient to see him, began to wonder at the time that he was taking. On June 13 Benjamin informed her that Billy had just received and forwarded to him a most unexpected letter, sent from Philadelphia, not by Jose, but by his eldest son, who wrote that he too was on his way to

Connecticut, yet made no reference to his father's journey.
Within the next day or two another letter came, this time
from Jose, excusing his own delay but giving no notice of
his son's impending arrival. Puzzled and uneasy, the family
,could find out nothing and heard nothing more for over a
week. On the morning of June 20 Benjamin returned from
the college to his rooms to find his nephew waiting for
him, a handsome, tall, and upright youth, though poorly
dressed and bearing marks of recent suffering. When he
had eaten and drunk, he unfolded a story that struck his
uncle, unprepared by any previous communication to hear
it, quite dumb with astonishment.

Two years of unremitting toil and hardship had left Jose
poorer than ever, and since Amelia's death the family's living conditions had deteriorated more. All the children were
miserable, but young Joseph had reached the breaking point
when he suffered a disappointment in love. Benjamin
recorded what had followed:

On the 19th May, without taking leave of his father or
brothers, and without their knowledge, *wholly destitute
of money,* clad in a short jacket & pantaloons & moca-
sons, with one change of linen, 3 cravats, a pair of leather
pantaloons, a great coat and a few biscuits in his pock-
ets, he left his paternal Mansion at 8.0c a.m., fondly
hoping that he should find the world as generous as his
own breast. Now, view a youth of eighteen accomplish-
ing in 18 days a progress on foot of 420 miles without
money, without friends, often for a whole day without
food, once lodging in the woods on the ground, obliged
to sell every article of cloathing except what he wore,
often ridiculed & abused, suspected of entertaining a
design on his own life, taken up and carried before a
magistrate and about to be committed to prison as a
suspected character, often worn down with fatigue &
hunger, with blistered feet and ready to sink under
such accumulated suffering, but at last arriving in
Phila[delphia], where indeed from the usual indiffer-

ence of great cities to the miseries of mankind he had
even less to expect than in the country.

He had gone there looking for friends of the family in
Connecticut, now living in that city, but had inquired for
them in vain. He then tried to obtain a working passage
to New York. Having failed in that, "he sat down on the
dock, famished, brokenhearted, and in despair."[60] There a
certain samaritan had noticed him, questioned him, fed
him, and delivered him into the hands of the family's
friends, who provided him with funds to continue his
journey to Connecticut. Not until Benjamin told him had
he known of his father's departure from home, the reason
for which was now clear.

When the boy had rested, Benjamin thought it best to
put him on a stage for Wallingford, where he might join
his brother in the house of his Uncle James. No more was
heard of Jose until the beginning of July, when, to Mary's
inexpressible relief, he appeared in Newport. His inquiries
after Joseph had led him on a long and tortuous journey;
weary and disheartened, he had come to seek his mother's
help, and from her, apparently, had learned for the first
time of his son's whereabouts. Mary did not describe the
reunion between herself and Jose, nor did she remark on
the difference between his colorful dispatches and the dismal truth except for a quiet comment in a subsequent letter
that "his pecuniary resources at present are small . . . altho
[he] has made the best of it and better perhaps than he
ought to have done."[61] As quickly as possible she prepared
to accompany him to Wallingford, but they arrived there
to find that Joseph, apprised of their intention, had fled to
his Uncle John in Norfield. Not until August did the
unhappy young man return to Wallingford to face his
father. Then, when Mary set eyes on him for the first time
in more than two years, she realized what no one else had
openly admitted: that her beloved grandson, though
handsome as described, was also mad.

The discovery shocked and grieved her more than the

discovery of the truth about Jose's circumstances. She immediately instituted the application of cold shower baths, engineered by having young Joseph stand half-naked outside the house while his Uncle James poured buckets of icy water on him from the garret window. This treatment she had learned about from Benjamin, who had submitted himself to a similar regimen during a time of severe depression, probably the period of his first year at Yale when he had described himself in letters to Mary as given to hypochondria and to fits of brooding on imaginary evils. Benjamin had certainly recovered, but Mary was forced to admit that Joseph made slow progress if any.

One evening a few weeks later Jose returned from an outing in a state of extreme agitation. He had received warning that he was about to be arrested for the debts of William Burr, a brother of Amelia's who had been raised apart from her. If he were, his farms in Ohio would be left with only his younger sons in charge. That night he fled on horseback, not stopping for anything, not even to call at John's house though he passed directly by it, until he crossed over the boundary line into New York State. His hasty departure had prevented him from repaying certain newly contracted debts, which forced him once again to ask his brothers for help while he hid out at a public house in New Rochelle. Once again his brothers, this time including Benjamin, opened their purses.

Toward the end of September he ventured back, though he paused no longer than necessary to gather his things for the return to Ohio. With him went not only Joseph but also a deeply reluctant James. Benjamin, who saw the three at New Haven, observed that James was close to tears, while Joseph, by contrast, "said he never felt so happy in all his life, and indeed he kept laughing all the time."[62] It was not an encouraging picture, and to make matters worse Mary knew that from now on it would be hard to take comfort in any representation of well-being that Jose might make. Apart from the fact that he had for two years gilded the facts with a lavish hand, the absence of himself and his eldest son, the only two grown men, throughout one entire growing and harvest season was bound to set him back still more. "It was indeed hard parting with them under existing circumstances," Mary wrote, "but providence called them and I must submit."

Besides her regret that they must return to a life which promised so little happiness, the thought that death might step between them and herself, to make the parting final in this world, came to Mary inevitably at this period of her life. The contemplation of death, though she had practiced it from youth, had occupied her meditations and her pen more and more since she had given up her house, as if the one act of divestiture symbolized for her the last and most solemn, the soul's departure from the house that had sheltered it since birth. It was true that she remained, at sixty-seven years of age, remarkably robust. That Thanksgiving she wrote of herself that "I enjoy perfect health and possess the vigor of youth."[63] In the context of her generation, however, she had almost reached her allotted span. "I have lived so long," she observed serenely, that "my contemporarys are few I find that are left."[64] Yet she was not quite the last leaf on the tree.

Early in 1804, oblique references appear in the correspondence to some affair too private for open discussion through the mail. On April 10 John wrote that he expected at any moment to hear "a decision of the important matter which has for some time agitated our minds," and we may presume that he did, for eight days later his mother was quietly married at Wallingford, by her son James, to Dr. John Dickinson of Middletown.[65]

Nine

ASCEND AND EXPLORE

WE know very little about the courtship of Mary and John Dickinson. When Benjamin came to collect and annotate his mother's letters and journals he remembered having seen a record of those events written in her hand, but he could not find it among her papers. Dickinson himself seems to have left few traces of his life, and most of what we know about him, as well as all of what we know about his marriage to Mary, was gleaned from her correspondence. A physician by profession and a judge by appointment, John Dickinson was undoubtedly the Dr. Dickinson whose house at Middletown Gold Selleck Silliman had visited during the special session of the general assembly in 1782, and who had subsequently carried a letter to Mary at Fairfield. Certainly the family had some previous acquaintance with the man that Mary married, for Jose responded to the news with a recollection of having spent "an agreeable afternoon with him" at the house of a distant relative in Hartford some years before.[1] But since the name appears nowhere in the family papers between 1782 and 1804, he had probably not become a close friend until recently.

Aged seventy-three in 1804, Dickinson was five years older than Mary. His first wife, Eunice Hall, had died a year before. A daughter of that marriage, Patty Dickinson, lived at home and kept house for him. His three other children had establishments of their own. John D. Dickinson, married and living at Lansingburg near Troy, New York, was a lawyer of some distinction, and would become a congressman. Eunice had married David Robinson of Bennington, Vermont, whose family had important political connections in that state. Abigail had married Elijah Hubbard of Middletown, who belonged to a wealthy mercantile family and who, like Dickinson, held an appointment as a judge.

The best picture that we have of Mary and John Dickinson at home comes from a letter that Benjamin sent his mother, obviously echoing back her own words:

> I need not assure you my dear mother that I find the most lively pleasure in contemplating you as surrounded by so many circumstances calculated to make you happy. The effectual care which Miss Dickinson is so good as to take of the family concerns frees you from no small trouble. . . . I view it also as a very happy circumstance that you are situated so near to such a worthy and cordial family as that of Judge Hubbard . . . [who] will do everything in their power to make Middletown as dear to you as ever New Haven or Fairfield has been. To crown all, I doubt not you are in the hands of a man . . . possessing the feelings of a gentleman and of a Christian, and distinguished by no small superiority of intellect and dignity of mind. . . . You think I shall say "this is honeymoon": let me add a wish that honeymoon may not be eclipsed, nor drop anything from its horn less pleasant than honey, during all its future phases and revolutions.[2]

The marriage quickly fell into the pattern that it would follow throughout its duration. At Middletown, the Dickinsons led a sociable life, counting all the most prominent local families among their friends. Middletown was a thriving port on the Connecticut River, and the society in which Mary now moved had perhaps a more commercial cast than any she had known before. She adapted with ease, delighted to "have a husband that is as fond of entertaining friends as I am."[3] Still more essential to her happiness, she noted that "my new Companion loves to have my family about him," and indeed her children and grandchildren made as long and frequent visits to Middletown as they had to Holland Hill.[4]

Since Miss Dickinson assumed a large share of the responsibility for running the household, Mary continued to enjoy ample time for intellectual pursuits. An avid reader, who had even chosen to be portrayed in the company of her books, she was delighted when Benjamin, soon to depart for a year in England, sent her his library to enjoy during his absence. She was soon "happily immersed," she told him. An examination of a book on the subject of Napoleon drew the wry comment that within the scope of Benjamin's library this volume and the one containing the sermons of Joseph Fish marked "perfect antipodes." For the most part, Dr. Dickinson had taken the history and left her the poetry as something for which he had no taste. Mary thought this a defect; on the other hand, she recognized that her own ignorance of history made the works of Pope, a poet she had not previously read, frequently incomprehensible. Indeed, the Augustan poets in general were strange to her, though "Milton I have been long acquainted with."[5]

The presence of Miss Dickinson, and the absence of responsibility for children, also gave Mary the freedom to travel with her husband. Sometimes she accompanied Dickinson when he rode to court; sometimes she made these occasions her opportunity to stay at Wallingford, Norfield, or Fairfield, where Dickinson would join her

when the sessions ended. When weather, health, and business permitted, they went on long, leisurely expeditions to
visit those of their friends and relations who lived at a distance. Thus, in her old age Mary embarked on yet another
stage of life. In it she combined the companionship of
marriage with a freedom from domestic care previously
known to her only in childhood and in those years of widowhood when she had lived as a part of her children's families rather than serving as the head of her own household.

I

ONE month after the wedding, while Dickinson "went to
judge within the gates of Haddam," Mary visited Wallingford.[6] Soon afterward, Dickinson joined her, and they
traveled on to Norfield. From Norfield they went to Newport, where they planned a lengthy stay with Sellek and
Hepsa, now the parents of a second child, Augustus Ely.
While they were there the pleasure of the jaunt received a
sharp check with the arrival of bad news from Jose.

Only a few weeks before, Jose had for the first time
admitted that his son, of whom he had previously written
reassuringly, had grown terrifying in his madness. He kept
the family awake at night with crazy talk, calling on them
to ring the bell and summon the people to a sale of effects,
apparently in a confused attempt to reverse the process that
had brought him to Ohio. Sometimes he broke out in
towering rages, threatening to kill his father and himself.
More than once, he had started out for Connecticut, only
to be found and brought back by search parties. Now he
had disappeared without a trace.

On April 16, two days before Mary's wedding, father
and son were cutting wood together when Joseph laid
down his ax and clambered over the fence that surrounded
the lot. Since he had left his jacket on a stump, Jose at first
thought that he had gone to relieve himself, or to break

the monotony of the work with a short walk. He took the precaution of checking the boy's belongings, but finding that he had taken no food, no money, and no clothes except the shirt and trousers he stood up in, Jose thought it almost impossible that he had run away. Hesitant to cry wolf, Jose waited too long. When at last he raised the alarm, friends and neighbors immediately downed tools and joined him in a search that lasted for days and covered "every point in the compass," but with no success. His last hope, he wrote, was that, as before, Joseph would turn up in Connecticut. Mary, however, told Benjamin that "as at this distance of time he has not, I fear the worst!"

Jose, who wrote "as if his soul were in bitterness about his son,"[7] told Mary that, before his disappearance, Joseph's most recent aberration had been to demand that his father give him, as eldest boy, the farm at Warren for his own. This had put Jose in the ironic position of arguing for the right of younger siblings to an equal share in the common stock. Joseph had apparently been driven to run off again by his discontent with this answer and perhaps also with the prospect of a change in his father's condition. On May 20 Jose too had remarried, taking as his wife a Mrs. Norton, a widow aged thirty-three. Her family, originally from Middletown, was known to Dickinson, though so slightly that he had nothing to say about it besides acknowledging the acquaintance. Jose's letter closed with a mere mention of this important event, which otherwise would have taken pride of place. As the weeks passed, while he assured Mary that "I am very happy in my new Connection & feel much richer for it," the greater part of his letters projected the misery of a man left in limbo.[8] Though he felt that his son's disappearance "comes almost as near to me as his Death," he could perform no healing ritual of mourning because "the want of evidence of his death also leaves hope of his Life."[9]

The pathetic image of Jose conjured up in these communications demanded and received the sympathy of his family in Connecticut. At the same time, he continued to try their patience and loyalty. He had made not the smallest attempt to repay his brothers, two of whom had large families to support on small clerical salaries, and even the temperate request that at least he protect them by giving them a mortgage on his property had met with refusal. "I consider you as perfectly safe without any Mortgage," he airily assured them, offering instead "to pay the whole note in land at the going price." Not surprisingly, they did not choose to take payment in unseen, unimproved lands five hundred miles away, but Jose seemed to consider that he had absolved himself, if not from the obligation, at least from any charge of negligence in attempting to meet it. Yet he complained bitterly of Billy Silliman's failure to repay a note that Jose had signed for him in 1790. "I have often spoken to Wm. about settling it . . . but he does not settle it tho it has lain fifteen years," he grumbled. "If all my Friends knew that man as well as I do they would despise him."[10]

This covert, somewhat unworthy invitation drew no response from his mother and brothers, who declined to judge Billy for the irresponsibility that they had forborne to condemn in Jose. Billy had in truth fallen in their estimation, but for political rather than moral reasons. He had been flirting with the Democratic party and participating in its political caucuses, a newfangled custom of which they decidedly disapproved. When Patty Silliman, who sometimes questioned her father's opinions, but never those of her favorite uncle, asked Benjamin what he thought of these proceedings, he replied:

> You ask me whether any good comes from democratical Caucuses. . . . No! I am not so uncandid as to believe that the democrats, *as a party,* are aiming at mischief; but I do sincerely believe that it is the genuine tendency of their principles & practices to weaken the religious, moral & sober habits of domestic life & to undermine the foundations of social order & good government. Multitudes of them are not aware of this, and while they

are fascinated with the sounds of republicanism, liberty &c, they do not dream that they are toiling to elevate a few ambitious men to power & emolument, while themselves remain, & will, as obscure as before.[11]

Confident that he had articulated his mother's sentiments as well as his own, he subsequently reported to her that his words had found their true mark. "Brother saw my letter," he wrote, "as I intended he should, and I find was, instead of being offended, much affected by it, and said that he had begun to think differently of the matter."[12]

Benjamin had spoken too soon, to judge from a comment of Mary's, made several months later, that "Bro. Wm. I believe is sorry he has changed his politicks, but dont know how to confess his errors." Even so, neither she nor her other sons would cast him out as Jose had hinted that they should. "Your Bros. John and James go there," she told Benjamin. "Tho they remember the *wormwood* and *gaul* given to yr. Br. at N.C. [New Connecticut], they think it not best to foresake him." The preservation of the family, as a sacred trust, obliged its members to transcend political differences as well as personal resentments, and to keep Billy, his wife, and children within the circle.

Mary's inability to extend the same protection to her own eldest son and his motherless children became in her last years one of the few painful feelings for which her faith provided no fully effective remedy. A death, even of a beloved infant, made no breach in the family stronghold but only set one more figure before her on the way that she herself would soon travel, and whose end in a heavenly home she never doubted now. As she wrote in 1805, when a grandson died, *"he* is safe in port, while survivors are *stemming* on the ocean of life."[13] The endless wheel of toil turning to failure, and love turning to loss, on which Jose seemed to be bound presented a far more rigorous test of her belief in a loving God. She turned frequently in her meditations to the question of why his afflictions should so far exceed his errors, and no answer fully sufficed. One

Sunday she sat at Middletown reading a sermon by John on a text from Isaiah, "For my thoughts are not your thoughts neither are your ways my ways, saith the Lord." The prophet's words and John's reflections on them, Mary wrote, "[have] comforted and instructed me under this dark leaf of God's providence in thus . . . driving my first born son into the wilderness and causing him to go through poignant trials while his relatives are enjoying the comforts of our own and his native land." But the images she employed of the "dark leaf," and of Jose as driven from his first home "into the wilderness,"[14] in addition to the contrast she expressed between the loneliness of his exile and the sense of belonging that sheltered his brothers, register more sharply on the reader than her profession of acceptance.

II

IN March 1805 Mary said farewell to Benjamin at Middletown, where he had called on his way to take ship at New York. "After following you with my eyes as far as I could see your sulkey, I retired into the house with the consoling thought that you was going where providence calls you, and the way of duty is the way of safety,"[15] she told him, echoing the phrase with which she had consoled herself when his father went to war.

A transatlantic voyage was fraught with danger even in a century of technological advance, and she had real cause to tremble for him. Soon after he sailed, word arrived that the *Jupiter,* a ship traversing the same route in the opposite direction, had collided with icebergs and sunk with twenty-seven aboard. When at last, some two months later, Dickinson came from the post office one morning bearing a letter whose cover alone announced that Benjamin had come safe to land, Mary was overcome by her emotion. As she recorded the scene, Dickinson, impatient to hear the contents, offered to break the seal himself.

"No, I want to monopolize even that."

"What do you cry for?"

"For joy sir."[16]

When she recovered sufficiently to read the letter aloud, she found that Benjamin's ship had encountered the same field of icebergs as the *Jupiter,* but had escaped her fate because there had been a full moon that night.

Benjamin, an excellent correspondent, sent Mary full and frequent letters describing his adventures abroad. At Liverpool he had made a tour of a slave ship. "My own country so nobly jealous of its own liberties stands disgraced in the eyes of mankind and condemned at the bar of Heaven for being at once active in carrying on this monstrous traffic, and prompt to receive every cargo of imported Africans," he declared.[17] He had kinder words for England. Though he had prefaced his departure with a solemn, not to say slightly pompous, declaration that he would not be "influenced by the infidelity or the splendid pleasures and gilded fopperies of the Old World,"[18] his first weeks there forced him to admit that "after making every drawback and deduction, England is a great and glorious example of the triumph of the arts, of learning, of arms, of commerce, of religious, moral and humane Institutions, and of freedom and law." He drew a picture of a country preparing to do battle with the formidable power of Napoleonic France which recalled his own country in the early years of her revolutionary war, except that here there were no dissenters: "The English are loyal and united, altho greivously taxed."[19]

In her replies, Mary strove to keep the remembrance of homely and familial things fresh and pleasing in his eyes. Jose, her "dear child of affliction in the wilderness,"[20] who had not been heard from for several months when Benjamin departed, had survived the winter with all his remaining children alive and well, and with an addition to their number named, at Mary's particular request, Benjamin Silliman Noyes. In August, Sellek became a father for the third time with the birth of a son named Benjamin Douglas Silliman in honor of the man who had probably introduced the child's paternal grandparents. Mary and Dickinson had their first sight of baby Benjamin that autumn, during a round of visits that encompassed Troy, New York, southern Vermont, and Newport, a 250-mile journey which they had accomplished with an ease that testified to their sound health.

In excellent spirits at all this good news, and particularly that part of it which indicated that his mother continued to "possess the vigor of youth," on September 29 Benjamin left England for the Continent. He landed in Holland, where Daniel Sillimandi had long ago set sail for America, expecting to make a short stay before traveling on to Paris. At Rotterdam, however, he made a scornful comment about the Dutch involvement in the business of building ships for Napoleon that was overheard and reported. As a consequence he found himself unwelcome where he was, and barred from entry into France. Disappointed (though unrepentant), he returned to England, then set out almost immediately for Edinburgh, where he planned to attend the University's lectures on chemistry and medicine. It was there, late in November, that he received a letter from his mother bearing the dreaded black seal. Augustus Ely Silliman, aged two and a half years, had died at Newport. His distracted parents had barely recovered from the first shock of bereavement when the baby had also fallen ill and seemed likely to follow his brother. Several more weeks elapsed before Benjamin heard that the baby had survived.

Benjamin longed to share with Sellek the pain of this first bereavement, but he had to complete the work he was sent to do, and not until May 2, 1806, did he embark for America. When he arrived twenty-five days later, after a remarkably speedy crossing, he found that the college which had funded his year abroad would now occupy enough of his time to render separate visits to all his relatives impossible. Most of the family came to Wallingford for a general reunion with him at James's house, while the rest called on him at New Haven. James and Anna had a newborn daughter, their ninth living child; Sellek and Hepsa had the baby Benjamin, their second living child, now almost a year old; and Patty Silliman Banks, Benjamin's junior by three years, had a new husband to display.

Benjamin looked with a wistful eye on all this change and increase. While the other members of his family had stayed behind in the small world where birth had set them, he had moved far beyond it, in intellectual and emotional development as well as geographical distance. Yet neither his new professional status nor the thrill of travel wholly compensated him for his failure to bear the fruit that Mary had taught him to prize. In his own words, he was "the only *childless* branch of her family," his name preserved not in a son of his own but in a brother's son.[21] At twenty-seven years of age, when he considered his bachelor state he began for the first time to speak not so much of his longing for romantic love as of his desire for fatherhood. His promising new career had put the means to marry and raise a family almost within his grasp, but its demands left him no time to search for a bride.

By contrast, John Noyes, after twenty-one years of labor in his chosen field, still received only the salary voted him at the outset of his ministry, and found it inadequate to support his numerous family. He had chosen the Norfield Society in the belief that their unanimity and goodwill toward him provided more security than the greater wealth of others who had offered him a church. This had proved a mistake. A controversy had arisen between himself and a part of his congregation over the question of baptism for the children of parents who had not acknowledged the covenant. Because of it the Society had never been able to agree on an increase in his original stipend of two hundred fifty dollars a year with forty cords of wood. Given inflation, this would have made a meager living for man and wife alone, and by 1806 John and Eunice were the parents of eight children. As a result, John acknowledged that "I have not been so devoted to my calling as I should have been, if I had not been necessitated to provide for myself and family, the means of subsistence, over and above my little salary." Nevertheless, he and his people might have rubbed along together for the rest of his working life but for a mysterious malady that suddenly attacked him early in 1806.

As John described his illness, "my powers of utterance failed me, and a general debility pervaded my system."[22] He could no longer preach, and no doctor could say whether or not he would recover. The Society saw an opportunity to dissolve the bond with honor, but, though John was ready to acquiesce, he had first to find some other way of making a living. His elder sons, too, were of an age when he must give some thought to their future. College was out of the question, at least for the moment, as was the ministerial calling followed for generations by the men on both sides of their family. Samuel was already serving an apprenticeship to an apothecary at New Haven, a member of the Darling family. John wanted to try farming, but there was no money to set him up in land. Both John and William also had opportunities to enter the mercantile trade; their father, however, preferred if nothing else offered to wait until further vacancies occurred with Dr. Darling, on whom he could rely to supervise their moral as well as their professional development. For, although business would undoubtedly prove more lucrative than medicine, "the *mere* man of business is not the character I wish for my sons."[23]

In this crisis, the collection of the money that Jose owed to him would have made a world of difference to every member of John's family. The amount had grown to more than seventeen hundred dollars, or the equivalent of almost seven years' salary. John had made several previous attempts to persuade his brother that some satisfaction was due him; now he sent word of his illness to Jose together with an appeal of unmistakable urgency.

A few months before, Jose had moved his family from the farm at Warren to the farm at Burton, where he described himself as much better off and "slowly ascending the hill again."²⁴ John and Samuel promised well as farmers and gave him invaluable help; James had a good post as a teacher at Youngstown; Rebecca, instructed by her stepmother, was working as a tailor; in short, everyone but the baby Benjamin was pulling together to rescue the family fortunes. In October 1806, after he received the news of John's illness, he wrote from yet another new address, this time in the town of Parkman. He had given up farming, had opened a "publick & boarding house," and at the same time had resumed the practice of law. "From my [boarding] house & Law Business," he wrote, "I find a small constant Stream of Mony coming in. . . . I never obtained my Bread so easy as I do now & meat is easier and cheaper raised here than with you." Prosperity was in sight; just at the moment, however, he had not a penny to spare. Though he acknowledged "the kindness and forbearance shown to me," and admitted that "requirements made of me from time to time have been perfectly reasonable & proper,"²⁵ his brothers must surely understand that he could not set himself up in business without committing all his resources and, in addition, borrowing money. Genuinely grieved to hear of John's misfortune, he suggested, with evident sincerity, that a voyage to Bermuda might restore him; but how his brother was to afford so expensive a cure he did not say. Between the lines the message was clear: Jose had gone deeper than ever into debt, and John should look for no help from that quarter. For the moment, uncomfortable as he was with his Society, he must cling to their obligation to support him.

A year later, improved, but not well enough to resume regular duty, John consented to his own removal from the church with a year's salary in hand. He thought of becoming a full-time farmer, but how to procure the land remained a problem. He was not at all tempted by Jose's eager suggestion that he "take a Ride into this Country with a direct view that, if you like it, afterwards to remove your family here either to preach or to farm . . . or to do both."²⁶ The vision Jose conjured up of an easy living to be made seemed likely to prove as ephemeral as the vision of Jose himself in the role of prosperous innkeeper-cum-attorney, a dream now apparently abandoned, for he had returned full circle to the farm at Warren. John, whose voice had recently grown stronger, decided that he would stick to what he knew. He continued to live at Norfield, and to farm on a small scale for his family's subsistence, while obtaining work as a temporary pastor at every opportunity.

III

MARY had kept close watch over the struggling family at Norfield, offering considerable moral (and possibly financial) support. Little disturbed the placidity of her own days at this period, except the happenings, for good and ill, in her children's lives. But in 1808 the focus changed when she suffered a potentially crippling accident.

On Sunday, January 18, as Mary descended from her carriage at church, she slipped on a patch of ice and fell, breaking her left wrist. A local physician set the bones, and she recovered from the experience quickly enough to write the letters herself that went out to inform her children. With her usual disposition to seek the good, she observed that "had it been my right hand I could not now be making a record of the event . . . [and] I have had more comfort in the society of friends than I could have had if I had been able to be about."

Mindful as ever of the principles instilled by her father in her youth, she saw to it that though "I cannot labor with my hands, which would be my duty if I were able and which I have practiced all my life . . . [I] spend my time . . . profitably." As part of that endeavor, while visiting James at Wallingford she transcribed for her grandchildren some of the many letters of spiritual counsel that Mr. Fish had sent her at various times. "Although he has been dead 26 years," she commented, "he still speaks to them in his writings." At Middletown again, she shared with a visiting granddaughter the letters "giving an account of the sickness and death of my dear only sister . . . [which] revived in my mind those days of trouble, affording a fresh inducement to me to follow those who I trust are now inheriting the promises." In her journal, too, this was a period during which she was drawn to reflect on the past more than to record the present. These excursions backward in time transcended simple reminiscence, and in no sense did she live in the past. It was more that past and present, good and bad, came together to light a way into the future:

> Never in all my life have I been under better advantages to pursue my Christian course. . . . My lame hand excludes me from labor. I am for the most part well in health and [possess] enough of the necessaries and comforts of life and a kind husband & children. In addition I have good books on every interesting subject. Among my mercies I have trying matters that heaven saw I needed and for which I ought to be thankful as for my daily bread.[27]

So cheerfully did she endure her disability that, though the weeks passed without a sign of improvement, no one questioned the efficacy of her surgeon's work until Benjamin came to visit her that May. He was then shocked to find that, four months after the accident, the small bones of the wrist were still visibly protruded into a knobby excrescence, while both hand and arm remained useless. He had called at Middletown on his way to Hartford, and while at Hartford he encountered Governor Jonathan Trumbull, Jr., the son of Mary's old friend, to whom he confided his growing suspicion that a botched job of bonesetting might have left his mother permanently disabled. Trumbull recommended a consultation with one Dr. Sweet, a surgeon who lived not far from his own home in Lebanon, and who possessed a quite extraordinary skill in treating broken or dislocated bones. Benjamin rode back to Middletown immediately and persuaded Mary to return with him to the governor's house.

There Dr. Sweet examined the wrist and gave it as his opinion that he could realign the bones. His confidence inspired trust, Mary "did not shrink from the pain which the Dr. said would attend the breaking up of the cartilage," and the procedure followed forthwith. "Stimulus was offered," Benjamin recorded, "but she declined, and this admirable woman, then 72 years of age and of a delicate and sensitive frame, resolved to endure the suffering with a firm and unclouded mind." While Benjamin grasped her arm above the wrist, and offered resistance, Dr. Sweet forced Mary's hand upward, then down, then to the left and right, each motion accompanied with a sound as of a bundle of sticks breaking. "In an instant after the last movement, the bones were in place," Benjamin wrote, "and the good lady made no moan nor did she faint, although she grew very pale, and then, for the first and only time I believe, she consented to swallow a few drops of gin."[28] Immediately afterward, at the direction of Dr. Sweet, Mary performed a series of maneuvers with her arm and hand which indicated a return to almost normal function.

After a brief stay in prearranged lodgings, Mary, at the insistence of the governor, returned to spend the next three weeks at the Trumbull family house, where Dr. Sweet supervised her convalescence. She hardly needed his attentions, or theirs, considering that she had felt entirely well almost from the moment following Sweet's procedure. Certainly she did not need the frequent visits made by Benjamin, for whom the long ride to Lebanon was a demand upon his time added to that already made by his profession. In June, she received a letter from him urging that she stay longer, but on that same day she looked out of the window to see her own chaise driving up, and exclaimed, "There comes Doctr. Dickinson!" In fact it was his tenant, Johnson, sent to see if she felt able to return. Dickinson, though he had Patty with him, had begun to miss Mary, and since by now she had fully recovered the use of her left arm and hand, she was willing to go. The next morning, having paid Dr. Sweet's bill for ten dollars and, she told Benjamin, "being intrusted with compliments to you from the G, his Lady and little Mastr, and the silent modest assent of ————, Johnson and myself set out for home."[29]

The blank space that Mary left was a teasing reference to Harriet Trumbull, daughter of the governor. Truly concerned as Benjamin was for his mother, his assiduous attentions to her at Lebanon, and his wish that she stay there still longer, had more than her welfare as their object. A few weeks later, when Harriet came to New Haven for a visit to friends, he invited her to attend a series of public lectures on chemistry that he was about to give. As he later described these occasions:

> It was my province . . . to explain the affinities of matter, and I had not advanced far in my pleasing duties before I discovered that moral affinities also, moving without my intervention, were playing a part. To this I could not object, and it was certainly the most gratifying result of my labors, that several happy unions grew, incidentally, out of those bright evening meetings.[30]

Among them was to be his own.

Benjamin's engagement to Harriet Trumbull, announced in August 1808, gave Mary nothing but satisfaction, though Benjamin seemed to require some reassurance on that point. He had spent more time with his mother since reaching manhood than any of his brothers, precisely because he had no family of his own to distract his attention. Since her accident, he had come still more often than before to Middletown to share with her both his work in chemistry and the journal of his travels that he was preparing for publication. Therefore, he feared that she might feel supplanted. "Believe me my dear mother," he volunteered, "the new attachment which now animates my heart can never diminish the emotions of filial love & veneration which I have felt ever since I remember anything: so far from this I feel the capacities of my heart rather enlarged & its sensibilities quickened, and if there is any change I love my mother more tenderly than before."[31]

Mary did not need to be told so. She had learned from her parents a concept of the family as an inclusive rather than an exclusive entity, and she readily assumed that one more daughter-in-law would increase, not diminish, the stores of affection from which she, no less than her children, drew sustenance. "[B]elieve me I am not jealous of a rival," she assured her son, "and the more reason you have to love and admire her on whom you have of late months set your esteem and affection, the happier you make me."[32]

In September 1809, Benjamin and Harriet were married. They rented a handsome house on Hillhouse Avenue in New Haven, and there, on June 16, 1810, Maria Trumbull Silliman was born. No longer the sole unfruitful branch, Benjamin still wanted one thing to complete his happiness: that Mary make all possible haste to visit the baby, "when you will have beheld the children of all your children."[33] For Mary's part, having come as desired, she counted her blessings crowned by the confirmation she received in Benjamin and Harriet's house that all her sons had now repeated her own happy experience of marriage.

Soon afterward, however, through the increasingly frank reports of travelers from Ohio, it began to dawn on Mary that, like his claims to prosperity, the bliss that Jose attributed to his second marriage had more to do with wishes than with facts. His wife emerged from the descriptions of others as "a sad termagant" who "scolds and drives at him, and cannot bear to have him read, but wants to have him at work all the time on the farm, &c."[34] Early in 1810 his son John sent Mary a letter, the first she had received from any of Jose's children in several years, in which he reiterated all that she had heard:

[H]e takes no peace nor the comforts of life when at home. . . . Never did a man pass through so many fiery

trials as my Honored Father constantly has to undergo;
when at home my stepmother is constantly teasing him
about one thing & another, she laufs at Him about his
religion & his God ... in one of her flurries when I
lived at home, & my father was gone from home, she
threw his bible & dream books out of the window, it
rained very hard & probable they would have been
spoilled if I had not got up of from a bed that I was a
shaking with the ague on & brought them in, not
because I believed in the dreams but I knew my father
did & it would have been a great grief to him almost as
mutch as if the bible had been spoilled.

The mention of "dream books," which Jose valued
almost as highly as his Bible, raises the question that his
"inthusiastical" tendencies had increased to the point
where he identified himself with the biblical Joseph,
whose gift of interpreting dreams had changed slavery to
riches and power, and exile to triumphant reunion with a
native land and a family long unseen. If so, Mrs. Noyes
had some excuse for her "flurries." John himself pointed
out, in fairness to her, that "she is very industrious & she
does a good deal towards supporting the family by her
trade," though it was a pity, he added, that she never allowed her husband to forget the fact. John and James
both lived elsewhere now: John was working on a farm
twenty miles from Warren, and well on his way to completing the payments on one hundred acres of his own.
James had done well as a schoolmaster, but had "injured
himself as to his own comfort in trying to help our father
with money from time to time."

John's letter incidentally reveals to us that, since the family's emigration, Mary had kept them supplied with pack-
ages of clothing. "I do not know how we should have stood
it through the winter without them," he wrote. He also
acknowledged the "unwearyed concern" she had shown in
the "numberless & affectionate letters" all the children had
received from her despite their own delinquency in writ-

ing, and begged her to continue, as her letters inspired him to keep striving and hoping for better things. "I have seen the want and still do of a kind friend to councel & direct me," he confided, "as I live far away from home and cannot receive those instructions from my father that I stand in need of, & when I see him his mind is wholly taken up with the hurrys & cares of his deranged affairs."[35] John knew enough of his origins to realize that he, with his brothers and sisters, had degenerated in both learning and deportment from the family standard and to wish for his grandmother's guidance in the only way that she could give it at that distance.

Though Mary could not violate John's confidence by revealing what he had told her, she began to urge Jose to return to Connecticut, where she might more effectively help him and his family. Jose, enraptured with a new, fair prospect that had arisen for "quitting farming . . . [and taking] my stand in some County Town, where I can practice Law, & at the same time instruct an Academy with James," would not hear of it. From his letter, with its closing assurance that "Mrs. Noyes joines me in best Love & Wishes,"[36] a casual reader would have thought that he was a happily married man on the verge of a great success. The family knew better, and Benjamin's comment exemplified the general response: "My only hope for saving Brother Joseph's old age from distress are founded on his sons."[37]

In the following spring, a traveler from Ohio called on Mary and reported that Jose "was not at his own house but went there now and then (to see his young children I suppose)."[38] This information, added to the news that James, now teaching at Pittsburgh, had obtained a post for his father at a school four miles from that city, suggested that a separation had taken place. The remainder of Amelia's children had also gone from home. Samuel had hired himself out as a farm hand, and Rebecca had apparently been packed off to live with relations of her stepmother. When James reported her situation as "very disagreeable and distressing" and stated that it was "absolutely neces-

sary for her future credit and honour that she remove,"
Mary immediately transmitted money with the specific
instruction that it "must be put to no other use than to get
Rebecca here."[39] James did his best to obey, but nothing
came of the attempt except, to judge from a scattering of
oblique references, that Rebecca returned a curt refusal to
leave.

Other troubles crowded in. Dr. Dickinson showed signs
of a sudden, rapid decline. In May 1811 came the shocking
news that an explosion in the laboratory had blinded Benjamin, for the moment completely, and whether permanently or not only time would show. Though Mary longed
to go to his side, and to lend Harriet her help and support,
she knew that her husband stood in greater need. Indeed,
Benjamin's youth and health had healed his injuries and
restored his vision so far as to encourage hope of a full
recovery when, in October 1811, John Dickinson died.

IV

MARY'S third marriage had held neither the freshness of
her first nor the passion of her second. While polite, friendly
relations had subsisted between the children on both sides,
they never formed the close attachment that time and pro-
pinquity had produced between the Noyes and Silliman
sons. Nevertheless, John Dickinson had given Mary seven
years of intelligent, warm companionship, and his passing
left her "tenderly affected."[40]

With no dependents—on the contrary, with children
able to take care of her if necessary—Mary felt no acute
anxiety about her financial position. Even so, widowhood
was not without problems. She and Dickinson had made
an informal prenuptial agreement to keep their estates separate, but in law he did have the right to dispose of her
personal property. Should he, without informing her, have
chosen to exercise that right, she would have found that

her third husband had infinitely more capacity than her second to endow his children at the expense of hers. Upon her marriage to Silliman, the greater part of her assets had consisted of land over which he had limited power; upon her marriage to Dickinson, her assets had consisted almost entirely of insurance and government stock which he could conceivably have claimed and willed to his heirs. Meanwhile, unknown to Mary, the Dickinson children had trepidations of their own. The marriage had lasted a full seven years, much longer than anyone had expected; Mary had rendered indisputable service as companion and nurse, even allowing for Patty's assistance; and if she laid claim to a dower right, the courts might well uphold her.

Happily, Dickinson proved to have kept his word, and to have left Mary's property untouched. He had also left her a legacy of three hundred dollars "in consideration of my esteem & affection,"[41] to which his children, thankful for his moderation (and, presumably, also for Mary's contribution to his comfort in old age), added another two hundred dollars in lieu of dower. Mary having expressed herself content, the matter ended there, with a cordiality creditable to everyone concerned.

Within three weeks of Dickinson's death, Mary removed to Wallingford. Miss Patty expressed some disappointment that she would not remain at Middletown through the winter, but James's wife tactfully explained that her children longed to have their grandmother return. Perhaps she left unspoken an additional reason, that Mary had formed no such strong tie to Miss Patty as would make her a substitute, in Mary's old age, for her own family. During her remaining years "she divided her time among her children [but] made Wallingford her principal home," Benjamin recorded. "To that house . . . she had a long established attachment . . . and there she felt more peculiarly at home." James had never fulfilled his early promise of brilliance, but as a good man pursuing a plain course of service to God he was very much the spiritual heir of his mother, and his home with its "gentleminded and devoted heads and chil-

dren" offered Mary "all those soothing attentions that were
so congenial to her own character."[42]

From within its shelter, she looked out upon a world
whose public events had less and less power to disturb her.
The War of 1812, it is true, raised memories of trials she
had hoped never to face again, and though she knew herself comparatively safe at Wallingford, there was one
scourge that no one could certainly escape. As at the start
of the revolutionary war, sickness ranged at large from the
army camps to the civilian population. Furthermore, James
did not live so far inland as to preclude the possibility that
an invasion might force him and his family to evacuate.
The operations of the British navy drove Sellek and Hepsa
from their home at Newport in 1814, while Benjamin's
family lived in fear of an attack on their part of the coast.
Equally distressing was the prospect that any of Mary's
sons or grandsons would be called upon to serve, perhaps
to die, in a war that she, as a Federalist, regarded as avoid-
able, a tragedy wrought solely in order to serve the ends
of the opposition party. Still, nowadays the longer view
prevailed with her, and she saw the greater peril in the
possibility that earthly anxieties, like earthly pleasures,
would grow strong enough to "cast out the thoughts necessary to prepare for a better world, as we are in less danger from an enemy we see, than from one who lurks out
of sight."[43]

She could not maintain the same composure in the face
of a private trial, that of Jose's slow descent into destitu-
tion. By November 1811 he had abandoned schoolteaching
and employed himself as a recorder of deeds in Allegheny
County, Pennsylvania. The family had heard that he was
drinking heavily. When John questioned him about this,
he responded with a cautious, almost cunning, request to
know the exact details of the report, and suggested that
there might be "degrees in guilt,"[44] which, to those who
knew him, effectively confirmed the charge. Without further inquiry, John dispatched a tract on the evils of drink
in which Jose recognized enough of his danger to draw

from him the eventual admission that "I have formerly found it a great Snare to me, & too apt to be indulged when great trouble presses, but we ought rather to be seeking for a very different kind of Spirit."[45] As always, however hopeless things looked, he was confident that something would turn up. "There is a Tide in the affairs of Men," he wrote, "who knows but my long & low Ebb may change to a flood. Mine and James whole time is absorbed in business, we are not seeking the *Dulce* but the *Utile,* we are anxious if possible to retrieve the Misfortunes of our Family, we rise with the light & retire to rest at Ten, he spends all the evening as well as the day in his School, & mine after my letters are finished will be spent in recording."[46]

A few weeks later, Jose was in prison and, in his son James's words, "out of all business." James had paid the sum for which Jose was arrested, but not before he had served thirty days, by which time other creditors were converging on him. Unable to help him further, James was forced to appeal to Mary for money, not only to clear his father of debt but also to pay off the debt on the Burton farm, for he had reason to suspect that one of the creditors "deemed it a good opportunity to put the matter in suit in order to get the farm for a mere trifle."[47] With Mary's assistance, Jose pulled through. He then became seriously ill, and for a while it looked as if the consumption that had carried off Amelia now held him in its grip. Six months later, fully recovered, he was again teaching school at Pittsburgh and writing with the optimism that seems at once admirable, infuriating, and heartrending.

By that time Jose's son John, now married and a father, had abandoned the long struggle to make good without the benefit of family connections. He had returned, with his family, to Connecticut, where Mary found cause for rejoicing, not only in the sight of her first great-grandchild, but in the proof that John presented of having grown up, despite his disadvantages, to be sober, industrious, and fond of reading. His Uncle James procured him a place with a local man of property, presumably as a farm worker, at a salary of twelve dollars a month, a modest beginning from which he went on in time to establish himself in business. Later, on John's recommendation, Mary appointed Samuel as her agent in managing the land that Jose had conveyed to her in partial satisfaction of the debt he owed to her. Thus, she was able to help two of Jose's children, if not to establish themselves as she would have hoped, at least to climb out of the slough into which they had sunk.

V

IN April 1814, Mary had a bout with pneumonia from which she did not recover with her usual resilience. This was the first clear signal she had received from the herald of death. In spite of it, within a few weeks she felt well enough to start out on her customary round of visits to the children.

Mary was aware that, for many in her present situation, their welcome on arriving to stay was far from certain. "An old person that I know," she wrote, her tone a nice mixture of disapprobation and amusement, "after being gone a year from her relatives and returning, they were asked if they were not glad to see her, [and] they answered, *that they were glad she stayed away so long.*"⁴⁸ Fortunately, of herself she could say, "I go from one family of my dear children to another, and tho I change my residence, I find the same disposition and ability to make me happy."⁴⁹

Their goodwill, of course, only reflected Mary's toward them, not forgetting her sons' wives, the "daughters of adoption" who, according to Benjamin, "were also the daughters of affection and confidence."⁵⁰ Though the pneumonia had left her weakened in body, her ability to perceive and respond to the needs of others remained unimpaired. That autumn, when babies were expected at

Newport, New Haven, and Wallingford, Mary recognized that the time had come when her presence would not lessen but increase the work of those households. In expressing to John her wish to come to Norfield she explained that "tho they [the other children] still desire that I would visit them, I fear I should add more to their care, than my visit would do them good."[51]

It was in the same spirit that, as soon as she had regained a little strength, she made certain preparations which she revealed to Benjamin when he visited her at Wallingford. She directed him to open a small traveling trunk in the corner of her bedroom and showed him her shroud and other grave-clothes, which she had provided to carry with her from this time forth so that when death came she would leave no more work to others than she must. Benjamin found these garments a mournful sight. "Mournful however they did not appear to be to her," he admitted, "for she added that death had no terrors for her and she contemplated the translation to another world as a bright and happy journey full of hope and promise."[52] Yet her confidence never degenerated into complacency. "I endeavor every day and night to realize death," she observed in a letter to John, "but God only knows how it will be when the time of trial comes. My children will pray for me that my faith fail not."[53]

Less than a year after she wrote these words, a tragedy occurred in her son John's family that shook her faith to its foundation. His son Benjamin, a bright, promising young man who had succeeded, in spite of his father's embarrassments, in gaining admission to Yale as a student of divinity, had become caught up in the religious revival then sweeping the college community. Since Mary had heard of no excesses to mar this latest "awakening," his fervor obtained her unqualified approval. During the spring of 1815, however, his observant Uncle Ben saw that something had gone awry. In a model of crisp, diagnostic prose, he informed Mary that "Benjamin is in a very unhappy state of extreme religious despondency joined with a good deal of bodily indisposition occasioned by the influenza, [and] I am endeavouring to persuade him to go home."[54] Still, he was disconcerted when his nephew suddenly packed up and left without a word of farewell.

On April 22 the young man appeared at Saugatuck, at the house of a maternal uncle. John, alarmed by his brother-in-law's report, went there at once, only to find that his son had gone. In a hasty letter sent first to Benjamin for forwarding to Mary, John wrote: "My son Benjn came last night in the stage to Brother Sherwood's and at usual bed time retired to rest. Between 7 & 8 in the morning his Uncle went to his chamber to call him to breakfast & found that the window was open & he missing. He got on to the Piazza & jumped off, leaving a deep track in the turf of both feet. Search has been made & is making for him."[55] Three days later the searchers received word that a young woman had seen the boy that night by a bridge over a stream. They went there and found evidence that he had dug for roots in an effort to feed himself.

Encouraged, but still apprehensive, John returned to Norfield in case young Benjamin should come there when hunger and exhaustion drove him, and while he shared with his wife the agony of waiting he turned naturally to his mother as an example of man's power, with God's help, to survive:

My dear Mother, your Son who now addresses you out of the depth of affliction, is not so overwhelmed as to forget that he has a tender & affectionate Parent yet spared to him, whose heart bleeds when her dear children are smitten with the arrows of the Almighty. . . . Oh my dear mother pray earnestly for your afflicted off-spring, your sorrowing son & daughter & their dear children that remain . . . that they may be prepared to meet what may still be before them. . . . I pray that God may support you under this stroke of his hand, as

he has done under great & repeated trials, and that his·
consolations may abound in you.[56]

But a darkness had descended upon Mary as deep as any
she had known. The accounts she had received of her
grandson's mental state, together with the manner of his
disappearance, made a certain terrible possibility all too
real to her. In a disjointed, poorly written, misspelled letter
to Benjamin she asked, "But will God leave and forsake his
own dear children? Shuch we had reason to think was, our
dear one we morn."[57] As the days dragged on, she lost all
but "a sickly dieing hope that it is *possible he* may be yet
alive." She strove to find a meaning in her pain, for since
God would not inflict a pointless suffering "it becomes us
with humble prostration of soul, to beg of God to teach
us all the good lessons such an event in infinite wisdom is
sent to teach us." Yet she found the workings of Providence "in this instance very misterious."[58]

On May 6 the blow fell. Young Benjamin's body was
found, floating upright, in the river at Saugatuck, not far
from the bridge where he had been seen. His Uncle Ben,
present at the awful moment of discovery, estimated that
death had taken place some ten days before, and that the
position of the corpse, a gruesome parody of life, came
about because it was "lifted by the gases of decomposi-
tion."[59] A letter found in the pocket left no doubt that the
young man had taken his own life:

> Pa & Ma do not grieve—be extremely careful to instruct
> your children in the great concerns of eternity. Use your
> utmost endeavours that they all know Jesus Christ &
> him crucified. Be very careful that they do not deceive
> themselves in the great matters of religion. . . . The
> Devil is very active & artful. He has got fast hold of me
> so that I am entrapped. . . . I know my case is distress-
> ing; my ruin was owing to my great negligence in the
> great matters of the soul. I feared when I ought to have

loved. I have been too dependent on others, not looked
so well to my own state as I should have done. Be careful that you come not to this place of torment—I do
not realize my own situation [60]

There the writing broke off.

If Mary, who had buried children and grandchildren,
had flattered herself that she had nothing further to learn
about the anguish of bereavement, the death of Benjamin
Noyes taught her otherwise. The fact of his suicide, and
his assertion of demonic possession, threatened to deprive
the family of the one consolation that had upheld them
through other losses. When Mary heard of his fate she knew
at once the dreadful question that would have arisen in the
minds of John and Eunice. For their comfort, she wrote,

> Now my dear Children you dont mourn without hope.
> Be thankful that you have had so much satisfaction in
> his life, and have so much reason to hope it is well with
> him; tho his exit was dreadful we have reason to think
> he was not in his right mind and therefore not account-
> able for that his last act.[61]

Privately, she had greater difficulty in accepting this death
than she had experienced for many years. To Benjamin,
some weeks after, she admitted: "The late distressing event
that has taken place, I believe, has had great hand in reducing my system, notwithstanding my feeble efforts to be
still and know who had and has the sovereign right of dis-
posing of our dearest comforts by the means he thinks
proper."[62]

In the midst of the search, Rebecca Noyes had sent word
to Norfield that she had arrived at Bridgeport. Uncertain
of her reception, she had gone first to the home of her Burr
relations, whence she wrote to her Uncle John apologizing
for her failure some years before to use the money sent her
by Mary for the purpose intended, that of bringing her to
Connecticut. The letters he and Mary had received at that

time, she said, though written in her name, were not composed by her. Benjamin and Harriet agreed to receive her
at their house, and she was there when her cousin's body
was found. Mary and her other relations met her soon
afterward, and all agreed that, though she had unfortunately inherited John Noyes's epilepsy, her appearance,
manner, and earnest desire to improve herself did her credit.
At the same time, she posed more of a problem for the
family than her brother John had done.

A young, single woman, though she might be asked to
make a living, could not be expected to live independent
of a family setting. Which family, then, should take Rebecca
in? A prolonged residence with either John or James would
embarrass them seriously since she had abandoned the
Congregational Church for Methodism. In addition, the
rural retirement in which they lived would severely restrict
her in the practice of the tailor's trade, her only means of
decent self-support. Benjamin offered "to do every thing
to the extent of my ability for Rebecca consistently with
my obligations to my own family," but he clearly did not
feel inclined to give her a permanent home.[63] When all due
praise had been rendered to her for her worthy attempt to
rise above the surroundings in which she had grown up, it
seems probable that a vast cultural gap separated her from
her relatives in Connecticut and that her continuous presence placed a strain on whatever family was housing her.
She visited them all in turn, and seemed prepared to remain
at John's house indefinitely, until "a very plain letter" from
Benjamin at last propelled her into an active search for
employment.[64] She then found a live-in position at New
Haven, did quite well for herself, and eventually made a
respectable marriage to a Mr. Lewis Lobdell, by whom she
had four children. The family always acknowledged her
right to membership, but it is clear that she never fitted
into it as naturally as her Connecticut cousins.

Just as Rebecca had begun to settle down, Benjamin
learned that her brother James, who had abandoned teaching for trade, was also thinking of coming to Connecticut

and resuming his first calling. Benjamin, however, thought it dangerous to assume that a position as a teacher would be open to him in the east, where educational standards were higher; especially since he too suffered from the seizures that had forced his grandfather to retire from the Hopkins school. Benjamin sent him fifty dollars toward the treatment of his disorder, but gave him no encouragement to proceed. Though the family recognized that James had shown "industry & frugality" in obtaining an education for himself while giving his struggling father frequent assistance, at the time they had reason to suspect that the son partook of the father's inability to settle to anything or to keep pace with his debts. Benjamin felt relieved when he eventually abandoned the idea of rejoining the family at Connecticut since "dependence, although among his friends, would have augmented his malady." In the end James "bought a farm [in Virginia], and occupied it and made some improvements, but sickened and died" while still a young man.[65]

John, James, and Benjamin, though they were touched by the plight of Jose's children, could maintain a certain emotional distance from it. Not so Mary. The "howling wilderness" had devoured a son, a daughter, and a grandson, for young Joseph had never returned. It had dimmed the bright promise that she had once seen in Amelia's remaining four children, while the three children born to the second Mrs. Noyes would probably never be known to her, separated as they were not only by distance but also by the hostility of their mother and her family. By the autumn of 1815, the succession of sorrowful and troubling events had reduced Mary's spirits so low that her sons in Connecticut persuaded her that she should make a visit to Sellek, who had recently moved with his wife and eight children to take up a legal practice in Brooklyn, New York. They pointed out that the institution of regular steamboat service between New York and New Haven would make it possible for her to traverse the miles with less fatigue than it cost her to ride in a carriage from Wallingford to

New Haven; but Mary, despite the encroachments of age, did not wish even now to miss the sights along the way. "The steam boat . . . is a great convenience," she allowed, "but if I should ever go, I should like well to go by land as I never saw the country that way further than Horseneck."[66]

One day, when Benjamin wrote his own Reminiscences, he would recall a journey that he and his brother John had taken in 1792, with Mary, to Stonington. She had not been there since her father's death eleven years before. As always, they traveled slowly, taking the time to make social calls and overnight visits as they went. They arrived to a welcome that astonished Benjamin in spite of his own high estimate of Mary's worth. "In our progress through Stonington," he recalled, "we were every where greeted warmly by the people, who were rejoiced to see the only surviving child of their revered and beloved minister with two of her sons." Once, when she rode past a house without stopping, he thought she must have overlooked it, for it seemed to him that she was known and honored everywhere. For the first time, he was struck by the gentleness and intimacy of the small community from which his mother came and by the "plain but welcome & cheerful hospitality" so readily extended. Even then, he perceived that in this sheltered place, where change came slowly, he was glimpsing the last days of a period in his country's history that had already passed away in many places. Looking back years later, he gave to the memory an elegiac tone:

> People in those days were not so much hurried as now; there was more leisure in the family, and personal friendships were cherished, often through long lives. . . . Those who were born and educated under the primitive influence of New England sentiments & manners, when population was yet sparse and personal friendships still partook of the simplicity & sincerity of colonial manners . . . appear to have felt and cherished the social sentiments as a part of their nature—and the

hospitality which characterized that state of society offered a welcome asylum to the travelling friend.[67]

Benjamin wrote these words from the perspective of one who had lived to see his world transformed by an industrial revolution which was only just beginning to make itself felt in 1815, when Mary at last consented to venture aboard the steamboat for New York. It was an alien experience to her. The long, slow hours of passage over rutted, rock-strewn tracks, pleasantly relieved by leisurely visits to the friends and relations she could claim in every town and village along the way, had yielded to a quicker, more comfortable transit divorced from the terrain and from familiar human contact. One day after her departure, in early November, she arrived at New York. She was happy to see Sellek's family, but showed little desire to see the sights in the rapidly developing metropolis, preferring to spend her days in the environment she knew, the home and the meeting-house. For the first time, she complained that she felt unable to read, write, or apply herself to any occupation for long, and soon after her arrival, despite the care that Sellek and Hepsa lavished upon her, she caught the influenza. Benjamin, on hearing of her symptoms, promptly dispatched a prescription that gave her relief, but she was clearly entering a decline.

In April 1816 Benjamin brought Mary home to James's family at Wallingford. In that dear place, she met with the last great sorrows of her life. During the summer, Billy, who had toyed for years with the idea of emigration, at last decided to remove his family (Phoebe and the two unmarried daughters) to Indiana. Within a few weeks of their departure he and his wife died, probably in an epidemic of typhoid fever. Mary had remained an affectionate mother to Billy, son of the man she had so passionately loved, and his fate cannot have left her unmoved, but as far as we can discover she made no record of her feelings.

Almost as blank a space exists in the account of Jose's death soon afterward. He was living in extreme poverty just outside Pittsburgh and received a summons to come into town as a witness at the court. When death overtook him, not one member of the family was there. John Noyes received an account at second hand:

> [The] Rev. Thos. Hunt, the Clergyman of the place, having been previously acquainted with him, he sent for him to come. . . . He had taken lodgings in a place where there were no conveniences for a person in his situation and was not able to be moved. He . . . requested some relief, which Mr. Hunt obtained from the humane society of the place, and by which he was principally supported until his decease [on February 6th]. . . . On his being taken ill he . . . expressed strong fears, saying that his life had not been regulated by the light which he had enjoyed. Afterwards, he expressed a strong hope in Christ. The day before his decease he appeared more comfortable and resigned . . . [and] much in prayer. The above was communicated by a letter from Rev. Mr. Hunt.[68]

A letter from Máry to John, written in July 1816, confirmed that she had received "the meloncholy news" and had also heard from Jose's sons, which relieved her mind of a fear she had apparently entertained that "*they* were dead, as well as their poor father."[69] She described herself as very feeble, and perhaps that is why she left her emotions mute. But if it is permissible to infer Mary's response from her past life and writings, then Jose's passing had replaced a long sorrow with a new hope. During his illness four years before, when she heard that he lay near death, she had comforted herself with the thought that "he will find mercy in that day when his flesh and heart shall fail him; if so, he enters the kingdom of heaven thro *much tribulation*."[70] Surely that same thought sustained her when the end did come.

Mary wrote very little as her life drew to a close, but she did produce two long documents. One, a religious meditation written in 1816, contained a vigorous attack upon

the decline of original standards, particularly those which
had to do with family prayers:

> They [the children] should be taught when family wor-
> ship is performed to lay all by and sit in a decent posture
> to read or hear God's word read, and not be looking
> out of the window or playing with any thing about
> them, and instead of bustle and motion about the house,
> it ought to be like that of Cornelius, who said to Peter
> "here are we all before thee to hear what thou shalt say
> unto us."[71]

The other was a seven-page eulogy written in early 1817 to
mark the recent death of President Timothy Dwight of
Yale. Mary had known Dwight since he had visited the
Noyes house as a student. During her second widowhood,
when he was minister at Greenfield near Fairfield, he had
often made himself helpful to her, and he had been the
moving force in giving Benjamin his professorship at Yale.
Yet Mary remembered him most affectionately of all for
the prayer that he had offered in chapel after the suicide
of her grandson Benjamin. Even now, remembrance could
revive the agony of that time in all its terrible strength;
even now, it seemed to her a trial greater than that which
God had made of Abraham when he commanded him to
sacrifice his son, for Isaac had been "spared and restored
. . . while our dear one died under awful and distressing
circumstances." Only the recollection of Dwight's charity
toward the dead boy and his grieving family prompted her
to happier, more hopeful thoughts. "It becomes us all to
be resigned to his departure from this world," she wrote;
"he is gone this vacation to explore celestial regions, from
whence he will not return to give us an account. . . . I
only wish you may all be prepared to ascend and explore
[them] with me."[72]

In early 1818, Benjamin brought his mother in a carriage
from Norfield to New Haven, "her first bridal home,"
where four grandchildren, two sons and two daughters,

now waited to welcome her. She was failing rapidly, and "one day under conscious weakness she exclaimed, O that I should have lived to survive my usefulness!" Benjamin wrote. "I replied, dear mother, you still teach us by your example & your heavenly temper and precepts, and you have not survived your usefulness!" Shortly afterward, at Mary's request, he took her back to Wallingford, where "the flame of life gently expired."[73] Five days before her death she began to refuse all sustenance except a little liquid. "It would be a matter of no surprise to us," a grandson wrote, "if she should drop away at any time. Her sun, to appearance, is already down, & is now only throwing a beam of light upon her horizon."[75]

She died on the second of July, 1818, and, appropriately for a woman of her generation, she was committed to the American earth on the anniversary of her country's independence. Yet she remained to the end of her life less a daughter of the Revolution than a child of the Puritans. "It fell to me to write an inscription for my mother's monument," Benjamin recorded in a note that he appended to Mary's journal, "but this book is her living record; she walked with God and was not, for God took her!"[75]

ABBREVIATIONS

| NFP-SNH | Noyes Family Papers, Samuel Noyes Homestead, New Canaan |
| SFP | Silliman Family Papers, Yale University Library |

MANUSCRIPT DOCUMENTS

BS Auto	Benjamin Silliman, "Origin and Progress of Chemistry, Minerology and Geology in Yale College, with Personal Reminiscences" (9 vols.), in SFP
BS Rem	Benjamin Silliman, "Reminiscences of my childhood and youth and of My Parents and other friends," home of Philip English, New Haven
JFMR	Joseph Fish, "Funeral Sermon on the Death of Mrs. Rebecca Douglas with some Memoirs of her Life" (1767), in SFP
M Accts	Mary's Account Book (1790s), in SFP
R + J	Benjamin Silliman's annotated copy of Mary's Reminiscences and Journal (1800 on: that is, the original begun by M in 1800 and the copy made by BS beginning July 5, 1856), in SFP

NOTES

NOTES are provided only to identify the source of direct quotations. Occasionally we have adjusted punctuation to make eighteenth-century texts more intelligible to twentieth-century readers. For further discussion of the materials from which this study was constructed, see the bibliographical essay.

CHAPTER ONE

1. M to BS, August 8, 1800, in SFP.
2. North Stonington Congregational Church Records, vol. I, 7, in CSL.
3. Stephen Hubbell, *A Discourse commemorative of the Rev. Joseph Fish* . . . (Norwich, Conn., Bulletin Job Office, 1863), 10, 11.
4. JF to RF, August 6, 1765, in SFP.
5. R + J, 3–4.
6. *The Works of John Robinson,* ed. Robert Ashton (Boston, Doctrinal Tract and Book Society, 1851), vol. I, 146.
7. JFMR, 53.
8. M to JF and RF, July 9 and November 23, 1763, in NFP-SNH; also August 7, 1776, in SFP.
9. Joseph Fish, *The Church of CHRIST a firm and durable House* . . . (New London, 1767), 114.
10. Ibid., 114, 115.

11. Ibid., 116-17.
12. Ibid., 139.
13. Ibid., 121.
14. Ibid., 119.
15. Ibid., 150.
16. Ibid., 132-33.
17. Ibid., 133-34.
18. Ibid., 134, 136, 136-37.
19. BS Rem, 27.
20. North Stonington Congregational Church Records, vol. I, 95, in CSL.
21. Fish, *Church of CHRIST,* 156-57, 158.
22. Ibid., 174, 172.
23. Ibid., 145.
24. North Stonington Congregational Church Records, vol. I, 126, in CSL.
25. Fish, *Church of CHRIST,* 124, 127, 128.
26. Samuel Hopkins, *Memories of the Life of Mrs. Sarah Osborn . . .* (Worcester, Mass., 1799), 58-59.
27. Ibid., 43, 49.
28. R + J, 5.
29. JF to Sarah Osborn, July 3, 1754, in SFP.
30. R + J, 7.
31. Ibid., 6, 7.
32. Ibid., 9.
33. Ibid., 10.
34. J to M, August 22, 1757, in NFP-SNH.
35. J to M, March 14, 1758, in NFP-SNH.
36. JF to J and M, December 5 and December 23, 1766, in SFP.
37. JF to J's father, Joseph Noyes, August 8, 1758, in NFP-SNH.
38. J quoting M in J to M, November 7, 1758, in NFP-SNH.

CHAPTER TWO

1. R + J, 11.
2. R + J, 9-10.
3. M to JF and RF, June 17, 1759, in NFP-SNH.
4. JF to J and M, August 17, 1759, in SFP.
5. J to JF, November 27, 1759, in NFP-SNH.
6. Joseph Fish, *CHRIST JESUS the Physician . . .* (New London, 1760), 36.
7. For this and what follows, R + J, 11-13.
8. J to JF, August 13, 1760, in NFP-SNH.
9. JF to M and J, August 4, 1760, in SFP.
10. R + J, 13-14.
11. BD quoting JF in letter to JF, October 5, 1762, in SFP.
12. JFMR, 53.

13. BD to JF, October 5, 1762, in SFP.
14. M to JF and RF, February 7, 1763, in NFP-NCHS.
15. M to R, March 21, 1763, in NFP-NCHS.
16. M to JF and RF, February 7, 1763, in NFP-NCHS.
17. M to R, April 15, 1763, in NFP-NCHS.
18. R to JF and RF, June 23, 1763, in JFMR, 71-72.
19. M to JF and RF, April 11, 1763, in NFP-NCHS.
20. J to JF and RF, April 20, 1762, in NFP-SNH.
21. M to RF, April 17, 1763, in NFP-NCHS.
22. JF to Sarah Osborn, September 13, 1761, in SFP.
23. M to JF and RF, March 28 and April 11, 1763, in NFP-NCHS.
24. JFMR, 69, 72.
25. R + J, 14-15.
26. BD's obituary of J copied by BS into R + J, 153-56.
27. R + J, 14-16.
28. JFMR, 83-84.
29. JF to M, December 5, 1766, in SFP.
30. JF to M, December 12, 1766, in SFP.
31. BD to JF, December 9, 1766, in SFP.
32. R + J, 27.
33. JF to M and J, December 23, 1766, in SFP.
34. JF to M, March 15, 1767, in SFP.
35. JF to BD, October 21, 1767, in SFP.
36. JF to M, March 15, 1767, in SFP.
37. JF to M and J, April 13, 1767, in SFP.
38. JF to M and J, September 29, 1767, in SFP.
39. R + J, 16-18.

CHAPTER THREE

1. R + J, 22.
2. Ibid.
3. M's account of administration of estate of John Noyes, New Haven Probate District, 1767, in CSL.
4. R + J, 22.
5. See note 3 above.
6. R + J, 23.
7. JF to M and J, September 29, 1767, in SFP.
8. R + J, 25.
9. M to JF and RF, March 9, 1769, in NFP-NCHS.
10. Ibid.
11. JF to M, April 11, 1768, in NFP-NCHS.
12. M to JF, June 28, 1769, in NFP-NCHS.
13. M to JF and RF, November 25, 1769, in NFP-NCHS.
14. M to JF and RF, June 28, 1769, in NFP-NCHS.

15. M to JF and RF, August 6, 1769, in NFP-NCHS.
16. Ibid.
17. R + J, 28–29.
18. Ibid., 31.
19. Ibid., 39–47 passim.
20. Ibid., 50–52.
21. Ibid., 52–66 passim.
22. Ibid., 85.
23. Ibid., 81.
24. Naphtali Daggett to JF, February 3, 1773, in BL.
25. Naphtali Daggett to JF, March 15, 1773, in BL.
26. JF to M, May 2, 1774, in SFP.
27. M to JF and RF, May 30, 1772, privately owned.
28. M to JF and RF, August 6, 1769, in NFP-NCHS.
29. JF to M, November 2, 1774, in SFP.
30. J to JF, March 17, 1759, in NFP-SNH.
31. JF to M, May 28, 1774, in SFP.
32. M to JF and RF, November 2, 1774, in Watkinson Library, Trinity College, Hartford.
33. JF to M, November 11, 1774, in SFP.
34. JF to M, January 10 and February 2, 1775, in SFP.

CHAPTER FOUR

1. M to JF and RF, March 8, 1775, in SFP.
2. R + J, 148ff. for this and following quotations from "Portrait of a Good Husband."
3. GSS to M, March 14, 1775, in SFP.
4. M to GSS, March 15, 1775, in SFP.
5. GSS to M, March 24, 1775, in SFP.
6. M to GSS, March 26, 1775, in SFP.
7. JF to M, March 14, 1775, in SFP.
8. GSS to M, March 31, 1775, in SFP.
9. GSS to M, April 19, 1775, in SFP.
10. M to GSS, April 20, 1775, in SFP, for this and following quotations from that letter.
11. GSS to M, April 22, 1775, in SFP.
12. GSS to M, April 24, 1775, in SFP.
13. M to GSS, April 25, 1775, in SFP.
14. JF to M, March 14, 1775, in SFP.
15. M to GSS, April 25, 1775, in SFP.
16. GSS to JF, June 15, 1775, in SFP.
17. GSS to JF, July 12, 1775, in SFP.
18. JF to GSS, June 25, 1775, in SFP.
19. R + J, 118, note by BS.

20. GSS to JF, July 12, 1775, in SFP; also JF to GSS and M, May 25, 1775, in SFP.
21. JF to GSS and M, May 25, 1775, in SFP.
22. JF to M, October 24, 1775, in SFP.
23. R + J, 106, note by BS.
24. GSS to JF, January 16, 1776, in SFP.
25. GSS to JF, September 12, 1775, in SFP.
26. JF to GSS and M, August 2, 1775, in SFP.
27. JF to GSS and M, September 5, 1775, postscript, in SFP.
28. JF to GSS and M, October 24, 1775, in SFP.
29. M to JosN and JnN, December 4, 1775, in SFP.
30. R + J, 97.
31. GSS to JF, December 22, 1775, in SFP.
32. JF to GSS, January 25, 1776, in SFP.
33. GSS to JF, March 14, 1776, in SFP.
34. M to JF and RF, March 18, 1776, in SFP.
35. GSS to JF, March 14, 1776, in SFP.

CHAPTER FIVE

1. M to JF, March 21, 1776, in SFP.
2. M to JF, April 11, 1776, in SFP.
3. R + J, 98.
4. GSS to M, April 8, 1776, in SFP.
5. GSS to M, March 29 and April 4, 1776, in SFP.
6. GSS to M, March 29, 1776, in SFP.
7. GSS to M, April 8, 1776, in SFP.
8. M to GSS, March 31, 1776, in SFP.
9. GSS to M, April 3, 1776, in SFP.
10. M to GSS, April 4, 1776, in SFP.
11. GSS to M, April 5, 1776, in SFP.
12. GSS to JF, April 15, 1776, in SFP.
13. JasN to JF and RF, April 17, 1776, in SFP.
14. WS to GSS, May 27, 1776, in SFP.
15. GSS and M to JF and RF, July 7, 1776, in SFP.
16. M to GSS, July 10, 1776, in SFP.
17. GSS to M, July 10, 1776, in SFP.
18. GSS to M, July 31, 1776, in SFP.
19. GSS to M, July 10, 1776, in SFP.
20. GSS to M, July 12 and 17, 1776, in SFP.
21. GSS to M, July 17, 1776, in SFP.
22. GSS to M, August 13, 1776, in SFP.
23. M to GSS, July 10, 1776, in SFP; also R + J, 103.
24. JF to M, August 14, 1776, in SFP.
25. JF to M, July 25, 1776, in SFP.

26. GSS to M, July 27, 1776, in SFP.

27. M to GSS, July 30, 1776, in SFP.

28. GSS to M, August 10, 1776, in SFP.

29. For instance, GSS to M, July 31, 1776, in SFP.

30. M to GSS, July 30, 1776, in SFP.

31. GSS to M, July 31, 1776, in SFP.

32. M to GSS, August 14, 1776, in SFP.

33. M to GSS, August 19 and 24, 1776, in SFP.

34. M to GSS, August 24 and 25, 1776, in SFP.

35. M to GSS, September 4, 1776, in SFP.

36. GSS to M, October 3, 1776, in SFP.

37. GSS to M, August 30, 1776, in SFP.

38. M to GSS, September 4, 1776, in SFP.

39. GSS to M, August 31, 1776, in SFP.

40. GSS to M, September 4, 1776, in SFP.

41. GSS to M, September 15 and 16, 1776, in SFP.

42. M to JF, June 21, 1776, in SFP.

43. JF to M, March 31, 1776, in SFP.

44. M to GSS, September 19, 1776, in SFP.

45. M to GSS, September 22, 1776, in SFP.

46. GSS to M, September 29, 1776, in SFP.

47. M to GSS, September 26, 1776, in SFP.

48. M to GSS, October 24, 1776, in SFP.

49. GSS to M, October 8, 1776, in SFP.

50. GSS to M, September 29, 1776, in SFP.

51. M to GSS, October 3, 1776, in SFP.

52. GSS to M, October 10, 1776, in SFP. The officers in the new army had adopted the "republican" style of wearing their own hair.

53. GSS to M, October 14, 1776, in SFP.

54. M to GSS, October 3, 1776, in SFP.

55. M to GSS, October 24 and 25, 1776, in SFP.

56. GSS to M, October 29, 1776, in SFP.

57. GSS to M, October 31, 1776, in SFP.

58. GSS to M, November 10 and 11, 1776, in SFP.

59. GSS to M, November 17, 1776, in SFP.

60. GSS to M, October 26, 1776, in SFP.

61. M to GSS, October 30, 1776, in SFP.

62. GSS to M, October 14, 1776, in SFP.

63. GSS to M, October 24, 1776, in SFP.

64. M to GSS, November 17, 1776, postscript November 18, in SFP.

65. GSS and M to JF, December 12, 1776, in SFP.

66. R + J, 103–4.

67. M to GSS, September 15, 1776, in SFP.

68. GSS to M, September 29, 1776, in SFP.

69. M to GSS, November 17, 1776, in SFP.

70. M to GSS, September 19, 1776, in SFP.

71. M to GSS, November 10, 1776, in SFP.
72. GSS and M to JF, December 12, 1776, in SFP.
73. JF to GSS and M, January 10, 1777, and GSS to JF, January 27, 1777, in SFP.
74. M to JF and RF, April 11, 1777, in SFP.
75. Ibid.
76. M to JasN, April 12, 1777, in SFP.
77. M and GSS to JF and RF, April 23, 1777, in SFP.
78. GSS to JF, July 1, 1777, in SFP.
79. M to JF, May 11, 1777, in SFP.
80. GSS to JF, July 1, 1777, in SFP.
81. JF to GSS, July 21, 1777, in SFP.
82. GSS to JF, September 30, 1777, in SFP.
83. GSS to JF, July 28, 1777, in SFP.
84. M to JF and RF, August 11, 1777, in SFP.
85. GSS to JF, September 30 and October 1, 1777, in SFP.
86. GSS to M, October 12, 1777, in SFP.
87. GSS to M, October 16, 1777, in SFP.
88. GSS to JF, November 10, 1777, in SFP.
89. GSS to JF, December 7, 1777, in SFP.
90. GSS to JF, January 27, 1777, in SFP.
91. GSS to JF, December 7 and 8, 1777, in SFP.
92. Ibid.
93. GSS to JF, January 19, 1778, in SFP.
94. GSS and M to JF and RF, July 31, 1778, in SFP.
95. JF to GSS, August 30, 1778, in SFP.
96. M to JF and RF, March 31, 1778, in SFP.
97. GSS to JF, June 8, 1778, in SFP.
98. GSS to JF, June 8, 1778, in SFP.
99. GSS and M to JF and RF, July 31, 1778, in SFP.
100. M to JF and RF, August 12, 1778, in SFP.
101. JF to GSS, January 10, 1779, in SFP.

CHAPTER SIX

1. BS Rem, 230.
2. M to JosN, May 11, 1779, in SFP.
3. JF to Jonathan Trumbull, May 17, 1779, in SFP.
4. JF to M, May 19, 1779, in SFP.
5. R + J, 110–12.
6. GSS to JF, May 12, 1779, in SFP.
7. GSS to M, May 10, 1779, in SFP.
8. Ibid.
9. M to JF, May 23, 1779, in SFP.
10. Copy of GSS to Jonathan Trumbull, May 21, 1779, in SFP.

11. GSS to M, June 12, 1779, in SFP.
12. GSS to M, July 17, 1779, in SFP.
13. R + J, 116.
14. Ibid., 117–19 passim.
15. M to GSS, July 26, 1779, in SFP.
16. James Beebe to GSS, August 9, 1779, in SFP.
17. GSS to M, August 27, 1779, in SFP.
18. GSS to JnN, August 27, 1779, in SFP.
19. GSS to M, August 20 and 23, 1779, in SFP.
20. M to JF and RF with postscript to JasN, October 9, 1779, in SFP.
21. M to JF and RF, October 28, 1779, in SFP.
22. M to GSS, November 1, 1779, in SFP.
23. M to GSS, October 4, 1779, in SFP.
24. M to JF and RF, October 28, 1779, in SFP.
25. M to GSS, November 11, 1779, in SFP.
26. GSS to M, November 11, 1779, in SFP.
27. R + J, 113–14.
28. M to GSS, November 16, 1779, in SFP.
29. R + J, 114–16.
30. GSS to M, December 1, 1779, in SFP.
31. GSS to M, December 31, 1779, in SFP.
32. M to JF and RF, January 9, 1780, in SFP.
33. M to GSS, March 12, 1780, in SFP.
34. GSS to William Franklin, March 6, 1780, in SFP.
35. William Franklin to GSS, March 6, 1780, in SFP.
36. GSS to William Franklin, March 10, 1780, in SFP.
37. GSS to M, March 14, 1780, in SFP.
38. GSS to M, April 13, 1780, in SFP.
39. M to GSS, March 12, 1780, in SFP.
40. GSS to M, April 13, 1780, in SFP.
41. R + J, 122–24.
42. GSS to JF, May 13, 1780, in SFP.
43. R + J, 104.
44. GSS to JF, May 13, 1780, in SFP.
45. GSS to JF, April 29, 1780, in SFP.

CHAPTER SEVEN

1. GSS to JF and RF, May 13, 1780, in SFP.
2. GSS to M, May 19, 1780, in SFP.
3. R + J, 141.
4. GSS to M, May 22, 1780, in SFP.
5. GSS to M, July 13, 1780, in SFP, for this quotation and material in following paragraph.
6. GSS to M, July 24, 1780, in SFP.

7. GSS to M, August 1, 1780, in SFP.

8. GSS to M, August 21, 1780, in SFP.

9. Ibid.

10. GSS to JF, November 1, 1780, in SFP.

11. GSS to JF, November 20, 1780, in SFP.

12. GSS to JF, December 23, 1780, in SFP.

13. R + J, 132.

14. GSS to JF, March 6, 1781, in SFP.

15. M to JF, March 18, 1781, in SFP.

16. R + J, 126–28.

17. Memo entitled "The last words of our Dear & HonD GD Father" in JnN's handwriting, n.d., NFP-SNH.

18. BS notation in R + J, 128.

19. R + J, 129.

20. BS notation in R + J, 129.

21. GSS to M, February 6, 1782, in SFP.

22. GSS to M, February 9 and 10, 1782, in SFP.

23. BS notation in R + J, 131–32.

24. M to Hannah Fellows, March 21, 1786, in SFP.

25. Ibid.

26. Taken from George P. Fisher, *Life of Benjamin Silliman* . . . (N.Y., Charles Scribner & Co., 1866), vol. I, 14–19.

27. BS Rem, 12, 7, 16.

28. BS notation in R + J, 133.

29. BS Rem, 172, 14, 18.

30. M to GSS Jr. and BS, March 17, 1793, in NFP-SNH.

31. R + J, 133–34.

32. Ibid., 136.

33. Ibid., 137.

34. Ibid., 138.

35. Ibid., 142.

CHAPTER EIGHT

1. BS to M, March 15, 1793, in SFP.

2. R + J, 139.

3. Gold Selleck Silliman estate, Fairfield Probate District, 1790, in CSL.

4. M Accts, 28.

5. JF to Eleazar Wheelock, December 9, 1763, in Dartmouth College Library.

6. JF to J and M with postscript by R, December 29, 1760, in SFP.

7. R + J, 29.

8. Ibid., 139.

9. Fisher, *Life of Benjamin Silliman,* vol. I, 22; M Accts, 68.

10. WS to M, n.d., in NFP-NCHS.

11. WS to M, December 9, 1790, in NFP-NCHS.
12. WS to M, December 16 and 17, 1790, in NFP-NCHS.
13. JasN to JnN, February 24, 1793, in NFP-NCHS.
14. M to JosN, undated copy (sometime in 1793), in NFP-NCHS.
15. R + J, 142, BS notation.
16. BS concluding note in R + J, 244.
17. BS to M, October 29, 1796, in SFP.
18. BS to GSS Jr., May 19, 1797, in SFP.
19. BS to GSS Jr., May 9, 1797, in Fisher, *Life of Benjamin Silliman,* vol. I, 63.
20. M to BS, March 8, 1798, and postscript, March 11, in SFP.
21. M to BS, March 6, 1798, in SFP.
22. M to GSS Jr., November 30, 1798, in SFP.
23. M to BS, March 8, 1798, in SFP.
24. M to GSS Jr., November 30, 1798, in SFP.
25. M to GSS Jr., October 24, 1797, in SFP.
26. Benjamin D. Silliman to "Cousin B," April 24, 1894, in SFP.
27. BS to Martha Ann Silliman, March 19, 1799, in SFP.
28. R + J, 145.
29. M to JnN, January 2, 1801, privately owned.
30. M to BS, June 19, 1798, in SFP.
31. M to GSS Jr. and BS, November 18, 1798, in SFP.
32. M to BS, March 2, 1800, in SFP.
33. BS Auto, vol. IV, 88.
34. BS to M, August 8, 1800, in SFP.
35. GSS Jr. to M, July 2, 1800, in SFP.
36. BS Auto, vol. I, 7.
37. M to BS, September 11, 1798, in SFP.
38. BS to M, June 14, 1801, in NFP-NCHS.
39. BS Auto, vol. I, 11, 14.
40. Ibid., 12.
41. M to GSS Jr. and BS, November 3, 1801, in SFP.
42. BS Auto, vol. I, 13.
43. M to GSS Jr. and BS, March 17, 1793, in NFP-SNH.
44. M to GSS Jr. and BS, November 3, 1801, in SFP.
45. BS to M, March 15, 1800, in SFP.
46. R + J, 170.
47. Ibid., 171.
48. M to BS, March 30, 1801, in SFP.
49. M to BS, June 5, 1801, in SFP.
50. M to BS, June 13, 1801, in SFP.
51. BS to M, June 14, 1801, in SFP.
52. M to BS, July 18, 1801, in SFP.
53. R + J, 171-72.
54. JosN to M, August 2, 1802, in NFP-NCHS.
55. M to BS, July 30, 1802, in SFP.

56. JosN to M, September 14, 1802, in NFP-NCHS.
57. Quotes taken from JosN to M and GSS Jr., September 14 and 16, 1802; to David Judson, October 2, 1802; and to WS, September 21, 1802, in NFP-NCHS.
58. M to BS, January 1, 1803, in SFP.
59. JosN to BS, May 8, 1803, in SFP.
60. BS to GSS Jr., May 20, 1803, in SFP.
61. M to BS, August 29, 1803, in SFP.
62. BS to M, October 7, 1803, in SFP.
63. R + J, 164.
64. M to BS, June 3, 1800, in SFP.
65. JnN to M, April 10, 1804, in SFP.

CHAPTER NINE

1. JosN to M, October 21, 1804, in NFP-NCHS.
2. BS to M, April 27, 1804, in SFP.
3. M to BS, June 22, 1805, in SFP.
4. M to BS, November 16, 1804, in SFP.
5. M to BS, April 8, 1805, in SFP.
6. M to BS, May 4, 1804, in SFP.
7. M to BS, July 9, 1804, in SFP.
8. JosN to JnN, October 21, 1804, in NFP-NCHS.
9. JosN to M, October 21, 1804, in SFP.
10. JosN to JnN, October 1, 1804, in NFP-NCHS.
11. BS to Patty Silliman, December 11, 1804, in SFP.
12. BS to M, January 3, 1805, in SFP.
13. M to BS, November 16, 1805, in SFP.
14. R + J, 177.
15. M to BS, March 26, 1805, in SFP.
16. M to BS, June 27, 1805, in SFP.
17. Quoted from John F. Fulton and Elizabeth H. Thomson, *Benjamin Silliman, 1779–1864: Pathfinder in American Science* (N.Y., Henry Schuman, 1947), 45.
18. BS to GSS Jr., February 21, 1805, in Fisher, *Life of Benjamin Silliman,* vol. I, 135.
19. BS to M, August 22, 1805, in SFP.
20. M to BS, March 26, 1805, in SFP.
21. BS to M, August 22, 1805, in SFP.
22. John Noyes, *A Discourse delivered in Norfield, May 29th, 1836* . . . (New Haven, Hitchcock & Stafford, 1839), 13.
23. JnN to BS, November 14, 1806, in SFP.
24. JosN to David Judson, April 7, 1805, in NFP-NCHS.
25. JosN to JnN, October 5, 1806, in NFP-NCHS.
26. JosN to JnN, November 29, 1806, in NFP-NCHS.

27. R + J, 201-11 passim.

28. Ibid., 212-14.

29. M to BS, June 15, 1808, in SFP.

30. BS Auto, vol. IV, 32.

31. BS to M, February 19, 1809, in SFP.

32. M to BS, March 1, 1809, in SFP.

33. BS to M, June 17, 1810, in SFP.

34. M to BS, March 1, 1809, and BS to M, March 19, in SFP.

35. JosN's son John to M, February 18, 1810, in SFP.

36. JosN to JnN, September 15, 1810, in SFP.

37. BS to M, November 29, 1810, in SFP.

38. M to BS, June 27, 1811, in SFP.

39. M to BS, September 8, 1811, in SFP.

40. BS to Harriet Trumbull Silliman, October 5, 1811, in SFP.

41. John Dickinson estate, Middlesex Probate District, 1811, in CSL.

42. R + J with BS note, 241.

43. M to BS, November 5, 1812, in SFP.

44. JosN to JnN, November ?, 1811, in NFP-NCHS.

45. JosN to JnN, February 25, 1814, in NFP-NCHS.

46. JosN to JnN, November ?, 1811, in NFP-NCHS.

47. JosN's son James to M, April 8, 1812, in SFP.

48. M to BS, September 24, 1814, in SFP.

49. M to BS, July 20, 1814, in SFP.

50. R + J, BS notation, 241.

51. M to JnN, May 17, 1814, in NFP-NCHS.

52. R + J, BS notation, 243.

53. M to JnN, February 21, 1814, in NFP-NCHS.

54. BS to M, April 18, 1815, in SFP.

55. JnN to M, April 23, 1815, in SFP.

56. JnN to M, April 26, 1815, in SFP.

57. M to BS, April 26, 1815, in SFP.

58. M to BS, May 4, 1815, in SFP.

59. BS Auto, vol. IV, 81.

60. BS's copy of Benjamin Noyes's suicide note, May 1815, in SFP.

61. M to JnN, May 18, 1815, in NFP-NCHS.

62. M to BS, June 27, 1815, in SFP.

63. BS to M, May 16, 1815, in SFP.

64. BS to M, July 21, 1815, in SFP.

65. "Family records furnished to me (BS) by my brother the Revd. John Noyes," 13-14, and BS to M, December 19, 1816, both in SFP.

66. M to GSS Jr., July 15, 1815, in SFP.

67. BS Rem, 31, 32, 38.

68. "Family records furnished to me (BS) by my brother the Revd. John Noyes," 12-13, in SFP.

69. M to JnN, July 31, 1816, privately owned.

70. M to BS, July 28, 1812, in SFP.

71. Dated June 18, 1816, labeled in BS's hand "Mother's Advice" and filed with BS correspondence, in SFP.
72. Labeled by BS "Mother's acct. of Dr. Dwight. This was written on loose scraps of paper by my mother + copied by her nieces. She was 81 years old the spring it was finished." 1817, filed with BS correspondence, in SFP.
73. BS annotation in R + J, 243.
74. JasN's son James to BS, June 27, 1818, in SFP.
75. R + J, BS's note, 244.

BIBLIOGRAPHICAL ESSAY

THIS life of Mary Fish is based first and foremost on the Silliman Family Papers in the Yale University Library, a collection that contains not only a large part of the correspondence by and relating to her, but also Benjamin Silliman's annotated copy of her Reminiscences and Journal, her account book for the period 1790 to 1799, and his own autobiography entitled "Origins and Progress of Chemistry, Mineralogy and Geology in Yale College with Personal Reminiscences." Important papers from the Fish and Noyes families are also to be found here, including Joseph Fish's diary and his "Funeral Sermon on the Death of Mrs. Rebecca [Fish] Douglas with some Memoirs of her Life." The collections of the Historical Society of Pennsylvania contain a large number of letters from Benjamin Silliman's professional correspondence together with a few family papers. Finally, some of Benjamin's direct descendants hold important manuscripts to which they kindly gave us access. More such private holdings may exist. George P. Fisher, *Life of Benjamin Silliman* . . . (New York: Charles Scribner & Co., 1866), 2 volumes, and John F. Fulton and Elizabeth H. Thomson, *Benjamin Silliman, 1779–1864: Pathfinder in American Science* (New York: Henry Schuman, 1947), quote from a few documents that we have been unable to locate despite the cooperation of a great many people.

The study would not have been possible without another important collection, the Noyes Family Papers, housed at New Canaan, Connecticut. These provided indispensable information about Mary's first marriage, her first widowhood, and the westward migration of her eldest son's family, and they shed further light on members of the Fish and Silliman families. The bulk of the papers was deposited by Mrs. F. Sherwood Guion with the New Canaan Historical Society, but a considerable number remain in the hands of her daughters, Judith Barlow and Mary Jane Miller, who currently reside in the New Canaan homestead of Mary's grandson, Dr. Samuel Noyes. An index of most of the privately held material, compiled by Mr. David Palmquist of the Bridgeport Library, is on file at the New Canaan Historical Society.

Other manuscript sources have helped us to fill in the background to our narrative, in particular the public records in the Archives Division of the Connecticut State Library, which include records of the North Stonington Congregational Church; of the probate courts at Fairfield, New Haven, New London, and Middlesex counties; of the petitions to the state legislature; of eighteenth-century land transactions; and of the Fairfield County Court and Superior Court (these last very fragmentary). We have also made use of the Ezra Stiles papers, to which Harold E. Seleskey, ed., *A Guide to the Microfilm Edition of the Ezra Stiles Papers of Yale University* (New Haven, Conn.: Yale University Library, 1978), provides useful access; the Naphtali Daggett papers; the Yale University Records of the Treasurer (all three collections in the possession of the Yale University Library); and Joseph Fish's correspondence and diary on the subject of his Indian Missions, which are deposited in the Connecticut Historical Society and the Dartmouth College Archives. The diary has recently been published under the title of *Old Light on Separate Ways: The Narraganset Diary of Joseph Fish, 1765–1776*, William J. Simmons and Cheryl L. Simmons eds. (Hanover: University Press of New England, 1982). Last, we have consulted some fragmentary materials in the Fairfield Historical Society and the Watkinson Library at Trinity College, Hartford.

Among the published sources we have used are J. Hammond Trumbull and Charles J. Hoadley, eds., *Public Records of the Colony of Connecticut* (Hartford, Conn.: Brown and Parsons Co., 1850–1890), 15 volumes, and Charles J. Hoadley, Leonard W. Labaree, et al., eds., *Public Records of the State of Connecticut* (Hartford, Conn.: Connecticut State Library, 1894–1967), 11 volumes. The published sermons of Joseph Fish, most notably *The Church of CHRIST a firm and durable House* (New London, Conn.: Timothy Green, 1767), and Samuel Hopkins's *Memoirs of the Life of Mrs. Sarah Osborn* . . . (Worcester, Mass.: Leonard Worcester, 1779), provided valuable details. Katharine Hewitt Cummins's *Connecticut Militia General: Gold Selleck Silliman* (Hartford, Conn.: American Revolution Bicentennial Commission of Connecticut, 1979) was of interest and help. We have also consulted with profit Franklin B. Dexter, ed., *Biographical Sketches of the Graduates of Yale College* (New York: Henry Holt Co. and Yale University Press, 1885–1912), 6 volumes; Clifford K. Skipton, ed., *Sibley's Harvard Graduates* (Boston: Massachusetts Historical Society, 1937–1975), 13 volumes; and Zephaniel Swift, *A System of Laws of the State of Connect-*

icut (Windham, Conn.: John Byrne, 1795), 2 volumes. Last, the experience of working together as author and editor on *Securing the Revolution* (Ithaca, N.Y.: Cornell University Press, 1972) and *Dear Liberty: Connecticut's Mobilization for the Revolutionary War* (Middletown, Conn.: Wesleyan University Press, 1980) strongly influenced our approach to the interpretation of the materials presented here.

INDEX